THE X-FILES™ BOOK OF THE UNEXPLAINED

by

JANE GOLDMAN

Based on the series created by Chris Carter

SIMON & SCHUSTER

A VIACOM COMPANY

First published in Great Britain by Simon & Schuster, 1995
An imprint of Simon & Schuster Ltd
A Viacom Company

7th impression 1996

Simon & Schuster Ltd.
West Garden Place
Kendal Street
London W2 2AQ

Simon & Schuster of Australia Pty Ltd
Sydney

A CIP catalogue record for this book is available
from the British Library.

0-684-81633-4

Design, Typesetting and Repro
by
The Imaging Business Ltd
1B Orleston Road
Islington
London N7 8LQ

Printed and bound in Great Britain
by
Butler & Tanner Ltd
The Selwood Printing Works
Caxton Road
Frome
Somerset BA11 INF

Dedication

This book is for Jonathan, Betty and Harvey, with all the love in the world.

Acknowledgements

Besides my perfect and beloved husband and children, who let me disappear into my study for months on end, there are so many others to whom this book owes its existence and I owe thanks.

Firstly, it's a delight to be able to thank Cleo Paskal without her being able to change the subject. She is one of the most exceptional humans I have ever had the fortune to know, and without her diligent research, intense work and unfathomable friendship this book would simply not have been possible.

I am also for ever indebted to the infinitely talented and thoughtful Jack Barth, who crossed the Atlantic to join me on the final week of my adventures in deadline hell, kept me sane with his humour and insight, worked like a demon and never once complained about sleeping on my uncomfortable sofa.

Of course, writing is only half of the equation. Equal credit must go to: the utterly wonderful Martin Fletcher whose calmness, trust, humour and patience have no doubt totally spoiled me for any editors I work with in the future; the tireless Gillian Holmes and the wildly dedicated team at Simon & Schuster; Steve Manners at Fox UK and Ian Downes at CPL for their constant support.

Thanks are due too to my fantastic family and friends for their love and help: Amanda Goldman and Stuart Goldman (whom I'm sure never reckoned that parental duties would include transcribing), Kinny, Bunker, Anny (who is always alive in my heart), Tara, Maureen Ross and Tony Phillips, Jacqui Deevoy, Max Ellis, Monica Rivron and Michelle Alexander. I'd also like to express my gratitude to the Paskal and Weisbord family for lending me their marvellous daughter for the summer, and to Suzanne McClintock and Mal Wharton for all their hard work.

Space does not permit me to individually mention all those who are the flesh and bones of this book, so I hope they will forgive me for making an enormous blanket thank you to all whose names appear in the text, and who gave of their time and wisdom.

However, I must also voice my heartfelt thanks to: Chris Carter, Howard Gordon and Glen Morgan for making time in their busy schedules to talk to me; the fabulous Bob Rickard for giving me so much time and invaluable assistance, and loaning me so many books; the wonderful Loren Coleman, for his immense help and kindness; the charming and generous Timothy Good; Claire Russell and Professor W.M.S. Russell for allowing me to pillage their library and their minds; Barry Karr, CSICOP and *The Skeptical Inquirer*; Eleanor O'Keefe at the Society For Psychical Research; Bob Oechsler; Mark Birdsall at Quest International; Tom Deuley, Walter Andrus, and MUFON; John and Anne Spencer; Tom Paskal; Joe Nickell; Professor Ray Hyman; Professor Paul Edwards; all at Prometheus Books and the *Free Inquirer*; Professor Wendy McGoodwin; Martin Lavut and Arnie Gelbart; Mark Chorvinsky and *Strange*; Richard Hall and FUFOR; Alan Woolworth; Stella Gallia; Professor Robert Morris and Cathy Dalton; Miles Ross; Dale Hinch and Robin Green.

Additionally, I feel it would be churlish not to acknowledge Lyall Watson, Jerome Clark and James Randi, with whom I did not have the pleasure of speaking, but whose work I found inspiring reading and invaluable reference.

I've no doubt forgotten several very deserving individuals in the above list, and hope that they will accept my sincere apologies and thanks.

INTRODUCTION

Don't worry. I'm not about to launch into a long ramble on why I love *The X-Files* (which I do), why it is such a significant and unique TV show (which it is) and why I think it speaks to so many people at different levels (which it does). After all, just about every publication on both sides of the Atlantic has done that already.

In the great sea of *X-Files* related print, the only thing that really bugs me is when I see *The X-Files* described as a show about the paranormal. Strange phenomena is only one element of the glorious *X-Files* equation. It's like calling *Citizen Kane* a film about a sledge. It worries me even more when I run across people who are still labouring under the misapprehension that *The X-Files* is a dramatic representation of real life events. And I want to make it known that this book does not buy into either of those fallacies.

Still, I think it's fair to say that *The X-Files* is responsible for piquing the viewer's interest in the weird, the wonderful and the sinister . And that's where I hope this book will come in handy. The aim of *The X-Files Book of the Unexplained* is to provide further reading on the subjects raised in the episodes and on the inspirations behind them. And occasionally, I have used the episodes as jumping-off points to dive into other pools of mystery and study.

Inside this book you'll find facts, theories, folklore and a lot more besides – but I promise you'll never find one masquerading as another. Whether – like Fox Mulder – you want to believe, or – like Dana Scully – you prefer the comfort and stability of consensus reality, all of us desire the truth.

X-Files creator Chris Carter has often said that Mulder and Scully are both parts of him. In a way, I think they are both parts of all of us – we want to believe, but we demand proof. And however we approach the enigmas of the universe, we're all fascinated by what might be out there.

JANE GOLDMAN

CONTENTS

Acknowledgements   VII

Beyond the Grave

Unfinished Business   1
Reincarnation   32
The Borrowers   48

Unnatural Abilities

Beyond the Five Senses   64
Up in Flames   82

Biological Oddities

Weird Nature   92
Human Enigmas   108
Feral Humans   136

Ancient Beliefs

The Shapes of Fear   152
Leaps of Faith   170

20th Century Threats and Paranoias

Artificial Intelligence   182
Genetic Tampering   200

A Cosmic Conundrum

The UFO Experience   218
Alien Territory   236
Trust No-one   244
A Celestial Fleet   260
Fallen Angels   276

Investigating the Unexplained

In Search of the Truth   294
The Real X-Files   308

X-File: Shadows

Case notes by Agent Dana Scully

There are many aspects of this case which remain unexplained.

We still do not know who killed the two men (later identified as members of the extremist group the Isfahan) who attacked Lauren Kyte on 22 September, nor the armed intruders who were subsequently found dead at her abode. Nor can I find any medical rationale for the highly anomalous post-mortem findings on their bodies.

It would seem impossible, for instance, that comminution of the hyoid bone and crushing of the larynx and oesophagus could take place without any evidence whatsoever of external abrasions and tissue damage, and yet this was the case with all four victims.

Furthermore, I am unable to explain the photograph taken by Agent Mulder of the upper window of Lauren Kyte's house, which clearly depicts the figure of her former employer and friend Howard Graves – a man who had died three weeks previously.

I found Lauren Kyte to be a sincere and credible source of information. Despite my inability to accept that she gained knowledge of the murder of Howard Graves through paranormal means (allegedly by communication with Graves himself) I believe that this is her honest perception of the situation, and not a ruse to conceal her complicity in any criminal undertakings.

Although I participated in the warranted search of HTG Industrial Technologies' premises, I was not present in Robert Dorlund's office when the carefully concealed micro-disk was discovered.

I am therefore unable to corroborate Agent Mulder's claims that its whereabouts were revealed by a spontaneous supernatural occurrence.

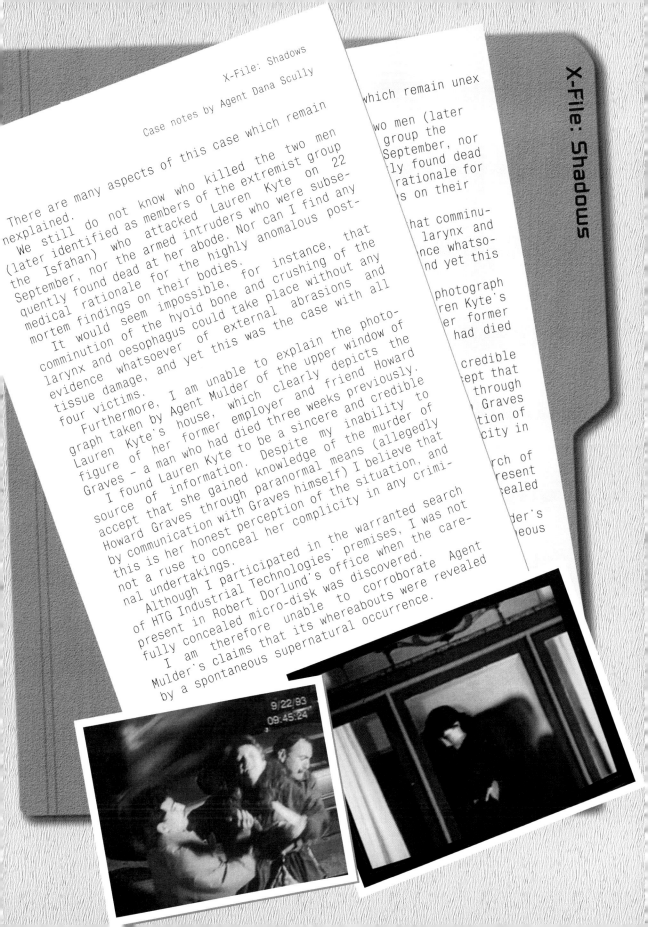

UNFINISHED BUSINESS

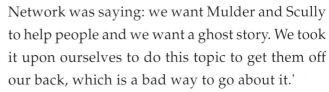

hadows is *The X-Files* take on the classic camp-fire ghost-story format: a chain of weird events, followed by the revelation of a restless soul with a motive, making everything slip tenebrously into place.

According to co-writer Glen Morgan, who has reservations about the episode, its birth was utilitarian. 'The Network was saying: we want Mulder and Scully to help people and we want a ghost story. We took it upon ourselves to do this topic to get them off our back, which is a bad way to go about it.'

Morgan does not believe in ghosts, but finds poltergeist phenomena intriguing. 'That there could somehow be energy in the body that could cause you to throw something across the room without even knowing it, and then it's interpreted as being a ghost. . .' But Morgan resisted the temptation to make the heroine of *Shadows*, Lauren Kyte, responsible for the spooky goings-on. 'Romantically, in my mind, it was her boss,' he confirms. And so *Shadows* got its tormented soul: murder victim Howard Graves.

Of course, a ghost story's primary purpose is to chill us, spook us, gross us out, and the horrible-untimely-death element serves that end deliciously.

But it is interesting to consider it as a crossover with another timeless literary theme: triumph over adversity. In ghost stories, the adversity is death, and the triumph is that the wronged person refuses to allow the small matter of being six feet under to get in the way of pursuing their goal

– whether it be attaining justice or just hanging out scaring the pants off people. Even when we throw in lines about being 'condemned to walk this earth for eternity. . .', you can bet that, if only subconsciously, we still figure it as an option that beats oblivion hands down.

So here in *Shadows* we have that element too. Howard Graves is essentially the little guy, the disadvantaged hero (and you can't get much more disadvantaged than being dead) fighting against the towering evil – in this case corporate treachery and violent political terrorism. He watches over his beloved surrogate daughter, taking her tormentors in hand and meting out justice fairly and squarely: the crotchety domineering co-worker gets hot coffee in her lap; the parade of morally bereft hit-men get their larynxes crushed. He makes it known that his suicide was murder, exposes his company's terrorist liaison, and makes damn sure his duplicitous colleague pays. His unfinished business settled, he is, it is hinted, rewarded with eternal peace.

Just as most ghost stories are essentially chronicles of somebody's life after death, most real-life 'ghost' encounters get pegged with the same interpretation.

But, before we can even begin to ask whether the existence of ghosts proves that death is a doorway rather than a brick wall, we have to ask whether ghosts exist.

Henry Habberley Price, a respected Oxford don and former president of the Society for Psychical Research (SPR) described the question 'Do you believe in ghosts?' as 'one of the most ambiguous which can be asked'. He felt that one should ask instead, 'Do you believe that people sometimes experience apparitions?' To which his own answer was a resounding affirmative. He asserts: 'No one who examines the evidence can come to any other conclusion. Instead of disputing the facts, we must try to explain them.'

John Spencer, along with his wife Anne Spencer, is one of Britain's leading researchers in this field. Together they work with the SPR and the Association for the Scientific Study of

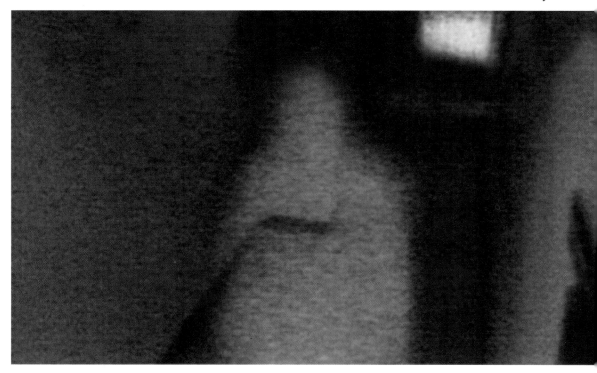

Anomalous Phenomena (ASSAP), investigating claims, logging data and hoping for the breakthrough that might begin to bring explanations to light.

Spencer feels that, like UFO sightings, a high percentage of 'ghost' phenomena have a logical explanation. 'I think we can be pretty sure that there are some genuine mysteries out there,' he asserts. 'But right now, we have no answers, only questions.'

One major problem is that the data itself suggests many, many different phenomena which may not even be related to one another, and provides little insight into understanding *any* of them, let alone into understanding the mystery of death itself.

Even if we choose to study only the manifestations which seem to suggest a clear connection to the dead – which means leaving out other 'ghost' phenomena such as apparitions of the living, ambiguous 'presences' and poltergeists (unseen forces which appear to manipulate their environment) – we are still left with a truck-load of categories.

CRISIS APPARITIONS

Scully's experience at the start of the episode *Beyond the Sea* – seeing an image of her father moments before receiving news of his death – is a classic representation of a crisis apparition. The surprise appearance of a loved one or friend which later turns out to have roughly coincided with the moment of their death may well be the most common kind of 'ghost' experience reported. Because these apparitions are usually seen by a single witness, it is impossible to discount the possibility that they are merely subjective experiences, perhaps triggered by some obscure function of the human mind, as opposed to being physically present. However, because these apparitions are so time-specific, it is quite impossible to study them in any kind of scientific way.

'RECORDINGS' GHOSTS

A ghost which is repeatedly seen by multiple witnesses in a specific place, and sometimes on specific occasions, obviously provides much better scope for investigation. It is likely, then, that this phenomenon will be the first to be fully understood.

A typical 'recordings' ghost appears to have no relationship with its surroundings (it passes through solid matter, sits where there is nothing to sit on etc.). Its behaviour is repetitive and limited, and it appears to have no interest in those who witness it. These forms are generally attached to specific locations, and most 'historical' ghosts fall into this  category. For instance, an apparition of President Lincoln has been seen at The White House on numerous occasions, by the most level-headed of witnesses, including Winston Churchill and John Kennedy.

The degree of perceived 'realness' varies greatly from one apparition to another. Some seem to take an almost translucent form, while others may appear solid, but still have that spectral *je ne sais quois.* As one witness interviewed by Spencer succinctly put it: 'I got the impression it was no more of an intrusion than people on TV. Real, but only to a certain degree.' On the other hand, there are those which appear to be so thoroughly mortal that the witness initially believes that they are looking at a real person. The former leader of the Liberal Party, Jeremy Thorpe, encountered an apparition of this kind while staying with friends in Trethevy, Cornwall. Returning to the dinner table after answering a call of nature, Thorpe looked back down the corridor and saw a monk in a brown habit entering the bathroom. The monk ignored his polite salutation, but Thorpe was still under the impression that he was real, and even asked his hosts who the monk was. It transpired that he was known as 'the Prior' and had been in residence for several centuries.

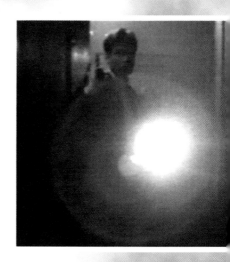

Sometimes the supernatural nature of an apparently 'real' person can be revealed in a more surprising way. John Spencer recalls an incident in the summer of 1995 which took place during the investigation of an allegedly haunted building and which involved a new and fairly sceptical member of his team. 'He looked up and saw this girl in front of him and just thought she was a member of the team that he hadn't been introduced to. He started to say hello and she just disappeared. . . That shook him up quite badly.' Along similar lines, Spencer chuckles at the memory of a group of witnesses who saw a ghost purported to be that of Lady Jane Grey. 'She was dancing through the corridors, and really happy. Everyone thought she was a genuine little girl, thought it was lovely. . . until she went straight through this iron door.'

Spencer, like most other psychical researchers, leans towards the belief that 'recordings' ghosts are a kind of natural hologram, recorded and played back by mechanisms we don't yet understand. 'I don't think,' he muses, 'that if someone sees Sir Walter Raleigh, it proves that there's life after death. . . I don't think there's anything of his "soul", just a picture, like a video.'

The key to understanding the 'recordings mechanism', if such a thing exists, is in discovering what triggers it. Says Spencer: 'Logic demands that there must be a combination of things, some of which are always there, and some of which are not. For instance, if it was just a matter of a particular combination of geography – a room constructed in a certain shape, say – then everyone who went into the room would be recorded and you wouldn't be able to move in there for ghosts flying all over the place. So it might be the combination of geography and atmospherics – a partic-ular type of location and a particular humidity or temper-ature – which might embed or play a recording. But again, you might suppose that it would happen more frequently. So you need another rare factor and that's where you bring in the human mind. Perhaps it takes a particular type of mind to embed the recording, and later, to press the replay button. That, I think, has a certain logic to it, because it would explain why not everything gets recorded and not everything gets seen.'

Anne Spencer posits that a recording might not be trig-gered by the person whose image is recorded, but by someone seeing them. She cites a recent case of a witness who looked out of a window on to a view of a pond and saw someone lying in the water. 'He rushed down to save him, but when he arrived, there was no one there. When he was back at the window again, he saw the same image. It suggests that the image could have been recorded by someone seeing him – and to experience the recording, you need to be in exactly the spot where the original sighter was.'

TIME-SLIPS

A time-slip is the rather suggestive term used to describe another kind of experience we know little about – a sighting not only of an anomalous figure or figures, but of their entire surrounding environment, too. Although less common than simple ghost sightings, these experiences are by no means rare.

The most famous 'time-slip' case concerns two women who, in 1901, visited the Petit Trianon gardens at the palace of Versailles and claimed to have encountered both an altered landscape and people in period dress. George Russel, a friend of the poet W. B. Yeats, had a similar experience in the ruins of a chapel: around him, he suddenly saw the chapel in a state of fine repair, with a small service taking place. And in 1988, John Spencer logged a report from a woman holidaying in Burra, Australia, who returned from dinner to find the lights of her rented cottage on. Peering through the window, the room appeared quite different and a woman was clearly visible sitting on a couch, smiling and talking to someone out of sight. Once inside the cottage, however, everything was back to normal.

Are these experiences a more elaborate recording? A glimpse into another time or dimension? Momentary transportation into the body or mind of someone present at the original scene? A hallucination or some other trick of the brain? The possibilities are endless, the answers – for now anyway – are not forthcoming.

One interesting point raised by this category of experience, however, is the fact that it cannot always support the after-life hypothesis. Sure, time-slips often feature human apparitions, but there are also cases – often referred to as 'Phantom Scenery' cases – where only buildings, trees and other presumably 'soul-less' structures are encountered.

This, along with the numerous reported cases of spectral trains, ships and cars, suggests that whether or not the after-life hypothesis is a sound one, there is undoubtedly something else going on.

INTERACTIVE GHOSTS

Apparitions and presences which display cognition and intelligence are in many ways the most intriguing, certainly the most rare and, it must be said, the most suggestive of the idea that the human spirit can, in one way or another, survive death.

Accounts of interactive ghosts often appear to suggest that they have a purpose. Comforting the bereaved seems to be the most typical, but sometimes, as with the presence in *Shadows*, their agenda is far more elaborate. . .

Don Repo, whose spectral life after death was witnessed by many of his colleagues

'He's watching over you, isn't he?'
MULDER TO LAUREN KYTE
Shadows

The L-1011 passenger plane was due for take-off, and the flight engineer was mid-way through carrying out the routine pre-flight inspection. 'You don't need to worry about the pre-flight, I've already done it,' Second Officer Don Repo told him. Under other circumstances, the engineer might have gratefully received this comment. But Repo was not the appointed second officer on the flight. Nor, for that matter, on any flight. Don Repo was dead.

Don Repo and his colleague Captain Bob Loft are the most intriguing interactive, protective ghosts on record. Their story begins where their mortal lives ended: on the evening of 29 December 1972 when Eastern Airlines flight 401 crashed in the swampland of Florida's Everglades, killing 101 people.

The flight had been uneventful and was preparing to land when Captain Loft became concerned that the nose-gear might not have locked into place. Second Officer Repo, the flight engineer, agreed to carry out a visual inspection, and duly climbed into the 'hell-hole', a small compartment beneath the cockpit. There, he was faced with the dismaying sight of watery marsh just below him – the last thing he saw before the plane plunged to its destruction.

It transpired that a far more serious fault had occurred than Repo and Loft could have imagined. The plane's

Loft and Repo's last flight? The remains of the rear jet engine and part of the tail assembly of Eastern Airlines flight 401

autopilot system had a mechanism which caused it to switch off if the steering column was pushed in a certain way. The autopilot had been set to keep the plane at an altitude of 2,000 feet, but as the men had moved about the cockpit, one of them had unwittingly disengaged the system. Within a minute, the plane had descended to just 500 feet above ground level, although the autopilot readout had continued to display an altitude of 2,000 feet. A warning signal had sounded, but was not loud enough to be heard by Loft through his headphones, nor, obviously, by Repo in the hell-hole. Twenty seconds later, it was all over.

Claims of encounters with Captain Bob Loft (above) and Don Repo after their deaths involved not just fleeting glimpses but coherent conversations

Loft and Repo were among the dead, but the airline industry had by no means seen the last of them. Although Eastern Airlines refuses to discuss the matter, researchers have interviewed numerous individuals claiming to have encountered the ill-fated pair on L-1011 aircraft – and, oddly enough, usually on the very planes utilising recycled parts of flight 401.

As the the reports would have it, Bob Loft and Don Repo have devoted their after-lives to watching over the passengers and crew of these little Lockheed passenger planes.

Many of the testimonies are extremely persuasive. Many come from people in highly responsible positions – pilots, flight officers, even a vice-president of Eastern Airlines, who allegedly spoke with a captain he assumed was in charge of the flight, before recognising him as the late Loft. Other sightings are convincing because they have multiple witnesses: a flight's captain and two flight attendants claim to have seen and spoken to Loft before take-off and watched him vanish – an experience that left them so shaken they cancelled the flight; a woman passenger made a concerned enquiry to a flight attendant regarding the quiet, unresponsive man in Eastern Airlines uniform sitting in the seat next to her, who subsequently disappeared in full view of both of them and several other passengers, leaving the woman hysterical. When later shown a sheet of photos depicting Eastern flight engineers, she identified Repo as the officer she had seen.

But Repo and Loft are apparently not content merely to be present. Often their style is far more hands-on – particularly in Repo's case. Aside from his appearance to a preflight engineer whom he appeared to have been assisting, there is a testimony from a flight attendant who observed a man in flight-engineer's uniform, whom she later recognised as Repo, fixing a galley oven. The insistence of the plane's own flight engineer that he had not fixed the oven, and that there had not been another engineer on board, would seem to lend weight to her claim. Repo has also been seen in the hell-hole by a flight engineer who had accessed it in order to investigate a knocking he heard coming from below the cockpit. On another occasion, Faye Merryweather, a flight attendant, saw Repo's face looking out at her from an oven in the galley of Tri-Star 318. Understandably alarmed, she fetched two colleagues, one of whom, the flight engineer, had been a friend of Repo's and recognised him instantly. All three heard Repo warn them to 'Watch out for fire on this airplane'. The plane later encountered serious engine trouble and the last leg of its flight was cancelled. It is interesting to note that the galley of Tri-Star 318, had been salvaged from the wreckage of flight 401.

The sightings were all reported to the Flight Safety Foundation (an independent authority) which commented: 'The reports were given by experienced and trustworthy pilots and crew. We consider them significant. The appearance of the dead flight engineer (Repo)... was confirmed by the flight engineer.' Later, records of the Federal Aviation Agency record the fire which broke out on that same aircraft.

Many of the accounts concerning the phantom airmen would seem to suggest that they have an agenda, but one testimony spells it out. An L-1011 captain reported that Don Repo had appeared and told him: 'There will never be another crash of an L -1011... We will not let it happen.'

John Spencer recently made enquiries and confirmed that there have indeed been no accidents involving that model of plane since that fateful December day in 1972.

'Howard showed me how Dorlund had him killed'
LAUREN KYTE

If many allegedly true reports are to be believed, the old adage that dead men tell no tales is a fallacy. History has numerous stories of spectral entities helping the living to locate wills, deeds, treasure and such. Other accounts infer that 'get someone to discover my mortal remains' is at the top of many a ghost's 'to do' list. Countless famous (supposedly) true hauntings begin with seemingly purposeful disturbances and end with the discovery of a skeleton concealed in some fashion suggestive of a wrongful death. Borley Rectory in Essex, Britain's most notorious haunted house, had its mournful nun apparently yearning for a sacrosanct burial after countless decades bricked-up in the cellar. The Great Eastern, an ocean liner plagued by a run of bad luck and the perpetual sound of ghostly knocking, turned out to conceal the skeleton of a hapless riveter, accidentally entombed alive between the iron walls of the vessel's double hull during its construction.

The passage of time has allowed most of these cases to slip into the twilight world between fantasy and reality, making serious research into any of these claims difficult. However, there is one historical case in this category in which there is proof that the tale has not been twisted in the retelling.

Sergeant Arthur Davies, 30-year-old leader of the English platoon stationed at Dubrach, Scotland, was last seen alive on the morning of 28 September 1749. Taking leave of his platoon, he set off into the hills for a spot of hunting and never returned. After four days, the search for him was abandoned, but foul play was not suspected given the notoriously treacherous Highland terrain: its crags, bogs and powerful water-currents could do for a man and easily conceal his corpse.

In fact, Davies was almost certainly murdered at the hands of Duncan Clerk and Alexander MacDonald, a deer-stalker and a forester whose motives were wrapped up in the acrimonious atmosphere between the Scots and the English which had pervaded since the English brutalities of 1746. Without witnesses, a body or even a suspicion of murder however, the chances of the case ever coming to court should have been non-existent. But today, anyone caring to visit the General Register House archives in Edinburgh can peruse the Court Record book for the years 1752 – 1754 and read about it for themselves.

Ten months after the disappearance of Sergeant Davies, a young shepherd named Alexander McPherson, who lived a couple of miles south of Dubrach on the slopes of Christie Hill, had a very weird experience. As he lay in bed, he saw the figure of a man who announced that he was Sergeant Davies and spoke to him at some length.

On 11 June 1754, McPherson took the stand in high court, as a witness for the prosecution. An excerpt from the court transcript of the prosecutor's declaration reads:

'...the Deponent rose from his Bed and followed him to the Door and then it was as he had been told that he said he was Serjeant Davies who had been murdered in the hill of Christie aboute near a year before and desired the Deponent to go to the place he pointed at where he would find his Bones...'

The terrified McPherson followed the spectre's instructions and found some skeletal remains. Not knowing what to do, he left the cadaver and fled. The court records report that the apparition returned to McPherson's home on a second occasion, an account corroborated by Isobel McHardie, the wife of McPherson's employer, who was also present. This time, the spectral sergeant asked McPherson to give his remains a proper burial and to contact his friend Donald Farquarson. And for good measure, Davies named his murderers.

Farquarson's court testimony asserts that he was initially sceptical of McPherson's story, but he allowed the young stranger to lead him to the remains, which he positively identified as those of his friend, the hair colour and tattered remnants of clothing being a definite match. For many reasons – the atmosphere of political tension, the reluctance to admit involvement in ghostly goings-on and the lack of any concrete evidence being but three – although the men fulfilled Davies's wish for a burial they agreed not to report the murder.

Many months later, the court heard, McPherson was sacked from his job and found himself employed instead by Duncan Clerk, one of the men Davies had fingered. During a row with Clerk, McPherson accused him of the murder, and was surprised when the man offered him twenty pounds to keep it quiet.

It was not long before village gossip reached the ears of the authorities, who brought the case to court, since, aside from the rather out-there ghost story, there was the more acceptable evidence of McPherson's hush-money (which had taken the very tangible form of a written and signed IOU from Clerk). Also there was the fact that two distinctive rings which had belonged to Davies were found on the fingers of Clerk's mistress. The authorities even found two witnesses to the murder. MacDonald and Clerk were eventually acquitted.

Ironically, it was not the legally ground-breaking ghost testimony which led to the acquittal, but a complex bout of hostility between the British prosecutor and the Scottish

defence advocate which started with one of the witnesses being hanged for an unrelated felony and ended with charges of intimidation which brought the trial to a close.

Davies may not have succeeded in having his murderers put away, but he achieved the distinction of being the first ghost to have his testimony tacitly admitted as legal evidence in court.

But does this story, or any other like it, prove the after-life hypothesis? Not necessarily. As John Spencer asserts: 'You could never absolutely say: this one proves that ghosts *must* be coming from beyond the grave. There is always another possibility. Albeit another paranormal possibility. But there *is* always another thought.'

There are certainly contemporary cases which purport to tell the tale of the dead revealing their secrets to the living, but more often these involve a medium or psychic acting as a go-between. There is, of course, something to be read into this trend – the business-like clairvoyant replacing the pleading spectre... A hint, perhaps, that the key to the mysteries of the paranormal lie with the percip-

ient? After all, the same kind of information seems to be coming through, albeit in a different way. Fashion and trend regarding what is acceptable seems to be in play here, but *acceptable to whom*? Either the deceased have mutually agreed that turning up as an apparition is oh-so-*passé* and that everybody who is anybody in the spirit world goes through a medium these days, or we have to look at the fact that the percipient is the common denominator.

There is no more or less proof to support the theory that information of the how-else-could-I-have-known-that? kind is received not from beyond the grave, but telepathically –

by thoughts somehow transferred from the mind of another *living* person. Davies's death, for instance, may not have been known to McPherson, but if he was indeed killed by MacDonald and Clerk, then we can be sure that there were at least two living people who knew the details of the murder.

Perhaps the figures 'seen' imparting information are actually hallucinations, a waking dream, a subconscious attempt by the human mind to rationalize a function that we don't accept or understand. In other words, we might be alarmed if we suddenly 'knew' something for no apparent reason, but if we perceive the information as being imparted to us by someone else – a ghost, or a religious vision, say – the whole experience fits in more comfortably with our belief systems.

Nowadays, it would appear that mediums – people who *do* accept the idea of suddenly receiving information from nowhere – form the majority of claimants. And, of course, the mediums who believe that their information comes from dead people absolutely perceive it that way. Those who don't, don't.

If we can gain better understanding of the human mind – the greatest mystery of all – we may yet find the key to comprehending a plethora of other enigmas.

'You believe in an afterlife, Scully?'
MULDER

*'Sure. But personally the jury's still
out on revenge from the grave'*
SCULLY

L ike Sergeant Arthur Davies, the fictional Howard
Graves of *Shadows* wanted legal justice exacted
upon his enemies. But he wasn't averse to getting
a little handy too, racking up an impressive body-count of
four in his quest to protect his mortal accomplice, Lauren
Kyte. However, there are few cases outside TV or movies
in which supernatural forces are fingered as the perpetra-
tors of injury or death.

A quick glance at claims of death or injury by supernatural causes reveals a clear trend: the older the case, the
more outlandish its claims. Go back a hundred-odd years,
for instance, and you'll find the 'Ghost of 50 Berkeley
Square' a London spectre which was allegedly responsible
for more than five deaths, three of which are unfortunately unchronicled. Go back another half decade or so to early
19th century Tennessee, and you'll find the story of the
Bell Witch, a malevolent unseen force which persecuted
the Bell family with an onslaught of bizarre pranks: slap-
ping, hair-pulling, choking and other unpleasant acts
which culminated with the fatal poisoning of the Bell
patriarch. Now go back further still, a few hundred years
at least, and behold the rather wonderful legend of 'The
Black Dog of Newgate'. There was this gentle academic,
see, who got locked up in the debtors jail with a bunch of
ruffians who got peckish one night and ate him. No,
honestly. And the next morning, do you know what the

guard found? The cell was empty, except for this enormous black dog, and the bloody remains of the academic's cell-mates. Oh and by the way, the black dog can still be seen, prowling in the shadows of Newgate.

Zip *forward* in time now, to the present day. Ah-ha, what have we here? A woman who claims to have been scratched on the arm by a poltergeist.

As a wonderful dramatic device and a rich compost for the seeds of glorious folklore, the homicidal ghost is worthy of a respectful salute. But it has no place or use in the serious study of ghostly phenomena. John Spencer observes: ' We've got cases of *something* picking up a four-wheeled truck and moving it across a field, and of picking up a sixteen ton concrete water tank and throwing it. Now, if you could do that, you could dismember a person. . . But it doesn't happen. . . I've got one case where someone bent down, and a chisel from his tool-box whizzed over and

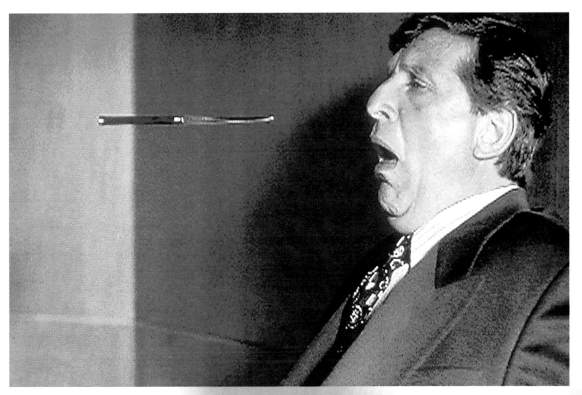

buried itself in the wall just above his head. But the point was, it buried itself *above* his head.'

'It's Howard Graves. He's alive'
SCULLY

'Not necessarily'
MULDER

Photograph taken by William Mumler of Moses Dow with unidentified extra

Despite the cliché, the camera lies with some regularity. Faults can create strange effects, double-exposures can superimpose one picture on to another, long exposures can faintly capture someone's image as they briefly move into and out of frame. Other times it is not the camera lying, but the person holding it.

Back when photography was in its infancy, the very concept of photographing anything at all was astonishing enough. There simply was not enough wide spread knowledge of the intricacies of photography for anyone to be in a position to question whether what they saw was real or not. Those with entrepreneurial spirit will always spot a chance to make a fast buck, so it was a safe bet that before long, someone, somewhere, would figure that bereavement plus technological naïveté equals rich pickings. If you were within travelling distance of Boston, Massachusetts in the 1860s, and you wanted one last picture of yourself with a now-departed loved one, William Mumler was your man – provided you had the cash to spare. At the zenith of Mumler's career he was fêted by the rich and famous, and boasted the patronage of President Lincoln's widow. Her custom provided Mumler with some very valuable credibility, not merely through her good name, but also by virtue of a cracking good yarn associated with her visit: she was said to have arrived wearing a veil and assuming a false identity, but – lo and behold – when she was presented with her portrait (complete with Abe lurking behind her), she broke down and 'fessed up. Mumler may have been a fine entrepreneur, but as a self-publicist, he was obviously quite pitiful. The Lincoln photograph clearly shows Mrs. L *sans veil*, thus destroying any credibility Mumler might have gained from the story by its intimation that he didn't know who he was photographing until the late President popped up on the print. He was eventually charged with fraud after being set up by the Mayor of New York.

Today, it seems crazy that the early anomalous photos could have been considered anything *but* bogus, but we must consider not just the inherent trust in photography, but the dearth of available knowledge on exactly how a photo could be faked.

It seems bizarre to us now to conceive that Sir Arthur Conan Doyle, the well-respected author and intellectual, could have been taken in by the 'Cottingley Fairies' affair. At the centre of this was a set of photographs taken by two young girls, purporting to show fairies at play. What had started in the summer of 1917 as a charming prank concocted by ten-year-old Frances Griffiths and her fifteen-year-old cousin Elsie Wright, came to public attention in the December 1920 issue of the *Strand Magazine*, in an article whose headline read: 'Fairies photographed. An epoch-making event described by A. Conan Doyle.' One of Doyle's major assertions was that two little girls would not have had the technical knowledge to fake such

Sir Arthur Conan Doyle: a classic example of how the will to believe can fool even the sharpest intellect

remarkable photographs. The girls had been quite astonished that so many adults had been convinced by their efforts – five photographs which in reality showed small cardboard fairies, beautifully drawn by Elsie and propped up with hatpins. Terrified of embarrassing those who had trusted them, the girls kept their secret for almost three quarters of a century before setting the record straight. Elsie said in 1986, 'The joke was to last two hours. It has lasted 70 years'.

Of course, awareness grew and today we are thoroughly savvy to visual trickery. All of us can watch *Jurassic Park* without becoming convinced that the

Top: Francis Griffiths with 'fairies' photographed by Elsie Wright at Cottingley Glen, West Yorkshire, July 1917

Below: The hoax continues. Cottingley Glen, August 1920

dinosaurs are back from extinction. Most of us can read the tabloids without baulking at the mock-ups of a bald Madonna ('how the star might look if she doesn't follow her trichologist's recent warning to kick the bleaching habit!') or a blood-spattered Nicole Simpson. Some of us can even check out the *Playboy* centrefold with full awareness that, on the day of the shoot, she might have had a face full of pimples and a huge bruise on her shin from walking into a coffee table.

Our savvy of photographic trickery has made us suspicious by nature. Says John Spencer: 'If someone just plonks a photograph down I don't think you can rely on it, no matter what it shows you. It has to be only part of the evidence. You have to consider the circumstances: if the story is a solid one and there's no obvious reason for faking.'

It usually stands that the most curious 'ghost' photos are accompanied by comments which include the phrase: 'and when the photo was developed. . .' In other words, the photographer thought he or she was snapping a normal scene, and the anomalous factor turned up on the print. This sometimes serves to lend the picture credibility, it can also make us more suspicious, particularly if the supposed original intent of the photo seems pointless i.e. 'I was just taking a picture of that empty staircase, and. . .' Yeah, right.

When there is a good story, on the other hand, the photo

'Old Nana's here'. Two-year-old Greg Sheldon Maxwell looking at the ghost of his great-grandmother. Or is it fogged film?

is often less distinct – which in itself seems to make it more believable, as we don't have to wrestle with the too-good-to-be-true factor. One of the most interesting recent pictures shows two-year-old Greg Maxwell gazing at a white mist. But it is the touching background story which makes the case more fascinating still. Greg's grandmother, Marina Jackson, wrote in a letter to the *Fortean Times*: 'About twelve months ago, he began saying "old Nanna's here", this being his name for my mother, who was no longer alive. We didn't take much notice of what Greg was saying until we saw this photo.' A fault in the film *could* have produced this effect, but the fact that Greg appears to be looking directly at the mist which was not visible to anyone else in the room, makes for a grand coincidence, at the very least.

Occasionally, a photo will turn up with a compelling story *and* a very clear 'spirit' image. The best known picture within this rare category is the 1959 photo taken by

Accidental double-exposure or back-seat-driving mother-in-law from beyond the grave

a Mrs. Mabel Chinery of Ipswich, Suffolk. The photo depicts Mabel's husband Jim in the driving seat of his car. Behind him is an old lady, who, claims Mrs. Chinery, looks exactly like her late mother. The photo was the last one taken on a roll of film which Mrs. Chinery had used mainly to photograph her mother's grave, and Mabel was certain that at the moment she took the picture, her husband was alone in the car. Both were shocked by

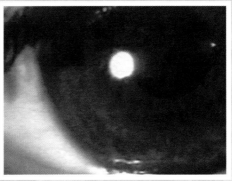

the photograph – so much so in Mabel's case that she had to take a week off work. Poignantly enough, Jim and his mother-in-law had apparently been close, and on the night before she died, she told him: 'Jim, you will never come to any harm. I shall still be with you.'

Mrs. Chinery's photograph was one of many put through rigorous computer analysis in 1984 by photographic experts Steve Gull and Tim Newton, who concluded that most of the photos they examined had quite rational explanations. Their main findings regarding the Chinery picture was that the light available in the car would have been unlikely to have caused such bright reflections on the old lady's glasses, and that she appeared to be illuminated by a different directional light source than the one present elsewhere. Moreover, they did not feel that the woman was in proportion, and concluded that the photo was likely to have been an accidental double exposure. However, the small matter of Mrs. Chinery's mother being dead anyway – double exposure or no – and the claims of another photographic expert, Bill Turner, mean that the case is far from being closed. Turner examined the photograph and also visited the location where it was taken, and eliminated the possibility of both double exposure and reflection. He says: 'I stake my reputation on the fact that the picture is genuine.' All of which goes to prove a saying that is well known in the paranormal field: wherever you find an expert, you'll find another expert who will tell you the opposite of what the first guy said.

Of course, double exposures *can* happen by accident, but a believer might argue that in the Chinery case, it would seem perhaps too remarkable a coincidence that the double exposure placed the old mum *perfectly* in the back seat of the car – her image might just as well have popped up above the car, balanced on the bonnet or smack dab on top of the image of Jim Chinery. But if you consider for a moment the sheer number of photos taken every year, the chances of a remarkable coincidence are pretty good. John Spencer cites as a fine example a picture taken of his wife when she was a baby. It shows the infant Anne Spencer reclining in her mother's arms, and apparently smoking a cigarette. Says John: 'It was a double exposure. There was another photo taken of someone smoking, and it just happens that the cigarette has come out right on Anne's mouth. It just shows you that pure bad luck can happen.' It is often the non-supernatural – such as the smoking baby

– which helps bring to light the more level-headed options in the spectrum of possibility.

Another fine example is the well-publicised British case of an elderly gentleman who collected his newly-developed snaps only to discover, to his horror, that all the photos he had taken were superimposed with scenes of rampant pornographic goings-on. It transpired that the film had been previously used by someone else. Through some strange twist of fate, the undeveloped roll had ended up being re-packaged in a sealed box along with a batch of brand-new films, and put on sale. As dismaying as the incident was for those involved (not only for the embarrassed man, but presumably also for the swingers who never got their prints back), the nature of it meant that there was an investigation and a solution. But had the strangers in the pictures not been sweaty, naked and doing the wild-thing, would the man have complained and demanded an explanation? If the anomalous figures had been fully clothed and standing serenely, would the man have taken them for ghosts? Muses Spencer: 'If the man had brought me a roll-full of ghost images, and I said to him, "Are you sure it's not double-exposed?", he would say to me, "But I bought this film sealed, from a reputable retailer." In other words, the case would have had every essential element of persuasiveness about it: a repeating pattern (the anomalous images appeared on almost every frame taken, ruling out many alternative explanations), a plainly sincere and innocent claimant, and no apparent explanation – given that it was only *since* this incident that the possibility of 're-cycled' film has been widely known.

With all sorts of new ways to capture images, we have all sorts of new ghost images. John Spencer recalls a wedding video captured on cam-corder which clearly showed the late father of the bride standing watching the happy proceedings, and predicts that with the proliferation of cam-corder ownership, this sort of anomaly will become more and more common. At present, though, it is still relatively rare, giving us some clue to just how much chaff gets cut away when you remove the possibility of double exposure and film faults.

Equally rare and interesting are images caught on security cameras – a medium which totally eradicates the scope for human error. Spencer encountered one such piece of footage, recorded on a camera monitoring the door of a provincial Conservative Club. He explains: 'A figure was seen approaching the door and the person who was working there though: "Oh, that will be nice, someone to talk to on a Saturday afternoon." He didn't turn up, so the guy went to the door, but there was no-one there. They reviewed the camera footage and you could see this person walk in. He doesn't come out again. But he definitely wasn't (in the building).' Additionally, Spencer says that there was something 'not quite right' about the figure itself. 'It's like he's only three quarters visible. . . He looks a bit iffy anyway.'

We have come a long way since the days of Mumler's spirit photographs and the Cottingley Fairies, but, as with every aspect of ghost phenomena, we still have more questions than answers. However, with our ever increasing technological know-how, this is one area in which we can reasonably hope that better understanding is just around the corner.

Bibliography
Sources and further reading

Books

Marvels and Mysteries of the Unexplained
Nigel Blundell and Alan Hall, McDonald and co.,
1988

Ghosts
Peter Brookesmith, Orbis, London, 1984

Hauntings
The Editors, Time-Life books, 1990

*Arthur C. Clarke's Chronicles of the Strange and
Mysterious*
John Fairley and Simon Welfare, William Collins
and Sons, 1987

The Ghost of Flight 401
John G. Fuller, Souvenir Press, 1975

I Saw a Ghost
Ben Noakes, Weidenfeld and Nicolson, 1986

Flim-Flam
James Randi, Prometheus Books, 1982

The Candle of Vision
George Russel, Macmillan and Co, 1918

The Encyclopedia of Ghosts and Spirits
John and Anne Spencer, Headline plc, 1993

Will you Survive after Death?
John and Anne Spencer, Imperia Books, 1995

Ghost Watching
John Spencer and Tony Wells, Virgin, 1994

Alien Worlds
Reuben Stone, Bookmart/Amazon publishing,
1993

Papers, Journals & Newspapers

Fortean Times (Issues 61-64)

X-File: Born Again

Case notes by Agent Dana Scully

It is difficult to weigh up the evidence in this case without being inexorably drawn to consider the theory of reincarnation. Michelle Bishop was born approximately nine months after the murder of Police Officer Charlie Morris, a man whose existence neither she nor her family were ever aware of.

Michelle's still unexplained presence at the deaths of two of Morris's former colleagues and the assault of a third would appear to transcend the realm of coincidence, as does the fact that Bishop was able to create a composite photograph which was positively identified as Officer Morris. Although Agent Mulder noted the presence of a photograph of Morris in close proximity to the scene of the first death, which he suggests that Michelle may have seen, I feel that this is an unlikely hypothesis, which in any event is certainly inefficient in explaining any of the other mysteries surrounding this case. Agent Mulder and I also disagree on the significance of Michelle's talent in the art of Origami (Japanese paper-folding), an unusual hobby at which Morris was particularly adept. However, neither of us can dismiss nor find plausible reason for our findings that, during the course of psychiatric treatment for various neuroses, Michelle had systematically disfigured a dozen dolls in a manner which exactly mirrored the mutilations suffered by Morris. In the light of our eventual discovery that Michelle's wounds had been inflicted post mortem, and that the cause of death was in fact drowning, Michelle's overpowering and irrational fear of water would appear to contribute to the weight of suggestive evidence.

REINCARNATION

s far as Mulder is concerned, the strange events which occur in *Born Again* are tantamount to evidence that Michelle Bishop, the disturbed little girl, is the reincarnation of murdered Police Officer Charlie Morris. And, try as she might, Agent Scully cannot find an alternative explanation.

Although Howard Gordon, *X-Files* writer and co-executive producer, liked the episode's theme of 'cosmic justice' – a theme Chris Carter has identified as running throughout the series – he says he was 'not overly happy' with *Born Again*. He feels that Scully didn't have a leg to stand on, so there were no questions for the viewer to ponder and hence the episode is 'ultimately not as interesting'.

Gordon, who his more of Scully than a Mulder, voices some of the arguments against reincarnation: 'The evidence is so scant. Everyone was either a chieftain or a princess. No-one was ever a dish-washer.' He also feels that claimed memories of violent death could 'possibly be a masking, or a metaphor for another trauma suffered. If you

think about it, dreams are incredibly powerful metaphors for things that are going on that we are unable to process consciously.'

On the subject of unexplained phenomena in general, he adds: 'It's intolerable, I think, for the mind not to know, and I think that's why people want an explanation. At some levels, I prefer the journey to the destination. I think the answers, especially when they are not supported, or when they are more the function of hope than empirical evidence, close one off to other possibilities.'

Howard Gordon is a rarity. When it comes to the paranormal, most of us find the journey uncomfortable without the security of preset ideas, and are, whether we realise it or not, are guilty of dogma to some degree. We are either believers or sceptics. Pay attention to how your mind processes what you are about to read.

'Do me a favour, Mulder, let me say it: reincarnation'
SCULLY
Born Again

Just one of the articles trying to get to the truth of Bridey Murphy's origins

In 1956, a book was published entitled *The Search For Bridey Murphy*. It was written by a Colorado hypnotherapist called Morey Bernstein and was about hypnotherapy sessions he conducted with a woman known as Ruth Simmons (the pseudonym of Virginia Tighe). According to the book, under hypnosis Mrs. Tighe regressed to a past life in 19th century Ireland. She spoke in a thick Irish brogue and described detailed vignettes of lower-class daily life. She named grocers and priests, villagers and relatives, she even danced a jig. When brought out of hypnosis, Mrs. Tighe could not say from where she had received her information if not from a past life. The book seemed to be an astounding document in support of reincarnation.

The Search For Bridey Murphy became a bestseller. A movie was made. People started throwing 'Come as You

Were' parties. A boy from Shaunee, Oklahoma, shot and killed himself, leaving a note which read: 'They say curiosity kills a cat and I'm very curious about this Bridey Murphy story so I'm going to investigate in person.' Newspapers competed with each other to prove or disprove Mrs. Tighe's facts. Some of her assertions were disproved, but others, including the obscure detail of the name of her grocer, were correct.

And that's when it all got complicated. The contention was that, even if the facts were true, she might have learned them some other way. The search became not for Bridey Murphy, but for the source of Bridey Murphy. More than one turned up, including a childhood neighbour of Tighe's who's maiden name was Bridie Murphy, and Tighe's aunt, Marie Burns, who had lived with her, and was, according to the *Chicago American* newspaper, 'as Irish as the lakes of Kilkenny'. However, Mrs. Burns was born in New York of Scottish-Irish descent and, as Mr. Bernstein writes in his rebuttal, 'You could say she was as Irish as the lakes of Kilkenny, inasmuch as *there are no lakes in Kilkenny*'.

A 19th Century Tibetan Wheel of Life

'Reincarnation is a basic tenet of many of the world's major religions'
MULDER

Reincarnation just keeps popping up. Over the millennia, various groups of ancient Greeks, Egyptians, Christians, Jews, Muslims, Hindus, Native Americans and Africans have all believed in some form of reincarnation. The Druids would even lend money with the stipulation that it be paid back in a future incarnation.

Many Westerners think of only one religion when they think of reincarnation: Buddhism. There are myriad branches of Buddhism, but the one most associated with (even founded on) reincarnation is Tibetan Buddhism. Like other forms of the religion, it believes that you keep being reincarnated, spinning the wheel of life, if you will, until you finally become enlightened and achieve Nirvana. Then it's game over, but in a good way.

'Which leaves us where?'
SCULLY

'One short step away from proving the pre-existence of the human soul'
MULDER

There is undoubtedly a rebuttal to Morey Bernstein's rebuttal of the Chicago American's rebuttal. This is the way debates about subjects like reincarnation tend to go: into ever tightening spirals of argument. And, at the base of that spiral is a single word – usually 'soul'. The problem is, human beings are so good at rationalizing that we often forget that we are covering up for some irrational belief. And, just in case we do remember, we invented a fall-back belief called 'science'.

Science contends that unless you can predict how something will behave under set conditions, then you cannot define what that something is. You can define what it is not, but that does not help very much. Not for nothing is 'category' the Greek word for cage. You must be able to box and label your quarry for it to exist.

People who study the paranormal have been wrestling

with the problem of proof for years. Many of the most respected ones have now adopted 'scientific techniques' to try to earn the respect of their lab-coated faculty cousins. There are 'double blind' ESP (extra-sensory perception) tests and cross-referenced computer data bases of reincarnation cases. And yet, every time their neatly typed reports are presented, they are greeted with a chorus of 'yeah, but. . .'.

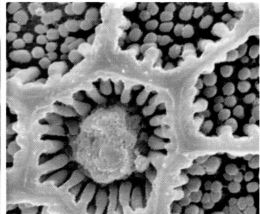

Should we eschew science and believe everything,? Worship science and deny all? Of course not. But we should realise nothing, including science, is as objective as it seems.

And so, stripped of the intellectual life preserver of 'pure' science, we now wade into the philosophical quagmire that is the reincarnation debate. . .

'Why is it still so hard for you to believe. . . even when all the evidence suggests extraordinary phenomena?'
MULDER

D r. Ian Stevenson, professor of psychiatry and neurology, founder of the Department of Parapsychology at the University of Virginia, is the godfather of 'scientific' reincarnation research. Since 1960, he has overseen thousands of individual case reports. The following is part of his list of 'types of evidence for which reincarnation is invoked as an explanation', combined with some counter–arguments:

'Inequities in the Distribution of Human Talent' (i.e. Pesky child musical prodigies)

Reincarnationists: The kid got the 'soul' of Mozart or Kurt Cobain, or someone.

Counter: Hey, some people are smarter than others.

'Statements made by Sensitives as to the Existence of a Person as Another Person in a Previous Life'
(i.e. A medium tells you who you used to be)

Reincarnationists: Not particularly valuable, but sometimes includes surprisingly accurate hard-to-come-by information about a dead person. Could be the result of ESP, though. (Reincarnation debates get tangled because many proponents also believe in other paranormal phenomena. This *really* bugs science people.)

Counter: They made it up.

'Special Predilections or Fears Possibly Related to Former Incarnations'
(i.e. In *Born Again*, Michelle liked origami, just like Charlie, and was afraid of water)

Reincarnationists: Proves survival of memory and personality.

Counter: Coincidence.

'Surviving Memories of a Past Life'
This is the big one and is composed of two sections: past life hypnotic regression, like that which Mulder recommends, and spontaneous memories.

Professor Stevenson is not all that interested in this last type but it is the sort most Westerners are familiar with and is worth a look.

'On the count of five, tell me where you are now? One. . . two. . . three. . . four. . . five. . . '

DOCTOR SPITZ

Since Bridey Murphy, hypnotism has been the vehicle of choice for those wanting to visit their past lives. Not everybody can be hypnotized and some scientists still claim the whole thing is a scam. It is uncertain what hypnosis actually is.

Most agree that some hypnotized people can be extremely suggestible, to the point of not feeling pain during an operation. Some can also be regressed to an earlier life. The first hurdle for sceptics is the words that get them there. In the Bridey Murphy case, Mrs. Tighe was sent back with the phrase: 'Go to some other place in some other time.' Many would say that would be enough to discount the entire regression. Due to extreme suggestibility, Mrs. Tighe might try to make up 'some other place in some other time' to try to satisfy her hypnotherapist's request.

The next question is: from where does she get that information?

'Sometimes. . . looking for the extreme possibility makes you blind to the probable explanation in front of you. . . This is where Michelle Bishop saw that face'

SCULLY

(pointing to a picture of Charlie Morris at the police station)

Cryptomnesia (literally, 'hidden memory') is a theory that says everything we see, hear, touch, smell and taste we remember – even if we don't remember that we remembered it. And many of our memories appear to be stored in such a way that we cannot access them under normal states of consciousness. A police witness who vaguely remembers seeing a car at the scene of a crime, can, under hypnosis, often recall perfectly the colour, make, model and licence plate number.

But what if the question asked is not so specific? A classic example of cryptomnesia was described by a Canadian

psychologist who put a patient into hypnotic regression. It ended with the patient writing lengthy passages in a strange language. When conscious again, he had no idea what he had written or from where his knowledge of the language had come. The psychologist took the writing to various linguists and finally identified it as Oscan, a precursor to Latin. It turned out, after much investigation, that years earlier the patient had been doing research in a library and sat next to a guy who had a book open to a page featuring an ancient Oscan curse. Just one look was all it took.

Regressions, then, may be just a mental re-jigging of memories – novels, actual events, movies, whatever – and cryptomnesia has been claimed to be at the bottom of quite a few famous regression cases. It is easy to remedy: all you have to do is ask the patients, under hypnosis, from where they are getting the information. Usually, they can name the source. Many sceptics will immediately dismiss cases in which this has not been done.

'The inconclusive results of Michelle's past-life regression do not shake my basic belief in hypnosis as a tool for psychological healing. Whether or not it offers us definitive proof of previous lifetimes is another matter'
MULDER'S FIELD JOURNAL

Which brings us back to the other type of memory, the Stevenson speciality, spontaneous memories.

'She's not like other girls, Agent Scully'
CYNTHIA

Every now and then, a little kid pops up who knows things they should not. Dr. Stevenson has flown all over the world to supervise the questioning and referencing of reincarnation cases. He uses scientific techniques and long words and is generally considered to be *the* expert.

The cases fall into a regular pattern. A kid of about two acts oddly and uses his first few words to say he is actually somebody else. The strongest 'memories' are of the (usually violent) way in which he died in a previous life. Others might include his name, where he lived, what he did, and details of his family. The kid's memories peak at about five- or six-years-old then start to disappear. As in (the fictional) Michelle Bishop's case, by ten they are mostly forgotten.

Spontaneous memory cases usually occur in cultures where belief in reincarnation is strong, but there have been plenty of Western cases too.

Since this is Stevenson's strongest 'type of evidence for which reincarnation is invoked as an explanation', let us now shift the focus to other things that might be happening and the recreationist's counter–argument:

Cryptomnesia

As discussed, it could be just things the kid picked up unconsciously. Most cases of spontaneous memory reincarnation happen within a couple of years and within 15 miles of the place where the dead guy lived.

Counter: In cases of children as young as two or three, it is possible to run through their past and determine what they have or have not been exposed to.

Fraud

Many of the kids live in poor families and claim to come from rich ones. Some parents could have coached the kids for financial gain.

Can the soul take over a body ?

Counter: Yes, it happens, but there are definitely cases where the poor families are intimidated by their rich 'relatives' and so hesitate to approach them at all. Also, kids that young cannot always be relied upon to accept 'coaching'.

Inherited memory

A favourite of Carl Jung. This claims that we inherit memory along with genetic components of our personality.

Counter: OK, prove it.

ESP, precognition, retrocognition

These claim that a psychically sensitive child might have picked up the stories tele-pathically from the people around him, or even from his mother while in the womb.

Counter: Does not account for cases where the families of the deceased and the reincar-nate have no connection and does not account for the kid not showing other signs of psychic abilities.

The telekinetic powers used by Michelle in *The X-Files* episode are not typical of reincarnation and might lead one to conclude it was actually:

Possession

Instead of a soul taking over the embryo, how about a spirit taking over the body?

Counter: So why does it always fade away before the kid turns ten?

Still following? How about two general

anti-recreationist arguments (basically scientifically-based 'yeah buts'), from the standard bearer (and very funny writer) of Sceptical Reincarnation Inquiry, Professor Paul Edwards. Followed, of course, by counter arguments:

The Evolution Question

If you believe that humans become humans again, what about the era, millions of years ago, when we were all swinging from trees? And how does reincarnation deal with the exploding population – how do you explain where all the new souls are coming from? And what about before the Big Bang when there was no life at all?

Counter: Perhaps this dimension is but one of many.

The 'Physicality' Question

Everybody knows that your 'physicality' affects your mind. In the extreme, brain damage makes you a different person. How could you still be the same person, with the same memories, after you leave one brain and enter a completely different one?

Counter: Our 'mind' or 'consciousness' or whatever, is not physically dependent, as proven with out-of-body experiences.

What you have just read are the bare bones of the incomplete skeleton of the recreation debate. Some very smart people have spent a lot of time thinking about this. Debate has not always been gentlemanly, but occasionally it has been very funny. Prof. Edwards, a sceptic, once reviewed a recreationist's work with the lines:

> 'Dr. Goldberg in his modesty has not realised that he
> himself constitutes the best evidence for reincarnation.
> His comic gifts are quite in the same league as Fatty
> Arbuckle and Ben Turpin. I do not for a moment believe
> that such a stupendous talent can be explained by ordi-
> nary genetics. The only adequate explanation would be in
> terms of one or more previous lives of assiduous labour
> or else the hand of God.'

Ouch.

All of which brings us back, appropriately, to the beginning. If you were paying attention to your thought processes as you read this, you probably noticed a mental 'trying on' of ideas and concepts. Some seemed to fit quite well and were flattering to thoughts you already had on the subject. Some were a new style that just might work. Some sucked.

Your brain, is reasonably hardwired to help you deal with the mass of information flooding in every day and has adopted concepts that reaffirmed established beliefs and ignored those that could potentially cause trouble. You remembered facts that could one day help you back up an argument and tried to discredit those that did not 'make sense'. This is normal. This is healthy. This is what everybody does all the time. Everybody including those who study paranormal phenomena. Whether we're using religion, science or a sort of à la carte belief in some aspects of the supernatural as a template, we are all thinking the same way. And all of us are struggling side by side on the journey towards the truth.

'End of field journal. 19 April 1994.
Agents of record: Fox Mulder and
Dana Scully
Status: Unexplained'

Bibliography
Sources and further reading

Books

The Search For Bridey Murphy
Morey Bernstein, Bantam Books, London, 1990

The Wheel of Life
John Blofeld, Shambala, Berkeley, CA, 1972

Psychic Voyages
The Editors, Time Life Books, 1990

*The Evidence for Survival from Claimed
Memories of Former Incarnations*
Ian Stevenson, M.C. Peto, Surrey, 1978

*Reincarnation: Field Studies and Theoretical
Issues*
Ian Stevenson (from the *Handbook of
Parapsychology*, McFarland & Company,
Fesserson, North Carolina, 1986)

Twenty cases Suggestive of Reincarnation
Ian Stevenson, University Press of Virginia,
Charlottesville, 1992

The People's Almanac
David Wallechinsky and Irving Wallace,
Doubleday, New York, 1975

The Tibetan Book of the Dead
W.Y. Evans-Wentz (ed), Oxford University Press,
1957

Mind Out of Time
Ian Wilson, 1981

Papers, Journals & Newspapers

The Case Against Reincarnation
(4 part series)
Paul Edwards; *Free Inquiry*; Buffalo, New York,
Autumn 1986, Winter 1986/87, Spring 1987,
Summer 1987

*Are Past-Life Regressions Evidence of
Reincarnation?'*
Melvin Harris; *Free Inquiry*; Buffalo, New York,
Autumn, 1986

*Empirical Evidence for Reincarnation:
Examining Stevenson's 'Most Impressive' Case*
Leonard Angel; *The Skeptical Inquirer;* Buffalo
New York, Autumn, 1994

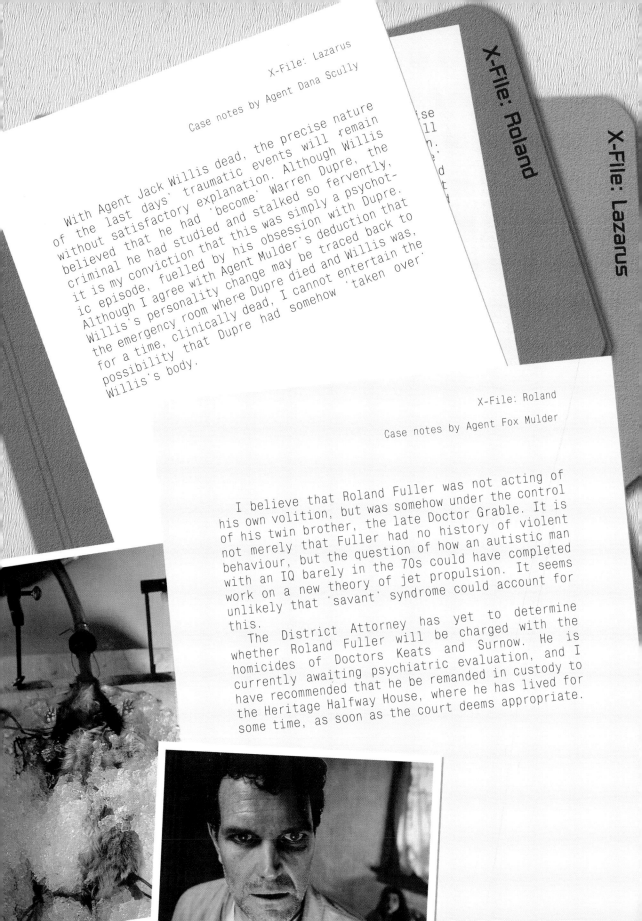

With Agent Jack Willis dead, the precise nature of the last days' traumatic events will remain without satisfactory explanation. Although Willis believed that he had 'become' Warren Dupre, the criminal he had studied and stalked so fervently, it is my conviction that this was simply a psychotic episode, fuelled by his obsession with Dupre. Although I agree with Agent Mulder's deduction that Willis's personality change may be traced back to the emergency room where Dupre died and Willis was, for a time, clinically dead, I cannot entertain the possibility that Dupre had somehow 'taken over' Willis's body.

I believe that Roland Fuller was not acting of his own volition, but was somehow under the control of his twin brother, the late Doctor Grable. It is not merely that Fuller had no history of violent behaviour, but the question of how an autistic man with an IQ barely in the 70s could have completed work on a new theory of jet propulsion. It seems unlikely that 'savant' syndrome could account for this.

The District Attorney has yet to determine whether Roland Fuller will be charged with the homicides of Doctors Keats and Surnow. He is currently awaiting psychiatric evaluation, and I have recommended that he be remanded in custody to the Heritage Halfway House, where he has lived for some time, as soon as the court deems appropriate.

THE BORROWERS

Dramatically, *Lazarus* and *Roland* are two very different episodes. But with regard to phenomena, they are essentially two approaches to the same question: Can the human spirit 'take over' a solid form belonging to someone else?

In *Roland*, it appears that the titular autistic janitor is being controlled by Doctor Arthur Grable, his late twin brother, whose brain has been cryonically preserved. In *Lazarus* (a brilliant study in carefully measured ambiguity) we must wonder whether Scully's old flame, Agent Willis, is delusional and simply believes that he has become Warren Dupré, the criminal he long sought to capture, or as Mulder suspects, whether something inexplicable happened in the emergency room where Dupré and Willis struggled for their lives? As Mulder puts it, two men died and one came back. . . but which one?

The X-Files co-executive producer Howard Gordon, who co-wrote *Lazarus*, notes: 'What was interesting here was the premise of someone who had been obsessed with a criminal and killed that criminal and took on his personality. And again, was that merely a psychotic episode? Or is there such a thing as a soul, and can it be transferred at that brief moment of death that everyone is so fascinated by?'

In 399 BC, Socrates, the father of philosophy, was executed by poisoning for his neglect of the gods. Plato recounts in his writings *Phaedus* that Socrates gaily swigged the deadly brew of hemlock because he believed that death was merely 'the release of the soul from the chains of the body' and he had spent much of his final day trying to convince his companions of this. Cebes, for one, was not so optimistic, pointing out: 'It requires a great deal of argument and many proofs to show that when the man is dead, his soul yet exists, and has any force or intelligence.' Hardly the most tactful comment he could have made under the circumstances, but a philosopher's gotta do what a philosopher's gotta do. And, let's face it, he had a point.

Two thousand, three hundred and ninety-four years later, mankind is no closer to settling the debate about whether the psyche can exist without the mortal body.

Rationalists are still waiting for proof. But, tens of thousands of people who have had near-death or out-of-body experiences claim to have experienced consciousness without physical presence.

In *A Farewell to Arms*, Ernest Hemingway describes his own experience on the Italian front, through the character Frederic Henry:

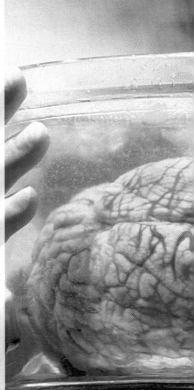

'I felt myself rush bodily out of myself and out and out and out and all the time bodily in the wind. I went out swiftly, all of myself, and I knew that I was dead and that it had all been a mistake to think you just died.'

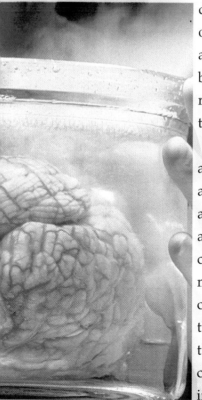

Believers in cryonics – like Doctor Arthur Grable – are so sure of the survival of the soul that they intend to wait in limbo until science has the know-how to make their bodies fit for use again, and bring them back. Cryonics is a dubious science the success of which depends on many permutations. Can the soul survive death? Can it re-enter the body? Will science be able to 'fix' dead and diseased bodies? Re-animate them? Clone new ones for all those cheapskates like Dr. Grable who have gone for the bargain 'neuro' (brain/head-only) option?

Proponents of cryonics often point to experiments on hamsters and dogs, in which the animals were cooled to just above freezing, their blood drained and replaced with a glycerol solution designed to prevent cell-damage at low temperatures, and held in suspended animation. These animals were successfully brought back to life. While this does not prove the possibility of bodily resurrection, (the animals were healthy and alive before they hit the chiller) it raises some interesting questions.

The animals' bodies were, for a time, entirely uninhabitable and disfunctional, so we must assume from what we know about death, that their conscious minds were not merely switched off, but dislocated from their bodies. When the bodies were reanimated, the 'spirits' of the animals came back. But what happened in between? And, hey – how

Could a human brain function without the body?

can we tell whether the 'souls' of the reanimated dogs and hamsters were the same ones that had inhabited the bodies before?

Just kidding, of course. Or maybe not. The idea of the body as something which can be borrowed, controlled or

A Cryonics experiment being conducted on a hamster in a laboratory in Berkeley, California

taken over by someone other than its rightful owner has been around since the dawn of time. It exists in the margins of belief systems and close to the heart of fiction the world over.

Many ancient cultural traditions divide the concept into 'good' and 'bad' possessions, and although in the West we don't share a common religious view on the subject, our attitudes seem just as clearly delineated – although, apparently, more by manners than anything else. We are all quite chuffed when Whoopi Goldberg lends her body to Patrick Swayze for one last smooch with Demi Moore in *Ghost*. But the idea that Warren Dupré may have challenged Jack Willis to a grim after-life version of musical chairs (last one back to the body is out) is scary. Ditto the possibility that Doctor Grable is forcing his hapless twin to do his dirty work.

Outside fiction, of course, things are rarely black and white, and the big question for us in the West is not whether possession is bad or good, but whether it is possible.

'Apparently in the process of dying there's a window of time during which the body is vulnerable'

Doctor Varnes

Lazarus

In India, 19 July 1985, a 17-year-old girl named Sumitra lay dead, her grieving family making preparations for her funeral. The shock of her sudden return to life was followed by puzzlement and dismay. She demanded to be called Shiva, and insisted that she did not remember anyone.

Sumitra – now claiming to be Shiva – said that she recalled being hit on the head with a brick during a family dispute, and that the next thing she knew, she had woken up in the body of Sumitra.

According to police records, Shiva was a 22-year-old woman who had died two months earlier, under suspicious circumstances. Her body had been found on a railway line, and despite severe unexplained head injuries, her husband's parents had claimed that she committed suicide. She had been cremated. Now it appeared that she was back.

'Reunited' with Shiva's family, Sumitra recognised relatives, friends and neighbours, places, belongings and items of clothing, despite the odd trick set up to test her. She also wrote letters in Shiva's handwriting and style – especially strange considering that Sumitra had been entirely illiterate.

In India, transmigration of the soul (though more usually in the form of re-incarnation) is a widely accepted belief and, rather sadly for Sumitra's family, Shiva's family welcomed her into their home and their lives, convinced that she was their own daughter, back from the dead.

'People die. They go away. . . and they're not supposed to come back'
ROLAND

MARY LURANCY VENNUM.

The extraordinary case of
Lurancy Vennum

While there is the possibility in cases like Shiva's and (the fictional) Agent Willis's that an 'unoccupied' body is ripe for take over – and the equal possibility that returning from a period of clinical death could trigger various unexplained psychoses – there are plenty of incidents without this element. In these, however, the 'take over' seems to be more temporary.

The classic example is 'The Watseka Wonder', chronicled in 1879 by physician E. Winchester Stevens, of Watseka, Illinois. Dr. Stevens first examined Lurancy Vennum when she was 14-years-old. She'd been suffering from fits for a year (possibly due to epilepsy) but was now showing signs of multiple personality disorder and claiming that she had spoken with the dead.

Under hypnosis, Lurancy told Dr. Stevens that an angel named Mary Roff wanted to come to her instead and had promised her freedom from 'the evil spirits'. The next day, she told her family that she *was* Mary Roff, and said that she was homesick.

Dr. Stevens, it turned out, had known the real Mary Roff. She had lived most of her life in Watseka and died in 1865, at the age of 18. It also transpired that the Vennums had lived next door to the Roffs for a short while in 1871.

In an act which seems extremely bizarre by today's standards of psychiatric practice, Dr. Stevens contacted the Roffs and told them about Lurancy's claims. Mary's mother and sister came to visit. They were adamant that they had never met Lurancy (although this seems strange considering that they had been neighbours), but nevertheless Lurancy recongnized them right away, weeping with joy and calling out the pet names that Mary had given them. When they left, she was inconsolable and begged to be allowed to go 'home'.

In an even stranger twist, an arrangement was made to fulfil her wish. Lurancy moved in with the Roffs for three months and ten days, during which time her numerous recollections convinced the Roffs that she was definitely their Mary.

The stay ended when 'Mary' burst into tears and told Mrs. Roff that Lurancy was coming back. She then looked frantically around the room and asked: 'Where am I? I was never here before.'

Lurancy returned to her own home and was not troubled by any further psychological problems, except that she would sometimes visit the Roffs, during which times 'Mary' would 'come back'.

Figure III

Psychic art:
Fred Thompson was no artist but claimed he was being compelled to paint. His sketches look remarkably similar to paintings by the dead artist Robert Gifford

Figure III

'But look. . . all these entries. . . Someone's been continuing to work on this for six months since he died'
MULDER

Figure IV

A third category of apparent 'possessions' seem to be an even less exclusive arrangement, not unlike Roland's situation – the personality of the original owner remains, but they periodically seem to be compelled to do someone else's will.

In the winter of 1907, a shy goldsmith named Frederick L. Thompson was referred to Professor James H. Hyslop, the head of the American Society for Psychical Research. Since the summer of 1905, he had felt an urge to paint, although he had never been interested in art. He turned out to be pretty good, but he always felt that the subjects he was compelled to paint were not his choice. Moreover, he said he would often black out and wake to find paintings completed that he could not remember executing.

Thompson became convinced that he was under the mental sway of Robert Swain Gifford, a fairly well-known landscape artist whom he had once met briefly. In 1906, Thompson went to an art gallery to check out Gifford's work (apparently for the first time) and was thoroughly spooked to learn that the painter had died the previous summer – exactly when his strange urges had begun. He claimed that he had heard a voice inside his head say: 'You see what I have done? Can you not take up and finish my work?'

Hyslop's initial reaction was that Thompson was 'demented', but his artistic skill and output increased, and he enjoyed some success. Many people compared his work to Gifford's.

'You believe he's predisposed to this kind of psychotic episode'
MULDER

'I believe it's a long way from saying Jack had a near death experience to saying his body has been inhabited by Warren Dupré'
SCULLY

These cases are hard to explain. At face value, they seem supernatural, but Howard Gordon is just one of many who feel that cases suggestive of possession are more likely to be psychiatric in origin. 'I believe there probably are physiological explanations for these extraordinary perceptions. . . Having experimented myself with a number of hallucinogens I know that the mind is capable of great imagination when given enough opportunity.'

Indeed, Scully was bang-on in her intimation that mental disturbance can cause very unconventional behaviour.

SCHIZOPHRENIA

Outlandish claims – and a belief that they are true – are a common symptom of mental illness and, without a doubt,

some cases of 'spirit possession' can easily be attributed to insanity. Then again, you have to admire the sheer balls of psychologist William James, who posited that some cases of insanity could be put down to spirit possession.

MULTIPLE PERSONALITY DISORDER

Although popular fodder for drama, this condition is rare – roughly 200 accounts of it have been published in international medical literature during the last 90 years.

The syndrome first came to the public's attention in 1957, courtesy of psychiatrists Corbett Thigpen and Hervey Cleckley whose bestseller *The Three Faces of Eve* –

later to become a movie – detailed their involvement with a patient named Eve White. A couple of decades later, the public's morbid appetite for real-life tales of psychosis was given a new lease of life by another page-and-screen offering: *Sybil*, the story of a woman whose mental smorgasbord of 16 personalities and backstory of savage abuse in her childhood, made the story of Eve look like something by Enid Blyton.

Abuse and trauma appear to have played a role in many cases of multiple personality, but not all. And it is still not a clearly delineated syndrome. It has been variously interpreted as psychotic role-playing in order to attract attention, an 'eruption' of the id – the part of the personality thought to control the 'base' emotions (sex–drive, hedonism, anger) - and as a particularly extreme example of:

DISSOCIATED PERSONALITY

Typically, 'dissociation' is a mental safety mechanism: something is too much to cope with, you become convinced that you are no longer you, and – hey presto – the trauma is no longer yours.

Victims of violence or abuse often experience a mild form of dissociation, hence the commonly heard claim: 'I felt like it was happening to someone else.' But if psychosis also comes into play, the sufferer ceases to be aware that they are *not* someone else.

Psychologist Dr. Thelma Moss recorded a case of a woman who believed that she was the Virgin Mary. The sad fact soon emerged that the disturbed woman had only turned into the Virgin Mary when her husband had returned from two years service in Vietnam, no doubt expecting a resumption of his conjugal rights.

Any of the above conditions could conceivably be mistaken for possession, but we are still left with the problem of knowledge that could not be acquired naturally – the same stumbling block we hit in cases suggestive of reincarnation.

As detailed in the *Reincarnation* chapter there are truckloads of alternative theories. On the rational side, there's fraud and cryptomnesia (Scully would no doubt have entertained the possibility that Roland, during his janitorial shifts, could have subconsciously absorbed Doctor Grable's computer pass-code and calculations. His natural mathematic aptitude could have done the rest). But there are elements of many cases which do not fit easily into either theory. For instance, Sumitra knew obscure and verified details of Shiva's death that had not been released to the media. Instant literacy is also difficult to account for.

There is also wish fulfilment. The families of Shiva and Mary Roff wanted very much to believe that their loved ones had come back. If we also take into consideration the simple human desire for proof of life after death, it is not hard to see how much the people involved had invested in their perceptions. And not impossible that the 'possessed' are sometimes subtly given a little help and encouragement in 'recognising' people and things and 'reporting' information.

Sceptic James Randi has made definitive studies of psychic readings which prove that the average person, when asked by a 'medium' whether they know someone called, say, 'Ann', will not give a straightforward reply, but will try to help the medium to be right. They will rack their brains, searching for a distant relative, anyone. They will suggest variations – Anastasia, Arnie, Mr. Anderson. They will do anything but break the fragile bubble of their own hope that there is something beyond the natural world. And, as with reincarnation, once we get into the paranormal options, all we can learn is that there are lots and lots of possibilities (channelling, mediumship, a 'collective memory databank') for which there is just as much definitive proof as there is for the phenomena of possession – i.e. none.

British psychologist Alan Gauld, who studied the Thompson/Gifford case, suggested Super-ESP, a phrase he coined to describe a potent concoction of telepathy, clairvoyance, precognition and retrocognition. He applied it to the case, and unsurprisingly, discovered that it fit very well indeed – but then, he wasn't exactly hedging his bets.

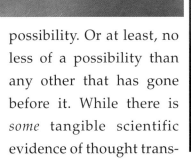

If you can dream up a phenomenon, bingo – it's a possibility. Or at least, no less of a possibility than any other that has gone before it. While there is *some* tangible scientific evidence of thought transference between the minds of living people, the question of contact with the dead remains unanswered and is, for now, an intellectual free-for-all.

'You are the spaceship. . .'
MULDER, HOLDING A REMOTE-CONTROLLED TOY

'Who. . . Who works the control?'
ROLAND

The counter-arguments against possession are not based on any proof that the soul does not survive death – there is none – but mostly on the infinite mysteries and possibilities of the human subconscious. So where does it leave us when we remove the human from the equation?

In December 1984, in Cheshire, Ken Webster and his girlfriend Debbie Oakes found a message of unknown origin on the screen of the BBC microcomputer they had borrowed from the school where Ken was a teacher. It appeared to be written in 16th century English, and was signed 'Thomas Harden', and turned out to be the first of over 300 missives.

Harden claimed to have lived in Ken and Debbie's cottage some 400 years earlier, and his messages appeared on every one of the 12 different computers that Ken borrowed.

Hoaxing was ruled out. Besides the fact that Harden was able to respond swiftly to questions left on file, the messages continued to appear even when independent investigators provided their own computer and sealed it in a locked room of the cottage.

The texts were studied by Peter Trinder, a linguist, who pronounced them entirely consistent with the claimed era, and noted that of the 2,877 different words used, 121 had never previously been recorded anywhere before. Trinder felt that it was extremely unlikely that, even if a hoaxer had been able to somehow feed the messages into the computers, they could have found and used the little-known linguistic details in such a fluid and appropriate fashion. In his words: 'The amount of effort involved in the process beggars belief.'

This is by no means an isolated story. There have been enough of its kind to merit the existence of a New York-based organisation which exclusively logs cases of 'possessed' computers.

This twist leaves us in an interesting position. Since computers are not sentient, we do not have the options of psychosis, crytomnesia or ESP. Even if we bring in to consideration the people sharing their homes with the computers, we are none the wiser. Certainly there has been some suggestive evidence that the human mind can influence electricity and machinery, but there has been no proof that anyone can produce a single character of type, let alone a lengthy message, on a computer screen by mind alone.

In these cases, the possibility of genuine spirit intervention is far harder to ignore. That Socrates was a smart guy. Who knows, maybe he had it right after all.

Bibliography
Sources and futher reading

Books

Souls on Ice: Cryo Science
Paul Bagne and Nancy Lucas, Omni, October 1986

Search for the Soul
The Editors, Time Life Books, 1989

Mediumship and Survival
Alan Gauld, Granada, London, 1982

Reincarnation: The Evidence
Liz Hodgkinson, Piatkus, 1989

Contact with the Other World
James H. Hyslop, The Century Co, New York, 1919

The Probability of the Impossible
Dr. Thelma Moss, Paladin, 1974

Flim Flam!
James Randi, Prometheus Books, 1982

Will You Survive After Death?
John and Anne Spencer, Imperia Books, 1995

The Nature of Things
Lyall Watson, Hodder and Stoughton, 1990

The Vertical Plane
K. Webster, Grafton, London, 1989

Papers, Journals & Newspapers

Deception and Self-deception in Cases of the Re-incarnation Type
Journal of the American Society for Psychical Research, January 1988, Ian Stevenson,
Satwant Paricha and Goodwin Samaratne

Love, Telepathy, Survival
Journal of the American Society for Psychical Research, April 1975, James Wheatley

Fortean Times

The Mind-Body Problem
Scientific American, January 1981, Jerry A. Fodor

Scientists In Search Of The Soul
Science Digest Vol 9, issue 7

The Unexplained,
Vol II issue 122, Orbis, London 1983

X-File: Beyond The Sea

Case notes by Agent Dana Scully

Although the information provided by Luther Lee
Boggs resulted in the resolution of the kidnapping
case, the authorities remained steady in their
refusal to grant him a stay of execution, and his
death sentence was carried out yesterday.

Agent Mulder continues to speculate that Boggs
obtained his information by conventional means,
and that his claims of 'channelling', telepathy and
other supernatural abilities were merely a ruse to
conceal his complicity in ongoing criminal activity and an attempt to secure himself a deal.
Despite a number of elements which remain extremely difficult to rationalize, I must concede that
this is the only reasonable conclusion that can be
drawn.

...ed by Luther
...tion of the
...s remained
...him a stay
...tence was

...late that
...conven-
...of 'chan-
...rnatural
...ceal his
...ity and
...Despite
...tremely
...de that
...n that

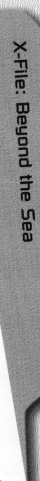

BEYOND THE FIVE SENSES

In one of the first season's finest, most resonant and disturbing hours, *Beyond the Sea* draws Mulder and Scully into a web of uncertainty.

Death row inmate Luther Lee Boggs claims that his extra-sensory abilities have given him insight into the whereabouts of two kidnap victims whose lives are in mortal danger. For once, Mulder takes the role of the sceptic, convinced that Boggs is merely scamming for a stay of execution. Scully, meanwhile, vulnerable after the sudden death of her father, finds his pronouncements to be chillingly accurate.

Boggs appears, to all intents and purposes, to have access to an extensive wardrobe of psychic endowments. Besides his claimed ability to 'channel', it appears that he is also able to 'tune in' to events taking place elsewhere, to accurately foretell the future, and to scavenge information from the minds of the living – mainly the haunted Scully.

Glen Morgan, who co-wrote *Beyond The Sea* with Jim Wong, says that even in his own mind, he was not sure whether Boggs genuinely had paranormal abilities. He is similarly uncertain of real life claims. 'I could believe in telepathy, some sort of senses that we have that aren't used any more or that are not developed. Jim Wong and I can sit in a room and I say, "well you know what that guy did and what happened there, we should have a thing like. . ." and he'll go, "right, right, right". It drives our wives nuts, because we never complete a sentence. When you know somebody so well, that is a form of it.

'Channelling, though. I've come to believe – and a great deal of this is from researching for *The X-Files* – that when you die, that's it. End of consciousness and they bury you. That's it. But that was Chris's most brilliant thing he ever did: to create the phrase "I want to believe". I believe everybody wants to believe. '

'He claims to have obtained this information through psychic transmission'
MULDER

'Mulder, do I detect a hint of scepticism?'
SCULLY

In the paranormal realm, channelling seems to fall somewhere in between possession and clairvoyance or mediumship.

Attitudes to people purporting to be mouth-pieces for the dead have swung violently throughout history. Early channellers were guaranteed a place at the stake or at least a room in the insane asylum. In the heyday of mediumship, they were big enchiladas, fêted by the rich and famous. The dawn of the scientific era saw them attacked by sceptics during the back-lash against spiritualism. Today? Well, it all depends.

Certainly, the phenomena has brand new connotations. When we think of channelling we usually think of people like Judith Z. Knight. Knight was a cable TV saleswoman from Seattle who claimed to have been contacted by Ramtha, an ancient Atlantean, whilst in her kitchen one day in 1978. She went on to make a fortune by allegedly allowing Ramtha to use her body to spread his words of wisdom on the mysteries of life, the universe and everything (including the subject of financial investment). She was made famous by Shirley MacLaine, and rich by her acolytes who called themselves 'Ramsters'.

In what must be a legal first, Knight was taken to court in 1995 by an Austrian psychic, Julie Ravel, who said she had been possessed by Ramtha whilst in a glass shop in Berlin and wanted exclusive rights to channel him. Judge Dr. Maria Friedinger ruled in Knight's favour and said that Ravel had 'infringed copyright' with her claims. Knight was awarded £600 damages. Apparently Ramtha didn't get a say in the matter.

'It was five hours of Boggs's "channelling". After three hours I asked him to summon up the soul of Jimi Hendrix and requested All Along the Watchtower. *You know, the guy's been dead twenty years but he still hasn't lost his edge'*
MULDER

Although Mulder's doubts lay more specifically with Boggs himself than with the concept of channelling, the phenomenon does have a rather dodgy reputation. In actuality, it is no more or less outrageous a proposition than many other paranormal claims, but its long-time association with financial gain and fraud has made everyone suspicious of anyone who announces that they can do it.

The more interesting aspect of the channelling phenomenon is where it occurs as a one off in people claiming to have no previous psychic ability.

In December 1993, an Indonesian newspaper reported a disturbance at the Dji Sam Soe cigarette factory in East

Java. It began when a young production-line worker named Lilik suffered a fit, after which she shouted: 'My name is Eva. I come from America. I am looking for my father.' Lilik/Eva continued to talk in fluent English despite the fact that, she, like her colleagues, had very little previous knowledge of the language. Stranger still, when Lilik recovered, another worker, Suryani, suffered a fit and subsequently announced that *she* was Eva. Other 'possessions' followed, and for two hours the factory was at a standstill. Several women suffered seizures, sometimes followed by outbursts in which they spoke at length in perfect English.

The situation was brought under control by a local shaman who rushed to the scene and – depending on how you choose to view the incident – either allayed the women's hysteria or sent Eva packing back to the spirit realm.

Another channelling-type case is much harder to explain away. Christine Silver is a well-balanced, well-educated, down-to-earth woman who worked for many years as personal assistant to a renowned psychiatrist. In December 1976, Christine, then aged 30, was driving to a friend's house in North London with her husband David when their car stalled without warning and would not re-start. Christine set off on foot, while David waited for an AA representative. The engine started immediately.

The Silver's car was fine until two weeks later when, on the way to visit the same friend's house, it stalled again – in *exactly* the same spot. This time Christine offered to call the AA while David went on ahead. However, she noticed something that he had not: a garage just across the road.

When Christine entered the garage workshop she was overcome with dizziness, and felt she might pass out. The owner of the garage, a middle-aged man, rushed to her assistance, bringing her a chair and a glass of water.

'Once I was sitting down, I started feeling less faint,' remembers Christine, 'but I still felt very peculiar. Then the guy asked me how old I was, and for some reason, that didn't seem like a strange question. I told him. And then he told me that his wife would have been about the same age as me, but she had died of cancer two years before. I suppose it was an odd thing to say, but it didn't really strike me as odd at the time. I felt very sorry for him. . . I was just about to tell him how sorry I was to hear it, and I opened my mouth to speak, but I heard myself saying: "I know you and the children miss me, but you are all doing so well. I'm very proud of you." '

Christine says that beyond this first comment, she has never been able to fully recall the rest of the conversation. She left the garage in a daze and found the car working normally again.

Although Boggs appears to be adept at both channelling and telepathy, the two could actually be one and the same. Innovative author Lyall Watson notes in his groundbreaking Supernature: '(Telepathy) is still so rare as to be considered abnormal, and it seems that in many subjects the fear of being able to do this type of thing produces a state of conflict that actively prevents them from doing it again. Many successful performers, whose livelihood or prestige depends on producing the phenomena resolve their conflict by dissociation. They enter a trance state in which their conscious minds can disclaim all responsibility for the events, or perhaps they become possessed by a spirit of someone else, who can be blamed for the goings on.'

'Luther if you really were psychic. . .'
SCULLY

'I'd have known you lied. That there never was a deal.
But I know you tried'
BOGGS

Telepathy has been the focus of many successful and fascinating studies in which some subjects have produced results far over and above the odds of chance. Many scientists reject the validity of these tests and refute the existence of the phenomenon, and yet apparent 'connection' with another person is one of the most frequent and wide-spread out of the ordinary experiences.

The experience of thinking about someone just before they telephone you is a common place occurrence. But if you are disinclined to believe in the existence of anything beyond the five senses, you are likely to write off any experience you have as coincidence. Or chance. After all, how many times have you thought of someone *without* the phone ringing afterwards? Or had the phone ring when you were not thinking of anyone?

Often we do not give chance its full dues. For instance, you only need 23 people in a room in order to have a 50:50 chance of meeting someone with the same birthday as you – a coincidence that most of us would react to with some surprise.

If you want to, you can stretch chance and coincidence a long way before they rip at the seams. And most of us *do* want to. Because if we do not at least try, we are left naked in a storm of unanswered questions.

The X-Files's Howard Gordon recently had to brave the storm. 'Just the other night I was working on an episode (for season III) in which a boy in Oklahoma is struck by lightning. He's one of those sort of slackers, he works in a garage, he's kind of a dressed up version of Beavis or Butthead. So what I'm trying to do to get involved in this character is listen to some of this headbanger music. So I'm sitting at my desk very late at night and I had Chinese food, and I was beating my chopsticks like drums for about 15 minutes, working myself up into a frenzy.

'The next day I got a call from my accountant, on completely unrelated business and he said, "Howard, I had a dream about you last night, you were playing the drums." And I don't play drums, that's the thing. And I don't often play chopsticks on my desk. But he'd had his dream about midnight and that's when I was doing it. So it was coincidence possibly, and you know, maybe not. I have to think that maybe there are parts of our brain that we have no idea what they can do.'

In a classic experiment by B.D.W. Morley of the Victoria Institute, ants were kept in separate jars, unable to communicate via sound, sight, smell or stridulation (a vibration effect common to ants). Yet they were apparently still able to convey information through a sense unknown to us, which Morley calls the 'ninth sense'. Insects with amazing abilities are clearly out there and communicating – and they don't need no Internet. Perhaps it is not so far-fetched that humans might also possess a hidden natural ability of the same type.

Japanese Macaque Monkeys, potato washers extraordinaire

'The dead, living. . . all souls are connected'
BOGGS

When we think about ESP or telepathy we tend to imagine thoughts transmitted from one mind to another. In cases where, say, a mother inexplicably 'knows' that her child is in danger, the idea of a direct thought transfer makes some kind of sense to us, because of the closeness of the two people and the importance of the information. But what about Howard Gordon and his accountant?

The traditional theory of telepathy can get murky. The good news is that there are other theories. The bad news is that they are no less murky.

Jung's Collective Consciousness theory says that all minds are connected. A twist on this idea is often tied to, and sometimes referred to as, the 'Hundredth Monkey' phenomenon.

The Hundredth Monkey refers to an alleged paranormal event which took place on Koshima island and involved a troop of Japanese Macaque monkeys who were being studied by primatologists. The story goes that one monkey learned to wash muddy potatoes in the sea before eating them, and taught others to do so. Once a number of monkeys had learned the secret, the knowledge spread spontaneously, not only throughout the rest of the troop, but to monkeys on other islands. Nice story. Unfortunately, there is no proof that this event really took place and plenty to indicate that it did not. It is safe to say that it is a myth. But, in fairness, it is used more often as a metaphor than as evidence for the existence of thought-transference.

Still, there are plenty of people who buy the basic hypothesis. In the 1980s, Dr. Rupert Sheldrake put forward the theory of 'morphogenetic fields' (energy emanating from people, animals, natural formations and even pieces of information, which can be received by other people). His claims may be radical, but his back-up experiments yielded bizarre results.

One involved an illustration containing a hidden image – one of those mind tricks that few people can solve immediately, but that once you've sussed out, you can't 'unlearn'. Sheldrake reckoned that once one or more people knew the secret, the knowledge would be collectively available to others. The image, along with its solution, was broadcast on TV in Britain, and tests took place in other countries, well outside the range of the broadcast, both before and afterwards. The difference was significant: people outside Britain who saw the picture *after* the broadcast identified the hidden image far more easily than those shown it before.

In another test, a well-known Japanese poet, Shuntaro Tanikawa, provided Sheldrake with three rhymes in Japanese which were identical in structure, meter and length. One was a nursery rhyme, known by generations of Japanese children, one was a new rhyme made up especially for the experiment, and the third was also new, but made no sense in Japanese.

Groups of volunteers in Britain and America, who had no knowledge of the language, and were not told anything about the rhymes, tried to learn all three by chanting them a fixed number of times, in no particular order. Asked to try and recall the rhymes half an hour later, 62% recalled the genuine nursery rhyme more easily and completely than the other two. By the laws of chance, each rhyme should score equally, around 33% each.

All this has, of course, been dismissed by science, but until someone investigates and tries some controlled experiments of their own, the results remain intriguing.

'Dana, Fox, please understand that from here we can return to the past, we can see the present, we can know the future'

BOGGS

We are an impatient bunch, us humans. For as long as history remembers, we have wanted to know *now* what will happen next. Also, in keeping with human nature, there have been no end of people and institutions willing to satisfy that craving. Most religions are based on prophecies, be they from the Oracles of ancient Greece, the I-Ching or the Book of Revelations. Through the ages, seers have conscripted everything from tea leaves, crystals, bones, cards, runes, bowls of water (Nostradamus's favourite) to entrails, in their attempts to peek into the future. By and large, though, they obtain success through the principle that if you throw enough mud at a wall, some is going to stick. From Nostradamus to Mystic Meg, the sheer volume of predictions guarantees by the law of averages a few 'uncanny' hits.

Nostradamus shows Catherine de Medici the future of the sovreigns of France in a mirror

But premonitions are something else altogether – an unsolicited dream, vision, 'spontaneous knowledge', or good-old-fashioned hunch concerning an event before it happens.

Small-scale precognitions happen all the time. Most people have had 'a funny feeling' before one incident or another. And like many who live in Los Angeles and other earthquake-prone areas, Glen Morgan says he often senses a quake shortly before it happens. 'It's not like I could tell you "there's gonna be one tomorrow", but I wake up or I pause right before they start.'

> *'Mulder. Don't go near the white cross. We see you down. . . And your blood spills on the white cross'*
> BOGGS

A desperate hunt for survivors at Aberfan. Hundreds of people claim to have had premonitions of this disaster

More dramatic premonitions usually concern death or danger relating to the percipient or to someone close to them. Some hunches appear to serve a life-saving purpose. From the Titanic to the Lockerbie tragedy, travel disasters have been preceded by last-minute cancellations by people who had a bad feeling about the journey. American mathematician William Cox carried out a survey of train accidents and discovered that there were always fewer passengers present on ill-fated trains than there were on the same trains in the preceding weeks, and fewer people in the damaged or derailed carriages. He calculated the odds against his findings happening by chance at over 100-1.

More specific cases of precognition usually take the form of dreams, which are often described as inordinately vivid. In Aberfan, Wales, on the morning of 20 October 1966, nine-year-old Eryl Mai Jones woke up after having a nightmare. She told her mum that she had dreamt that she had gone to school but when she arrived, it was not there because 'something black had come down all over it'. The next day, while Eryl was in class, half a ton of coal waste slid down a hillside and buried her school, killing at least 140 people, including Eryl.

London psychiatrist Dr. John Barker investigated the myriad premonitions that had preceded the Aberfan disaster and decided that around 60 were genuine. He set up the British Premonitions Bureau hoping that a centralized data bank of premonitions could help avert future tragedies. A similar idea was also tried out in the States, at the Central Premonitions Registry. Wanting to dispense with the preliminaries, they accepted only premonitions of general and national interest. Sadly, neither organisation managed to make the world a safer place.

Testing phenomenon is difficult, since – despite what prophets and fortune tellers would like to think – it appears to be something that cannot be done to order. An

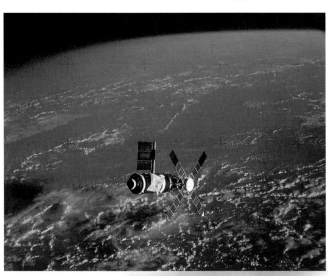

experiment called Project Chicken Little was launched in 1979 to see if anyone could predict the date and site of the Skylab space station's re-entry to earth. Over 200 people tried. None of them guessed it would be 11 June, in Australia. More specialised tests have also been tried. Starting in 1927, Dr. J.B. Rhine from Duke University oversaw a series of ground-breaking controlled laboratory experiments devised to explore precognition and other unusual human possibilities.

Skylab. Over 200 people tried to predict the date and site of the space station's re-entry to earth. Nobody got it right

Since then, all sorts of experiments have been devised to try to weed out some of the variables. One used rats, on the principle that 'simple' animals are somehow more in tune with primal gifts. The rats were put in a cage that was divided into two parts. Every now and then (randomly), one half of the cage would be electrified. The goal was to see if the rats would be able to predict which half and jump out of the way before it happened. The unfortunate beasts scored about 8% above chance.

Experiments with humans were slightly more humane. At the Maimonides Hospital 'Dream Laboratory' in New York, subjects were asked to dream about what would happen the next day. The next morning, another group of experimenters, who did not know the result, used a randomly generated painting to create a unique environment. One painting showed snow and ice. The corresponding room had white sheets draped over the furniture and, when the subject entered, ice cubes were dropped down his back and a fan chilled him. His dreams had, in fact, contained frosty elements. In one series of tests, eight nights of dreams produced five direct hits and two close matches.

For as long as there have been believers, there have been sceptics, adding a range of other possibilities to what might (or might not) be happening. Aristotle mentions coincidence and self-fulfilling prophecies. There is also a thin line between premonitions and intelligent, logical predictions. Leonardo Da Vinci foresaw many modern inventions. Was he a prophet or just a damn good engineer? Few people see anything mystical in the prediciitions of this century's science fiction writers, who wrote up just about every modern invention, from video phones to personal computers and the Internet, long before these things came into being.

Modern day debunkers have added the valid points that some accounts are altered after the fact by confused believers or unscrupulous attention-seekers, that only correct prophecies tend to be quoted, that many large-scale disasters and single personal tragedies go unprophesied and that many predictions turn out to be false. Scientific debunkers have also correctly noted the inherent flaws in the scientific analysis of data. But they have not succeeded in proving empirically that premonition does not exist.

So people continue to have disturbing dreams and hunches, and predictions still come true. Sometimes. One that did not was made by the dean of sceptics, James Randi: 'I predict that the 1980s will see us relieved of the burdens of astrology, flying saucers, Jeane Dixon (a well-known US psychic), the Burmuda Triangle and other idiocies.'

Bibliography
Sources and further Reading

Books

The Power of the Mind
Edited by Peter Brookesmith, Orbis, 1986

Biological Anomalies – Humans I
William R. Corliss, The Sourcebook Project, 1992

Predictions
Joe Fisher with Peter Comins, Van Nostrand
Reinhold, New York, 1980

*The Hundredth Monkey and other Pardigms of
the Paranormal*
Edited by Kendrick Frazier, Prometheus books,
1991

*Visions of the Future: The Definitive Study of
Precognitions*
Dr. Keith Hearne, The Aquarian Press, 1989

The Presence of the Past
Rupert Sheldrake, New York, 1988

ESP: Your Sixth Sense
B. Stieger, Award Books, 1966

The People's Almanac
David Wallechinsky and Irving Wallace,
Doubleday, New York, 1975

Supernature
Lyall Watson, Hodder and Stoughton, 1973

Papers, Journals & Newspapers

Fortean Times

Formative Causation: The Hypothesis Supported
New Scientist, 1983 (Rupert Sheldrake)

X-FILE: FIRE

Case notes by Agent Dana Scully

The arson suspect, Cecil L'ively, was admitted
to Boston Mercy Hospital with fifth and sixth
degree burns over his entire body. Military burn
specialists have been brought in to study the case
which they are calling extraordinary, not only for
the fact that the suspect survived, but for the
rapid regeneration of his basal cell tissue. Full
recovery is anticipated in as little as a month.
L'ively is being held in a high security medical
facility, confined to a hyperbaric chamber until
he can be tried for the murder of a Massachusetts
caretaker. His body temperature remains at a steady
109 degrees. Health technicians have removed
anything flammable from his room due to several
fires which have broken out in the vicinity.
    According to Agent Mulder, further incarceration
remains a problem for the Federal Penal authorities.
    While Cecil L'ively certainly presents a medical
anomaly, neither science nor law-enforcement
currently recognises the feasibility of pyrokine-
ses - the ability to generate fire by the power of
the mind; an ability with which Agent Mulder
suggests L'ively may be endowed.

UP IN FLAMES

In *Fire* Mulder is challenged with not one but two personal demons – his fear of fire, and his treacherous and libidinous old flame from his days at Oxford University, Phoebe Green – now Inspector Green of Scotland Yard.

Following a mysterious spate of British arson attacks, Green accompanies the family thought to be the next victim to a holiday refuge in Cape Cod. Mulder is enticed to join her.

The case even has the FBI's arson expert, Agent Beatty, foxed. But then the culprit, Cecil L'ively, is no ordinary arsonist – he ignites his blazes, it seems, by the power of his mind.

According to Glen Morgan the episode came about because fire is one of the basic things of which people are afraid. 'We actually wanted to explore spontaneous human combustion,' says Morgan, 'but it's hard to avoid it looking like a Monty Python sketch.'

> ## 'People don't normally just catch on fire'
> AGENT BEATTY

Agent Beatty is, of course, quite right. But in this strange world of ours, you never can tell.

The curious experiences of four-year-old Tong Tangjiang of Hunan, China, might also seem slightly Pythonesque if they were not so alarmingly real. One morning in April 1990, the tot's family noticed smoke pouring from his trousers and discovered that his under-pants had ignited for no apparent reason. He was rushed to hospital where he was treated for burns. He ignited a further three times in the space of two hours, injuring his hands, armpits and genitalia. Doctors suggested that Tong seemed to generate unusual amounts of electric current, which increased when he was excited or under stress. Tong also unwittingly set fire to his mattress and once narrowly missed igniting his granny's hair.

While Tong, and others like him, appear to be 'fire prone', this is a different phenomenon from spontaneous human combustion (SHC), which is usually fatal and generates heat capable of reducing the body to a pile of calcinated ashes in minutes. This is extraordinary when you consider that a body can burn for over eight hours in a crematorium at 1,110°C without any sign of that happening.

There is much dispute as to whether SHC exists at all, and the official line from doctors and coroners is that it does not. Opponents of the theory of SHC meet cases of apparent spontaneous ignitions with any number of everyday explanations, from dropped cigarettes, to flying sparks from a heater or fireplace. But, as *Fortean Times* co-editor Bob Rickard notes: 'Faced with the alternative – a nightmare out of the dark ages – it is not surprising that they are accepted'.

Intriguing though SHC is, perhaps cases like Tong's constitute an even greater mystery. Not only do they defy any of these explanations, but their varied nature seems to suggest not one, but several different phenomena.

A classic case, recorded by Charles Fort in 1929,

concerned the exotically named Lily White of Liberta, Antigua. Like Tong, she experienced frequent spontaneous ignitions, but, unlike him, her clothes would burn to a crisp while she remained unscathed. She wrote off clothing at a terrifying rate and had to rely on hand-me-downs from friends and neighbours.

Other spontaneous ignitions are, like SHC, one-off occurrences, although they do not start from within, as SHC appears to do.

On the evening of 25 May 1985, Paul Hayes, a 19-year-old computer programmer – and a non-smoker to boot – burst into flames whilst strolling along a quiet road in Stepney Green. Luckily, he was within staggering distance of The London Hospital which treated him for burns. He recalls the incident as 'indescribable. . . like being plunged into the heat of a furnace. . . my chest felt like boiling water had been poured over it. I thought I could hear my brains bubbling.'

'There've been reports of pyrokinetics. People who can conduct and control fire. . .'
MULDER

There is another breed of 'fire prone' person who does not burst into flames, but seems to set things ablaze by looking at them, thinking about them or by simply being near them.

An early example of a typical case is that of Jennie Bramwell, an orphan adopted in 1891 by a Mr. and Mrs. Dawson of Thorah Island, Ontario. Within just a few weeks of her arrival several hundred individual fires started spontaneously in Jennie's presence. Ceilings, walls, towels, logs, furniture and even the family cat caught alight. Needless to say, the Dawsons packed poor Jennie back off to the orphanage.

Pyrokinetic children have never had it easy. Twelve-year-old Willie Brough of Turlock, California, could allegedly start fires with a glance, and was turfed out by his family who thought he was possessed by the devil. A farmer in a nearby town took him in and sent him to a new school where he was expelled after his first day thanks to five classroom blazes, including one which started in the teacher's desk drawer.

More recently, a quiet and studious 16-year-old boy named Benedetto Supino came to public attention. Benedetto, from Formia, near Rome, discovered his strange abilities in 1982 when a comic he was reading in a dentist's waiting-room went up in flames. Since then both he and his family have been shocked by frequent fires. Furniture and objects sometimes ignite as he passes by them, and more than once Benedetto has woken to find his bed linen ablaze. Items ignite in his hands, (especially books), or when his gaze lands on them – a plastic object held by his uncle once ignited while Benedetto was staring at it.

The scientific community has been unable to help Benedetto, who says he finds his abilities embarrassing and

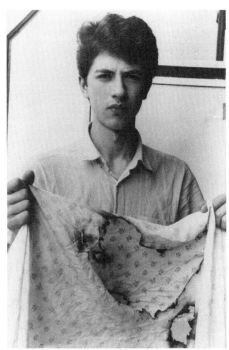

Bendetto Supino displays the results of his bizarre 'gift'

distressing. Professor Mario Scuncio of the Tivoli Social Medical Centre declared the boy 'perfectly normal' – a rather odd diagnosis. Dr. Giovanni Ballesio, Dean of Physical Medicine at Rome University, investigated the possibility of abnormally high personal electricity but could find no evidence of it. Benedetto is pinning his hopes on Dr. Demetrio Croce, a parapsychologist who is trying to teach him to control his abilities.

The cases detailed above could, under other circumstances, be interpreted as poltergeist activity. It really all depends on the beliefs of the family involved. But there may

be a connection between the two phenomena. It is widely believed that poltergeist activity (which frequently includes spontaneous fires) is generated not by mischievous spirit' but by

disturbed individuals, usually children and teenagers. Pioneering psychical researcher Dr. Nandor Fodor suggested taking a psychoanalytical approach to ridding a home of poltergeist disturbances, which he defined as a 'bundle of projected repressions'. He has achieved many notable successes.

Veteran anomalist Vincent H. Gaddis reviewed a great deal of scientific research carried out in the field of parapsychology and concluded in his wonderful 1967 tome *Mysterious Fires and Lights* that, 'One of the unsuspected powers of the mind seems to be the ability to release the vital energy that will speed up molecular agitation in a target object. As agitation increases the object becomes hotter. It requires only a hot spark to ignite a curtain, a dress, or any easily combustible object.'

> ### 'This one likes to burn his victims alive. Can't figure how he does it, either. Not a crumb of evidence left at the crime scene'
> #### PHOEBE

Carol Compton – witch or victim?

Although there are many cases suggesting that some humans can spark spontaneous fires, there are few, if any, which implicate the kind of conscious command and control over this talent that Cecil L'ively had. There are anecdotal accounts of yogis, lamas and other enlightened persons intentionally producing fire by meditation or chanting, but no one has yet turned up anything like L'ively's nice line in tricks and lethal implements for homicide.

Remarkably, though, there *has* been a person accused of pyrokinetic crime. On 12 December 1983, in Livorno, Italy, one of the decade's most bizarre court cases commenced. Carol Compton, a young Scottish woman, was led into court by armed soldiers and locked in a steel cage installed for use in terrorism trials. She was accused of five charges of arson and one of attempted murder.

Since early in 1982, Compton had worked as a nanny. She had lost her first job after three fires had broken out, the first destroying her employer's living-room, the subsequent two occurring in the house which they had moved into while repairs were taking place. Although there was no proof that Carol was responsible, she had been blamed.

Worse was to come. Carol had quickly found a new job looking after three-year-old Agnese, the daughter of a wealthy couple who worked in television. On the evening of 1 August, Agnese's grandfather's bed was discovered burning. The next morning Agnese's cot mattress burst into flames while she slept. Fortunately she was not hurt, but the police were called. Although Carol had been sitting downstairs with the rest of the family when both fires started, she was arrested, charged with attempted murder and arson (taking the previous fires into account), refused bail, and imprisoned for 16 months pending trial.

The lack of any solid evidence against Carol gave rise to talk of pyrokinesis, and the trial soon became a media circus, ably assisted by Agnese's superstitious grandmother who ranted on about witchcraft, and a well-known, elderly clairvoyant who told the Press that the spirit of an 18th century girl had given Carol the 'power of fire'. The clairvoyant turned up in court, shrouded in black, muttering incantations in Carol's face and brandishing an enormous Hammer-horror style crucifix.

The prosecution ignored the paranormal implications, (not to mention the fact that Carol had no criminal record, no previous history of pyromania and a clean bill of mental health). They laboured only the point that Carol was the common factor in all the fires.

The defence avoided the spooky element too, but it kept coming up. A fire officer with 38 years experience deemed the nature of the fires peculiar, unusually hot, and

Grandma Ceccini, Agnese's superstitious grandmother

appearing to have burned downwards. Another expert, Professor Vitolo Nicolo of Pisa University, agreed telling the court, 'In all my 45 years experience of this kind of investigation I have never seen fires like this before. They were created by an intense source of heat, but not a naked flame.'

The mattresses, although made of different materials, had both burned in the same strange way: on the surface only. Professor Nicolo declared that they could not have been ignited with matches, a lighter or any other naked flame. Forensic tests showed that no fuels or chemicals had been used.

The first fire was odd too. Its source appeared to be a wooden stool, but the stool was only slightly scorched while the rest of the room had been destroyed. The flames also seemed to have travelled sideways and downwards at one point, and into a cupboard drawer.

At the close of the case, the jury was out for six-and-a half hours. Despite the fact that Carol had not been seen setting the fires, had not been close enough to set them, and had been in full view of others when they started, she was found guilty on two counts of arson and one of attempted fire-raising. On the attempted murder charge, a verdict was returned of 'not proven' (a third option in Italian law). Carol was sentenced to seven years imprisonment and the court president reiterated that the case was not about witchcraft or the paranormal.

Certainly Carol was the only common denominator in fires in three separate homes, and yet there was not a crumb of evidence that she lit them. She is either extraordinarily crafty, a victim of cruel and bizarre coincidence, or embroiled in a phenomenon that transcends all that we currently know and understand.

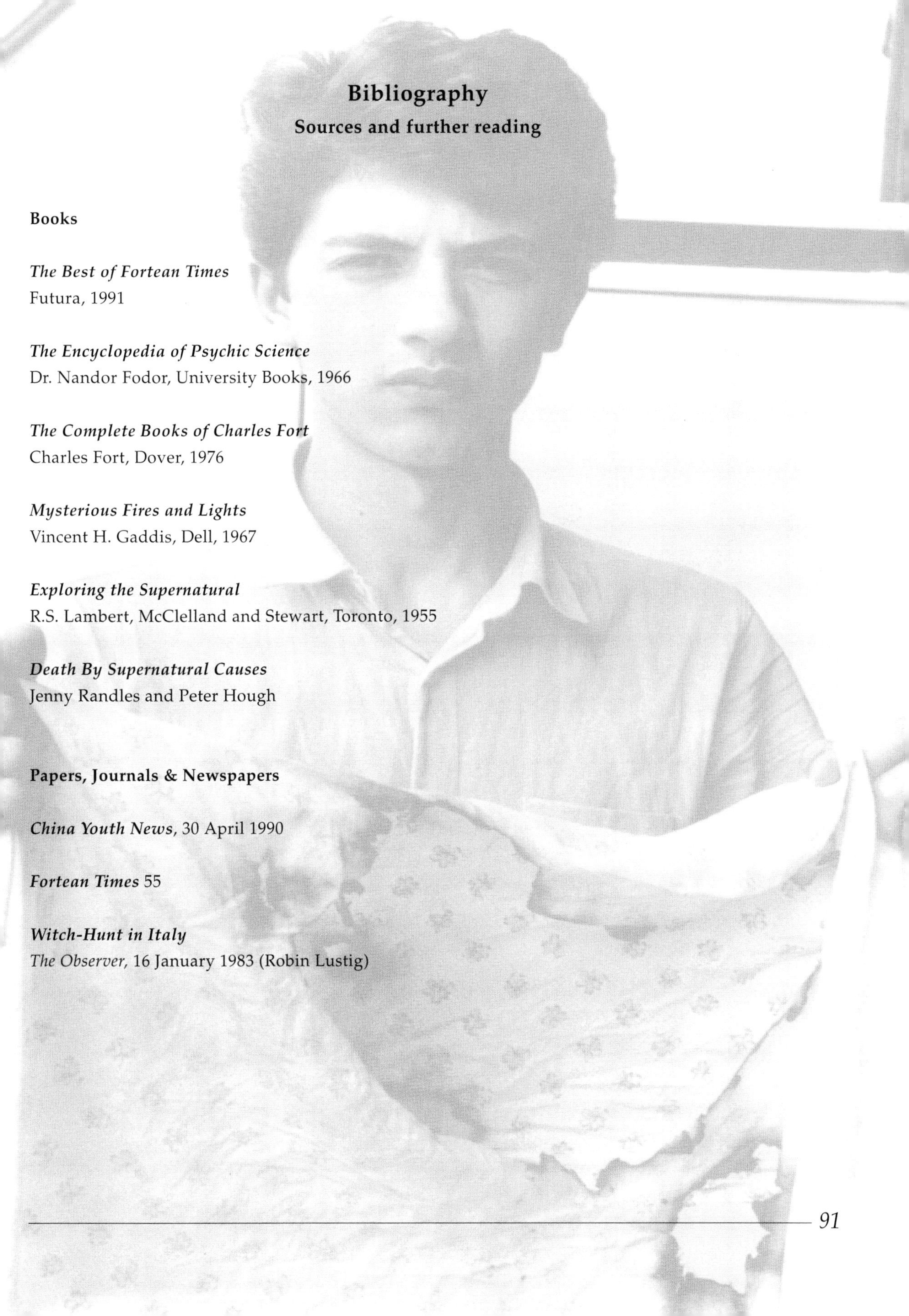

Bibliography
Sources and further reading

Books

The Best of Fortean Times
Futura, 1991

The Encyclopedia of Psychic Science
Dr. Nandor Fodor, University Books, 1966

The Complete Books of Charles Fort
Charles Fort, Dover, 1976

Mysterious Fires and Lights
Vincent H. Gaddis, Dell, 1967

Exploring the Supernatural
R.S. Lambert, McClelland and Stewart, Toronto, 1955

Death By Supernatural Causes
Jenny Randles and Peter Hough

Papers, Journals & Newspapers

China Youth News, 30 April 1990

Fortean Times 55

Witch-Hunt in Italy
The Observer, 16 January 1983 (Robin Lustig)

X-File: Ice

Case notes by Agent Dana Scully

The decision by the authorities to destroy the research centre an hour after our evacuation prevented us from further investigation. I acknowledge the gravity of the potential hazard, there was still a great deal of research to be done on the origin and genetic structure of the parasitic, worm-like, ammonia-based life-forms which were unwittingly freed from their habitat in the depths of Icy Cape.

The geographic profile of the excavation site strongly suggested that the Arctic Ice-Core Project team had unknowingly penetrated a meteor crater. If, as seems entirely feasible, these organisms had indeed been brought to earth 200,000 years previously and preserved in the ice, mankind has effectively been robbed of its first opportunity to study an extraterrestrial life form.

X-File: Darkness Falls

Case notes by Agent Fox Mulder

Prior to my discharge from Seattle's Human Rickover Naval Hospital, I learnt that my tests – like those undertaken on others present in the vehicle attacked by the unidentified swarm – had revealed excessive concentrations of luciferin, the enzyme produced by bioluminescent insects, although I have sustained no permanent damage. Agent Scully, by contrast, remains seriously ill, having lost a great deal of body fluid.

Entomologists are still trying to determine the specific epithet of the insects we encountered, and I was informed that the Government has initiated eradication procedures, with controlled burns and pesticides in the infested area of woodland. The implications of failure in this endeavour do not bear contemplation.

WEIRD NATURE

If there is one precept that encapsulates the very notion of *The X-Files*, it is that the world is a very strange place indeed. Nature is rich with weirdness.

Two episodes that deal with nature's fickle fury are *Ice* and *Darkness Falls*. In the former, ultra-deep exploration at a polar ice cap digs up a parasitic worm that crashed to earth on a meteor; excavated, the worm enters mammals and stimulates their aggression. The result is not a pretty sight. *Darkness Falls* sees ancient insect larvae (unleashed with the destruction of an old-growth tree) coming to life and swarming humans, cocooning them and draining them of all fluids.

The message of both is a staple of myth and legend. Mother Nature is basically benign and nurturing, but if you tamper with the natural order, she can be the Mother From Hell.

By now our planet has been pretty well trodden; but still we stumble across hitherto unknown forms of life with the most unusual origins. Natural mysteries arise in many ways, but they can be roughly divided into three categories: creatures not originally of this earth, creatures from the past lying dormant in suspended animation, and creatures living undiscovered by man for generations in extremely remote locales. Who knows what exotic beings lie beyond the purview of human exploration? The creatures uncovered in *The X-Files* are only the beginning.

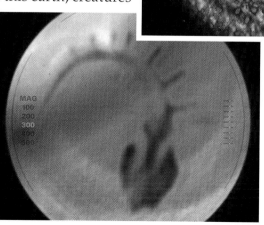

*'Looks like they were drilling
into a meteor crater'*
MURPHY
Ice

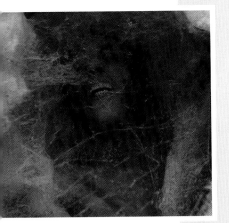

My biggest inspiration for *Ice*,' says Chris Carter, 'was *The Thing*.' This tense 1951 Sci-fi/horror classic and John Carpenter's vivid 1982 remake, were both based on John W. Campbell Jr's *Who Goes There?*, an eerie tale of scientists at a lonely Antarctic outpost terrorised by a thawed-out alien organism.

Glen Morgan and Jim Wong, who wrote the episode, had also come across a report in *Scientific American* on a Greenland expedition which had dug down into the ice to an all-time record depth. Says Morgan: 'That ice had been basically the same for a quarter of a million years and so we said, "Wow. What could be down there?" So with *Ice* it was that article, the fact that we needed a contained set because we were really over-budget, and also that worms are just horrible.'

Says Carter: 'It became an X File about the idea that something extraterrestrial landed, and living inside it were these creatures. The things that crash into earth (in real life) seem to be a little bare and uninteresting except for the destruction they cause. It's fun to think about, but I think the process of actually going through the atmosphere would probably kill just about anything.'

*'The meteor that hit a quarter of a
million years ago may have carried
that type of life to Earth'*
MULDER

Could a life-form survive the toasty trauma of a plunge through space? Many scientists doubt it, but there seems to be some evidence that, meteors have occasionally arrived with a few stowaways intact. Additionally, reports of pwdre ser, (Welsh 'rot from the stars') describe gelatinous blobs from the sky – possible alien matter in a form that looks nothing like the more commonly encountered meteorite.

One morning in 1979, Frisco, Texas, after a night during which a bright light seemed to descend over the neighbourhood, Sybil Christian found three purple blobs in her front yard. Analysis of the substance proved inconclusive. In 1989 it was reported in *The Times* that Dr. Ian Watson and colleagues from the Open University in Milton Keynes had detected 'organic materials' in a small fragment of an Antarctic meteorite they believed to be from Mars.

This leads to the question, does the presence of organic materials denote life? Ralph Harvey, of the Department of Geological Sciences at Case Western Reserve University, describes himself as, 'not only the guy in charge of recovering Antarctic meteorites, but a fan of *The X-Files* as well.'

According to him, 'Back in the 1880s, it was noted that a specific kind of meteorite called a "carbonaceous chondrite" contained organic compounds. Please note that to modern chemists and geologists the term "organic" does not in any way imply biological processes – the term is used for a wide range of hydrocarbon compounds produced both by organisms and by other non-biogenic processes.

'Almost any meteorite will show a molecule or two of "organics" here and there, but these are one in a gadzillion, and not meaningful indicators of biogenic activity.

'A debate surfaced recently over a possible sample-return mission to Mars. There's an active camp suggesting we shouldn't go, either because we'll bring back a killer virus or because our earthly viruses will contaminate Mars. Either way, it's a moot point. We know that giant impacts on the surfaces of planets and moons send pieces flying through space to land on another planet or moon. We've recognised pieces of our moon and of Mars among the Antarctic meteorites already, enough so that this kind of cross-cultivation must be occurring on a year-by-year basis!

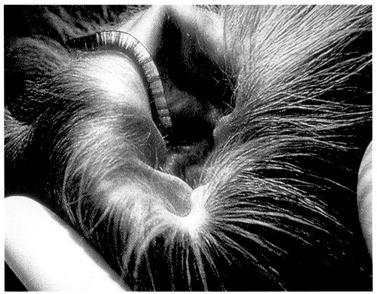

'The physics of these material transfers between planets also suggest that the delivered pieces come from planetary surfaces rather than from deeper localities, so the likelihood of transfer of biogenic material, if it's there, is increased. With 3.4 billion years of life on Earth, and all those impacts during that time, we've almost certainly invaded other planets ourselves already.'

Some scientists believe not only that Earth has received interplanetary biogenics, but also that some of that material has been pathogenic – and responsible for some of our most notorious diseases. Professors Sir Fred Hoyle and Chandra Wickramasinghe of University College, Cardiff, assert that diseases such as Black Death and Legionnaire's Disease are sprayed on Earth by passing comets, and are thus impossible to eradicate, since eventually another comet will cruise by and sneeze those same pathogens right in our faces. They extend this to hypothesise that life itself began on our planet with material sprinkled by a passing comet, and that, furthermore, comets – serving as interstellar bumblebees – are spreading life forms similar to ours all around the galaxy.

Hoyle and Wickramasinghe make a provocative if less than airtight case, citing diseases that seemingly sprout from nowhere after years or even centuries of eradication, or pointing to disease cycles similar to that of Halley's Comet (76 years), implying that the pathogens follow in the comet's wake.

Probably the best and most dramatic case for terrestrial life from outer space can be made for the Venus fly-trap (though we've yet to discover a gargantuan, *Little Shop of Horrors*-style man-eater). Mark Chorvinsky, editor of *Strange* magazine, lays out a convincing argument: This carnivorous plant exists as only one species and is the only plant with an active trap for catching flies; it's truly unique. Chorvinsky quotes botanist Francis Earnest Lloyd, who writes: 'How the highly specialised organs of capture could have evolved seems to defy our present knowledge'. The Venus fly-trap grows naturally in only one spot on Earth: a one hundred-mile radius around Wilmington, North Carolina. And in the centre of this circle is what appears to be a series of craters from a meteor shower that now comprises what are known as the Carolina Bays. Here's the kicker: the fly-trap seems to thrive on heat and fire and it is remarkably hardy overall, which just might have allowed it to withstand a plummet through space.

Awe-inspiring stuff. But let's get back to those worms.

The Venus fly-trap (Dionaea Muscipula). Did it descend to Earth from outer space?

'A parasite shouldn't want to kill its host'
SCULLY

'No. No. This won't kill you – unless you try to extract it'
HODGE

Parasites: Nasty or *Really Nasty?* Just as the worms in *Ice* stimulate their host's hypothalamus in order to cause aggressive behaviour and, presumably, aid in reproduction, so do some documented creatures. The sheep-liver trematode, for example, must first pass through an intermediate host, such as an ant, before  invading the sheep, so it alters the ant's behaviour to make it a more likely lunch. The trematode burrows into an ant's brain and forces it to clamp on to the top of a blade of grass that might be eaten by the sheep – yet it releases the clamp if not eaten, so that the ant can get out of the sun and live to try again another day. No parasite wants to kill its host before having secured another.

A nematode that infests queen bumble-bees alters the bee's hibernating behaviour so that instead of burrowing into the

ground, the bee is made to fly about and deposit nematode larvae in various spots, thus abetting nematode reproduction – and leading to the bee's demise.

'Maybe they've been lying there dormant for hundreds of years. Maybe they woke up hungry'
SPINNEY
Darkness Falls

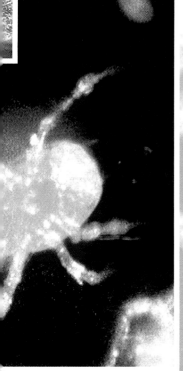

'**M**y original inspiration for *Darkness Falls*,' says Chris Carter, 'was my college science class, when we studied dendrochronology, which is the reading of tree rings. These trees are thousands of years old; they are time-capsules, they hold all the nutrients and/or critters that might have existed in those times lying dormant. Then there was a story in an Oregon news-

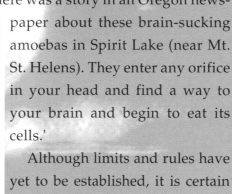

paper about these brain-sucking amoebas in Spirit Lake (near Mt. St. Helens). They enter any orifice in your head and find a way to your brain and begin to eat its cells.'

Although limits and rules have yet to be established, it is certain that *some* creatures have been able to survive for *some* length of time in a state of suspended animation, or metabolic abeyance. Entombed animals are surprisingly common. A toad in Eastland, Texas, survived for 31 years before being discovered sealed in the cornerstone of the town's old courthouse. The toad, subsequently named Old Rip, became a local celebrity and lived a long and happy life. As reported in an 1891 edition of *English Mechanic* science journal, two men sawing a tree came across a pair of wasp-like insects imbedded in the wood. Brought near a fire, they revived and began to crawl about, though they were never able to fly.

H.E. Hinton and M.S. Blum reported on the 'just-add-water' phenomenon in a 1965 edition of *New Scientist*. Their experiments with the larvae of a chironomid fly show that it can be *repeatedly* dehydrated then brought back to life by rehydration and heating. They could even chop the larvae into pieces while desiccated, and the individual pieces would spring to life – albeit temporarily – when water was added.

The ability of creatures to survive in a state of suspended animation is known as crytobiosis. Metabolism, it appears, is not a necessary function of life, as long as an organised molecular structure is maintained. Some dried nematodes have been revived after 39 years.

The freshwater fish parasite, Crustacea Copepod, whose eggs were successfully hatched after they had been buried for over 300 years

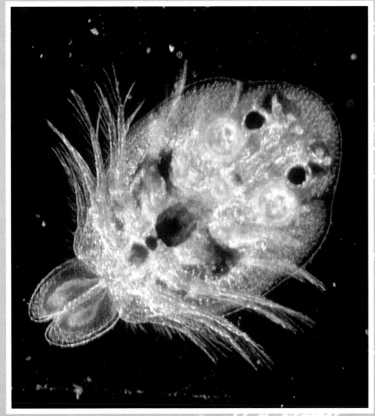

'These are obviously not your typical bugs. To say the least'
SPINNEY

B ut could insects be so organised and virulent as the ones Mulder and Scully encountered? For sure. For example, at Uganda's Lake Edward, and elsewhere, concentrated clouds of lake flies, sometimes hundreds of feet high, mass together to form a whirlwind effect. Fishermen who've strayed into the vortex are rumoured to have suffocated. And we're not just talking about the wilderness. On 14 August 1991, a swarm of millions of tiny black flies plunged the streets of Bonn into buzzing darkness, bringing traffic to a standstill. Similarly, colonies of ants are often described as acting very like a single organism and are well known for achieving remarkable feats.

'What if it's some kind of extinct insect larvae in that ring? Deposited there during a period of volcanic activity. Ancient insect eggs, thousands, maybe millions of years old – lying dormant'
MULDER

M ulder may have some out-there ideas, but it seems his explanation of the insects' origin may not be as unlikely as it appears. An experiment described in an 1837 issue of the *American Journal of Science* involved an electric current being passed through a volcanic rock bathed in solution. Over the course of a month, 50 white specks in the stone slowly developed into living insects, which resembled cheese mites.

Early in 1995, it was announced that the spores of single-celled organisms up to 135 million years old could be brought to life. And the first success with multi-celled creatures followed in August 1995, when scientists witnessed successful hatching of the eggs of a 17th century copepod crustacean, which had lain buried at the bottom of Bullhead pond in Rhode Island for over 300 years. Professor Nelson Hairston, writing in the journal *Ecology*, noted that secreted in the mud, there may also be the larvae of ancient, extinct creatures.

'Like I said thirty-two years, you see a lot of weird stuff'
PARK RANGER BROUILLET
Jersey Devil

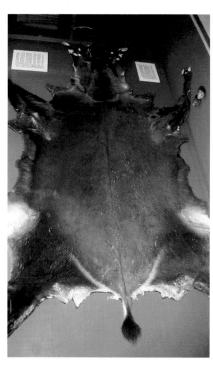

The skin of a newly discovered Vu Quang Ox from Vietnam

Not all the weirdness in nature involves little critters. The world abounds with fantastic, prehistoric-looking creatures, so why could there not also be a 70-foot anaconda, a sea monster or even a hairy hominid with a body-odour problem?

'At the turn of the century,' says Bob Rickard, co-editor of *Fortean Times*, 'it was generally thought that there were no more big animals to be discovered, only little ones – and they didn't matter. Yet, at the beginning of this year there was a new tree-kangaroo found in Papua New Guinea and a new kind of ox and a new kind of deer found in an area in Vietnam which had been bombed with agent orange. It makes you wonder.'

Cryptozoology (literally "the study of hidden animals") seeks everything from the maybe-extinct (i.e. the moa of New Zealand, the Tasmanian Thylacine) to the mysterious (the Mokele-Mbembe in Central Africa, said to resemble a Mesozoic sauropod). But the grand prize is an elusive creature known by many names, but commonly, Bigfoot.

'Just about every culture has one.
Yeti, Sasquatch, the Russian Almas.
The Dsonoqua. It's a kind of universal
Wild Man myth. A symbolic gear of
our dual natures as humans'

DR. DIAMOND

Bigfoot captured on camera
in 1967 at Bluff Creek
in Northern California

Unlike most folkloric entities, the evidence – sightings, footprints and other tangible clues – for the existence of a real, live, Bigfoot-like beast is persuasive. But as cryptozoologist *par excellence* Loren Coleman explains, the Bigfoot concept encompasses several different creatures: 'People who try to act like there is only one anthropoid or humanoid or hominid species that we are dealing with are foolish. For example, from the Himalayas, through parts of China, down through Sumatra, you definitely would have to classify these as ape-like, unknown anthropoids that may be related to orang-utans. The toe structure is the clue. If you have a creature leaving prints that resemble your hand, it is an ape. If the unknown's footprint looks like your track would look, it's more man-like, woman-like, hominoid.

'In the USA, I think you have two pockets of possibly "real" creatures, one of huge hominoids in the Pacific north-west and another of smaller anthropoids in the southern bottomlands.

'I do not believe that Yeti (an ape) or Sasquatch (a possible humanoid) are directly related to man. We are indirectly related to them, in the same fashion that we are indirectly related to gorillas or chimps.'

Although a Bigfoot has never been killed or captured, anecdotal encounters proliferate. In a 1941 report from Daghestan, USSR, a Soviet Army officer, Colonel Karapetyan, describes a creature that was captured and killed – but not submitted for scientific study – as 'doubtlessly a man', but whose 'chest, back and shoulders were covered with shaggy hair of a dark brown colour. His eyes were dull and empty – the eyes of an animal'. Wait. Jeremy Beadle?

One of the oddest tales ever is that of Albert Ostman of British Columbia who, in 1957, described an encounter 33 years earlier in which he was scooped up in his sleeping

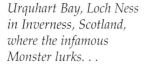

Urquhart Bay, Loch Ness in Inverness, Scotland, where the infamous Monster lurks. . .

bag and carried several miles to become the prisoner for six days of a friendly nuclear Sasquatch family: mum, dad, brother and sister.

Canadian Bigfoot expert John Green has combined all credible sightings, which date back at least one hundred years, into a composite Bigfoot: seven-and-a-half-feet tall, solitary, covered almost entirely with reddish-brown hair, ape-like in bodily structure, broad-shouldered, no neck, flat face, sloped forehead, ridged brow, and a cone-shaped head.

There is no cryptozoological search today anywhere near as intense as the hunt for Bigfoot. In April 1995, a 30-member team of anthropologists, biologists and geneticists from the Chinese Academy of Science, Beijing University, and Beijing Normal University set off for the Shennongjia Nature Reserve in central China on a year-long expedition to investigate centuries-old reports of a

seven-foot, 'half-man, half-ape' creature.

Peter Byrne, an Irish-born Bigfoot hunter, has at his disposal two helicopters, a Jeep, Toyota Land Cruiser, International Scout, snowmobile, and van, called the Bigfoot Mobile Base. His pistols are loaded with biopsy darts, which take blood samples and allow the target to walk away. If that Bigfoot guy expects to have a peaceful year, he can forget it.

Cryptozoological legends are not just a long-standing part of many cultures, they are also a major tourist draw. Sightings of England's Beast of Bodmin Moor and Scotland's Nessie have repeatedly cropped up this century, but do not let a lack of press make you think the following aren't also much feared and beloved:

- The Changbai Queer Animal, a sea monster in Tianchitianchi Lake (formerly Dragon Lake), China.
- Ogopogo, Canada's most famous lake monster, in Lake Okanagan, British Columbia. (Also, along the Pacific coast, the sea serpent Cadborosaurus, known as 'Caddy'.)
- Nahuelito, the sea monster of Lake Nahuel Huapi, Argentina.
- Champy, of Lake Champlain, on the New York Vermont border.

Yes, large creatures do fire the imagination. But if Chris Carter could devise any biological mystery for a future X-File, he'd prefer to think small. 'You know, I'd love to do an episode where the whole mystery takes place under a microscope. And it would be very difficult to do, but every time you bend down and look in a microscope you would be terrified of what you would find.'

Bibliography
Sources and further reading

Books

Meteorites in History
John G. Burke, University of California Press, 1986

Unexplained!
Jerome Clark, Apogee books, Detroit, M1, 1990

Incredible Life – A, Handbook of Biological Mysteries
William R. Corliss, The Sourcebook Project, 1981

Diseases from Space
Fred Hoyle and N.C. Wickramasinghe, Sphere, 1981

The Carnivorous Plants
Francis Earnest Lloyd, Dover Publishing, New York, 1976

Papers, Journals & Newspapers

Fortean Times 62

Flytraps from Space
Mark Chorvinsky, Strange Magazine 12

The Telegraph, 26 August 1995

The Times, 20 July 1989

X-File: Squeeze

Case notes by Agent Fox Mulder

Besides the liver extraction, the most notable element connecting the crimes is the undetermined port of entry. Many victims were found with their doors and windows locked from the inside. Fingerprints at 7 of the 19 crime scenes match Eugene Tooms's.

I contend that, perhaps through a genetic mutation, Eugene Tooms is capable of contorting and elongating his body in order to gain access to his victims so that he may extract their livers, which provide him with sustenance for a hibernation period of 30 years.

A preliminary exam at the time of his arrest revealed abnormalities in Tooms's striated muscles and axial bones. However, his attorney blocked further investigation.

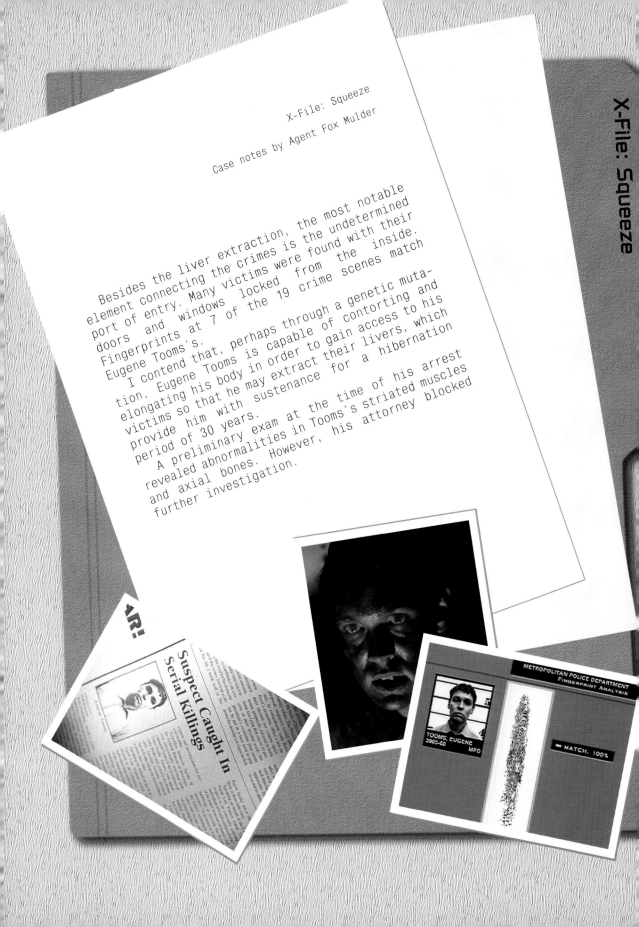

Suspect Caught In
Serial Killings

TOOMS, EUGENE
5205-60   MPD

METROPOLITAN POLICE DEPARTMENT
FINGERPRINT ANALYSIS

MATCH: 100%

HUMAN ENIGMAS

Squeeze and *Tooms* are horror stories, pure and simple. Eugene Victor Tooms, the agent's adversary in these episodes, is not only a biological anomaly, but also something of a literary anomaly: free from any fictional ancestry, a true innovation.

In the quest to create a villain who would challenge the Agents and terrify the viewers, writers Glen Morgan and Jim Wong drew on their love of the macabre inlcuding Jack the Ripper and a story in the LA Times about a retired detective obsessed with a 30-year-old homicide case. 'But most important,' recalls Morgan, 'was this hideous, bizarre almost - as-big-as-a-building ventilation system

outside our office. Jim and I were there late one night saying, "it's kind of weird here. Jesus, look at that vent, what if a guy was crawling around in there?"

Tooms himself, the agents guess, has a genetic mutation which not only facilitates remarkable feats of contortion without pain, but also gives him the urge and ability to hibernate and regenerate his cells - a process for which the bile from human livers is a necessary factor. He is, it is hinted, not your run-of-the-mill sadistic serial killer, but a hominid animal without regard for law or morality, simply driven to harvest that which he needs to survive.

But while Tooms's crimes may be fuelled by an uncontrollable animal urge, his faculties of intellect and reason are perfectly intact: he is cunning and thoroughly cognizant of the ways of the world. This sets him apart from a real animal or any literary man-beast. We can put his atrocities down to animal instinct and physical need, but only up to a certain point. His collection of 'souvenirs' from his victims suggests another, altogether more sinister and human element. Moreover, he is careful not to get caught and appears to know exactly what will constitute a risk: as Mulder correctly predicts, he does not kill the couple who give him a home when he is released from psychiatric confinement, although presumably their livers are just as good as the next guy's. As is Mulder's - and yet we see Tooms in the sleeping agent's apartment, passing up the perfect opportunity for a hassle-free bile-feast in favour of executing the cunning scheme that is on his mind. Never are Tooms's actions more evidently premeditated and intellectually driven than in the plot twist that has him frame Mulder for assault. Tooms might share an animalistic hunger with the werewolf or any other traditional man-shaped monster, but there the comparison ends. These blood-thirsty behemoths are simply not cred-

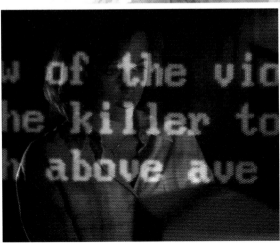

ited with the savvy and determination needed to voluntarily submit to a beating (even a self-administered one) in order to have the attack blamed on an adversary. Tooms is animal enough to be terrifyingly uncontrollable and unpredictable, and man enough for his actions to be unforgivable. Perhaps this is why Tooms' eventual demise -- squished in the dank mechanical underbelly of a shopping mall escalator – is allowed to be so deliciously, unashamedly visceral, and is refreshingly free of the bathos which usually accompanies the slaying of a fictional killer who is part-man part-animal.

'We wanted the series to do stuff you could relate to,' says Glen Morgan. 'You see a lot of shows where blood pours from the walls or something and it's kind of scary, but you go:"I really don't believe that's going to happen ."'

Sadly, it is almost too obvious to state our awareness of the possibility of human monsters – at least in terms of an unfathomable capacity for evil. But besides Tooms' s homicidal drive, what makes him so fearsome is his unusual physical abilities. He looks like us, he acts like us (when he's not gouging out people's internal organs with his bare hands) and yet he is not like us.

While most people readily accept that the capacity of the human mind remains an unknown quantity, scientific dogma would have us believe that we have the human body thoroughly sussed.

Certainly, the last century has seen many of its mysteries solved. It is entertaining to note, for instance, that a weighty and wonderful 1896 tome entitled *Anomalies and Curiosities of Medicine* by Doctors George M. Gould and Walter L. Pyle includes a section on allergic reactions. This syndrome, which is commonplace today is referred to as 'Idiosyncracy' and sits cheek-by-jowl with entries on such esoteria as males with the ability to produce milk and successfully nurse a baby, and women who experience regular menstrual bleeding from the eyes, ears, breasts and (as in the case of a young lady who injured her leg with the broken steel of her crinoline) the site of a previous wound.

Sure, a modern catalogue of medical anomalies would be somewhat slimmer, but the human body still generates plenty of unsolved mysteries. We may not be sharing the planet with a liver-scoffing centenarian who can distend his limbs to squeeze through the U-bend of a toilet, but there is definitely some high weirdness afoot, and it would be arrogant and foolish to ignore these enigmas. As Gould and Pyle sagaciously offer in their introductory pages, 'Possibly, indeed, it was the anomalous that was largely instrumental in arousing in the savage the attention, thought, and investigation that were finally to develop into the body of organised truth which we now call science.'

Serpentina - the boneless woman

'The preliminary medical exam revealed quite abnormal development of the muscular and skeletal systems...'

SCULLY

If Eugene Tooms had been around in the morally dubious heyday of the freak show (and who knows, perhaps he was: Mulder and Scully never did ascertain when he was born) he would have been extremely popular – until he started murdering people, of course. He might also have found plenty to chat about to a young lady best known as Serpentina. Allegedly born without any bones in her body – whatsoever – apart from her skull – Serpetina was an extremely unsual woman. Her lack of internal structure may have been overstated for dramatic effect – her publicity shot showed her leaning coquettishly on a suspiciously steady- looking elbow – but, had she wanted to, she would have been capable of making some grand Eugene Tooms style entrances through air vents and the like.

In the 1880s, any kind of physical deviation from the norm was a ticket into showbiz. Charles Warren was a man born with an abnormal skeletal structure which meant that his joints could barely live up to their title. Contemporary accounts reveal that 'when he was but a child he was constantly tumbling down, due to the heads of the femurs slipping from the acetabula'. The eight-year-old Charles was dubbed ' The Yankee Dish-Rag ' and was packed off to join a company of acrobats and strolling performers. To his credit, he acquired an astonishing control of his muscular system, far surpassing that of a normal man. Not only could he walk perfectly well without his legs popping out of their sockets at inconvenient moments, but he could dislocate any bone at will - which was great for business at any rate.

Charles allowed himself to be studied by many medical men over the years, but no explanation was ever found for his strange bodily construction. It is interesting to note that he fathered two children, both of whom could readily dislo cate their hips, which seems to suggest a genetic element in the conundrum.

By the 1930s both the medical profession and the public had become rather blasé where dislocationists were concerned. Doctors figured that there was little to be learnt from them, and the man in the street felt that once you'd seen one joint pop out, you had seen 'em all. If you were the proud owner of an out-of-the -ordinary skeletal structure, just about the only place you could get any attention was Robert Ripley's world famous, syndicated *Believe It Or Not!* newspaper features. But even there, you needed to do something a little bit different. A perusal of Ripley's archives reveals a generous collection of sensible and digni-

*Alice Penfold
demonstrates
her unusual
strength*

fied-looking people doing silly and undignified things: doffing a hat with a double-backed arm, kneeling with feet in front, turning the lower torso or feet in the opposite direction to the rest of the body. All harmless fun, but a strange reminder that mankind seemed to have given up asking *why* some people could achieve these feats while others could not.

Another common type of skeletal/muscular curiosity is unusual strength. Although working-out was still well over half a century away from being a popular pastime, the classic 'strong-man' was far from rare. Hence, if you were a buff guy who wanted to get into *Believe it or Not!* you would have to cook up some unusual way of demonstrating your strength: holding a chair aloft with someone on it – and preferably someone playing a mandolin – was a popular option. But there were genuine medical curiosities in this area too. In 1953, Alice Penfold, a 21-year-old from Bury, England, demonstrated her ability to hold her older sister aloft on a stool using only her teeth. A decade earlier, an eight-year-old strong-girl by the name of Patricia O'Keefe was the crowd-puller *de jour* around the beaches of California, given as she was to offering piggybacks to hefty volunteers. Weighing a mere 4 st. 5 lbs, there was definitely something out of the ordinary about her ability to dash around with a 14 st. man on her back, but as always, everybody was having far too much fun to wonder what it was.

'It's not where he lives. I think it's where he... hibernates'
Mulder

Hibernation in animals is well known, and many species hibernate as a matter of course. Countless others have the ability to hibernate but may not use it within their lifetime. The domestic hamster is one of these, and the lack of human knowledge about the hibernation state – with its barely perceptible breathing and lack of response to stimuli – has led to a grisly Edgar Allen Poe style burial for many a hapless hamster. Thankfully, not all unexpected hibernations have such tragic endings. In 1845, a 'dead' snail brought from Egypt spent five years glued to a label in the British Museum before springing back to life in March 1850, after which it heartily feasted on a meal of cabbage leaves offered by the curator and went on to live as happy a life as you'd care to imagine a snail can.

*Human hibernation:
A Yogi buries his head in
the sand at Agra, India.
His breathing stopped
and his pulse reduced to
two beats a minute.*

By and large, humans do not hibernate. Anxious doctors once toyed with the idea that comatose patients might be hibernating, but soon discovered that, unlike a dormant animal which can survive for long hibernation periods without food, a person in a coma will expire relatively swiftly without regular intravenous feeding.

This is not to say that humans cannot hibernate. For centuries Indian Fakirs have fulfilled every basic criterion without claiming that hibernating was their game. At first science was extremely sceptical of this. The first controlled scientific investigation into the phenomenon concentrated more on whether it was indeed taking place, as opposed to how.

The Indian Journal of Medical and Physical Science published the results of this experiment in their August 1836 edition. It had taken place in Jaisulmer and involved a 30-year-old man who – for a fee – submitted to being buried alive for a month. (Oddly, he said that he travelled around the country making his living this way - it seems that there were enough curious people around who felt that paying a guy to let you bury him alive was quite a dandy thing on which to blow your wages.)

On the appointed day, the volunteer was sewn into a cloth bag before being interred in a 3ft by 6ft grave lined with masonry and cloth (to help keep the nasty local white ants at bay). The grave had been dug into the floor of a small (12ft by 6ft), secure building. Two large slabs of concrete were placed over the hole, the door of the building was bricked up, and two guards were placed outside at all times. After a month, the research team broke through the door and dug up their subject. He was still in the sewn-up bag, and still asleep, and apart from looking a little thin, he appeared just fine. His jaw had stiffened somewhat, though, and had to be prised open with an iron instrument before the team could force water down his throat. Once this had been achieved, the man awoke and showed no particular ill effects.

Human 'hibernation'.

A 1922 edition of *Scientific Monthly* included a report on a Colonel Townsend of Dublin, who could 'die or expire when he pleased, and yet... by an effort he could come back to life again'. A well-known physician, Dr Cheyne recounted: 'I found his pulse sink gradually, till at last I could not feel any by the most exact and nice touch.' His observations were assisted by two colleagues, and Cheyne records: 'Dr . Baynard could not feel the least motion in the breast nor Dr Skrine perceive the least soil on the bright mirror he held to his mouth... We began to conclude he had carried the experiment too far, and at last we were satisfied he was actually dead.' But the colonel came round at 9.00 the next morning: there was, for all to see, a very extreme case of anomalous body control, with not a trace of the religious shenanigan about it.

A subsequent case suggested that body control was not necessarily only a natural gift (like Townsend's) or something that needed to be learnt and practised (like the Fakirs did). On 26 June 1930, the reigning US Navy wrestling champ, Joe Reno, allowed himself to be hypnotized by a mystic named Rajah Yogi in Dallas, Texas. He slept, buried in a coffin, for nearly 17 days – 406 hours – without food or water and awoke in perfect health. It was reported that a mere 15 minutes after being roused by Rajah Yogi, he wrestled Shreveport, Louisiana champ, Red Lindsay to a 10 minute draw.

Many years and numerous studies later, we are closer to fully understanding the phenomenon of human hibernation. It is facilitated by a conscious control of supposedly involuntary functions – principally breathing, blood circulation, digestion and metabolism. Laboratory tests on adepts of yoga, zen and various other doctrines have proved that these functions can be somehow influenced at will. With this kind of control, it is possible to kick the whole organism into neutral, making live burial for fun and profit a perfectly safe option.

The main difference between a dormant human and a hibernating animal is that although we can exist without nourishment for longer than we could in a conscious state, we are still talking about days rather than months – our fat stores just do not cut the mustard. But who knows, perhaps one day we will hit upon something that does. Did someone say human bile? Now there's an idea...

'What's going on in there? Mobile? Do you read me? Mobile!?'
DOCTOR RADIOING AMBULANCE CREW
The Erlenmeyer Flask

Chris Carter and *The X-Files* writing team always keep a look out for strange stories in the news. Although no episode has been based on any real-life event, weird reports can sometimes provide inspiration or a smaller element within the main story.

One such element appeared in *The Erlenmeyer Flask*: the toxic blood of the human-alien hybrids, inspired by an extremely arresting headline story.

The story itself is one of the oddest biological mysteries of the decade. As anyone who has ever worked in a hospital will attest, Saturday nights typically herald more mayhem than any other time, except perhaps New Year's Eve. On the night of Saturday 19 February 1994, the casualty department staff at Riverside General Hospital in California had steeled themselves for the usual onslaught. But nothing could have prepared them for the arrival of Gloria Ramirez.

Ramirez, a 31-year-old mother of two, had been brought to the hospital by ambulance, experiencing chest pains, breathing difficulties and repeated vomiting. She had a strange oily film covering her body, which a nurse later described as being 'like you see on the ground at the gas station'. Thirty-six minutes after reaching the medical room, Ramirez went into full cardiac arrest.

The attendant medical team leapt into action. Sally Balderas, Susan Kane and two other nurses took up standard procedure along with respiratory therapist Maureen Welch, under the supervision of Doctors Julie Gorchynski and Humberto Ochoa. Within 15 minutes, all but one of the team were unconscious.

It was Sally Kane who unwittingly started the night's horrific chain of events when she drew a blood sample from Ramirez. A strong smell of ammonia emanated either from the sample itself or the puncture wound and Kane collapsed. Dr. Gorchynski took over, but it was not long before she too was out cold, along with Welch and two of the remaining nurses. Nurse Balderas passed out shortly afterwards, leaving Ochoa as the only member of the original team left standing. Bizarrely, he had not responded to the fumes, nor been affected by them.

Ochoa was a lucky man. Whatever it was that had affected the others had extremely grim consequences. Following the incident, Dr. Gorchynski suffered such severe breathing difficulties and muscle spasms that she required a week in intensive care. By the end of February she was discharged from hospital, but remained extremely unwell – unable to draw a full breath or walk without crutches. Impaired blood circulation threatened to destroy her leg bones, and on 13 April she underwent surgery to try to save her knees. Nurse Balderas, meanwhile, spent ten days in hospital and never stopped being plagued by headaches, frequent attacks of vomiting and violent stomach pains, all of which prevented her from sleeping for more than an hour at a time. Both women also suffered from sleep apnoea – a syndrome which has been tentatively linked to cot death, where breathing stops during sleep.

So, what had caused this lethal miasma? Ramirez's medical records revealed that she had been diagnosed with cervical cancer two months before the incident, and that she was routinely using both painkillers and Compazine, a prevalent anti-nausea drug. However, none of these facts explained the release of toxic fumes from her blood. Nor did they account for the peculiar signs of contamination in the blood itself: the original sample contained clearly visible particles of yellow crystalline matter. Stranger still, a blood sample taken from Gorchynski was found to contain the same unidentified particles – suggesting that the fumes were not merely a result of the contamination, but also carried the contaminant.

The human body can produce toxic fumes after ingestion of cyanide, strychnine or organophosphates (chemicals found in pesticides and military  nerve gases), but Ramirez's blood tests showed no sign of any of these and her family insisted that she was certainly not suicidal. The results of the tests done on Doctor Gorchynski and Nurse Balderas again raised the possibility of organophosphate poisoning. Meanwhile, the California Department of Food and Agriculture issued a statement declaring that they knew of no organophosphate that could 'cause the kinds of things reported in that hospital'.

Sadly, Gloria Ramirez died shortly after the incident, but it was hoped that an autopsy would clear up the mystery once and for all. It took place on 24 February, and could have been a scene straight out of *The X-Files*. Personnel wore air-tight 'moon' suits and breathing equipment and communicated through two-way radios. First, air samples and remote camera pictures were taken through tiny holes poked through the closed body bag inside an aluminium casket. When the hands-on examinations began, they took place with a team of pathologists each working 30 minute shifts, followed by 12 hours of precautionary quarantine and medical observation. The whole procedure was carefully monitored by paramedics on closed circuit TV .

In the following weeks the body was kept in a sealed container. Further tissue samples were taken and an independent forensic examination was carried out. Ramirez was finally laid to rest on 20 April , but the murky enigma surrounding her was not. On 29 April , the Riverside County coroner declared that she had died as a result of kidney failure (caused by cancer), and that there was no sign of any toxins or other factors that could explain the events of that fateful Saturday in February.

With the constrictive cage of scientific study removed, the lurking beast of groundless speculation was allowed to run free. Despite inspections of the Riverside General's ventilation and air conditioning systems which had ruled  out any environmental causes, Ramirez's family continued to insist that the fumes had come from the hospital, not from Gloria's body. The media toyed with the idea of mass-hysteria, conveniently ignoring the thoroughly tangible facts of Gorchynski's and Balderas's continuing illness. Conspiracy theorists pointed out that Riverside County had been sprayed with Malathion, an anti-fruitfly pesticide, in the week prior to the incident. However, the coroner's office took the biscuit by proposing that the fumes may have been simply 'the smell of death' – a remark that *Fortean Times* magazine correspondent, Edward Young shrewdly described as 'positively medieval'.

Further investigation by the *Fortean Times* turned up an

anonymous police source, who alleged that Ramirez had used Phencyclidine (PCP or 'angel dust'), and had a theory to go with it. This kind of substance can be self-administered using DMSO, a liquid which can carry substances through the skin and into the blood stream. They volunteered that DMSO could account for both the strange film on Ramirez's skin and the noxious smelling fumes. One odd property of DMSO is that its smell varies according to the user. As reporter Young notes: 'On one person it might smell like fish, on another like garlic. Why not ammonia?'

However, even this hypothesis leaves many questions unanswered. Why were the fumes lethal? DMSO had once been sold over the counter for the treatment of bruises. If it could trigger this effect, it would surely have caused wide-spread carnage. What were the yellow crystals in the contaminated blood samples? Tests would have revealed any link with a familiar substance like PCP. Could something within Gloria Ramirez's own body have triggered an irregular chemical reaction? Who knows?

It looks like the events at Riverside General only serve as a further reminder that for all our medical knowledge, we still have a long way to go before we fully understand the human body.

'...An in-depth analysis of Tooms's injury would show my foot was not in the shoe at the time of impact'
MULDER

'Mulder... Are you suggesting Tooms is framing you?'
ASSISTANT DIRECTOR SKINNER

Among Eugene Tooms's catalogue of unusual abilities, he appears to be remarkably tolerant to pain. We hear some unpleasant wrenching and cracking noises as he distends his body; we see him gouge his cheek, drawing blood; we see the results of the violence he inflicts on himself in order to frame Mulder. But we never see him flinch.

Every year in the Kataragama temple in Sri Lanka a religious festival is held where members of the sect inflict severe injury on themselves, apparently without harm or pain. Nailing your tongue to a plank of wood is particularly popular, as is walking in clogs whose inner-soles are studded with sharp nails. Other participants spear their faces with knives or hang for hours from hooks driven through the muscles of their backs, thighs and buttocks.

But public demonstrations of apparently pain-free mutilations are not limited to the realm of religion. In the western world 'human pincushion' acts have always been popular, as have 'heat-resistant' performers such as '50s side-show star Theodore Kaufman who could lick a heated, soldering iron, and Leona Young of Norwich, New York, who called herself The Devil's Daughter and wowed the crowds by applying hot lead to her flesh and aiming a lit blowtorch into her mouth. These enchanting traditions are kept alive today by the charismatic Jim Rose (who makes an arresting guest appearance in the season two episode *Humbug*). The huge success of Rose and his gloriously grungy troop of travelling performers (including the 'Torture King') further proves that there is just as much satisfaction to be gained from revelling in a mystery as there is in solving it.

'Human Pincushion':
A dancer spears his face
during a magical trance
dance at Prambanan, Java

This is just as well, really, since we are a very long way from understanding why it is that some people do not feel pain. But then, we have yet to discover how to measure pain, or indeed what exactly pain is.

At one extreme of the mystery there is a rare congenital medical condition which causes a complete absence of pain. This condition was only recognised well into this century, and must have puzzled the doctors of bygone eras. We can only guess that it might lend an explanation to a case recorded in 1887 in which a patient's leg was amputated without anaesthesia, during which he showed no sign of distress and 'only remarked that he thought the saw did not cut well'.

Then again, it is an extremely rare affliction, and could not begin to account for the thousands of cases of pain-free people. It is beginning to look like we may be dealing with two or three separate phenomena.

The first category is people whose responses are usually normal but who find themselves pain-free under unusual circumstances, and who claim to have no control over the situation.

One of the first recorded cases of this kind concerned one of Napoleon's generals, who had a particularly nasty run-in with a cannon ball. He underwent impromptu surgery on the battlefield, where both of his legs were hastily hacked off and the stumps thrust into a cauldron of boiling tar for disinfective purposes. He was said to have smoked a cigar during the proceedings and been delighted to find that he felt no pain.

Battlefield bravery is by no means rare. A survey undertaken in the seventies revealed that 70% of soldiers injured by bullets or fragments of metal felt no pain at the time of injury – only later. It is well known that the human body produces endorphins – a pain-suppressing agent often referred to as 'the brain's natural opium', and many believe that an especially horrific incident can trigger the brain to produce enough endorphins to block pain altogether.

It has been suggested that certain people may be able to control the release of endorphins, in much the same way that adepts can control the body functions which facilitate 'hibernation'. The endorphin hypothesis may account for people who are aware of their ability to suppress pain. But then again, it appears that there are other factors at work – namely the brain and its receptors.

In the early Seventies, American researchers Elmer and Alyce Green tested Jack Schwarz, a man who claimed to be able to stab himself without bleeding. Wired to the EEG, a device which measures patterns of brain activity, Schwarz registered Beta waves (the state of mental activity and concentration) before the experiment, which immediately turned to Alpha waves (awake – but-relaxed) when he shoved a six inch sailmaker's needle into his bicep. It seemed that Schwarz was somehow able to switch his thought patterns away from the pain and into a more relaxed state. However, the Greens were puzzled by the nature of the wounds themselves. Elmer Green reported that after deliberately interrupting Schwarz's concentration during one repetition of the

The arresting Jim Rose - keeping the side - show tradition alive in grand style

experiment, blood began to pour from the wound. Green then watched amazed as the man said softly 'Now it stops', and the hole closed up 'as if drawn by purse strings'.

If we are prepared to believe that an individual can control the secretion of endorphins, or change his brain patterns as if by the flip of a mental switch, then presumably it might also be possible to suppress the sympathetic nervous system in order to prevent bleeding. Understanding of these abilities is improving all the time, and laboratory studies indicate that there is nothing supernatural about them.

Perhaps one day selective pain control will truly be within anybody's capability. But that day would seem to be a long way off. For now, we should simply sit back and enjoy the mystery.

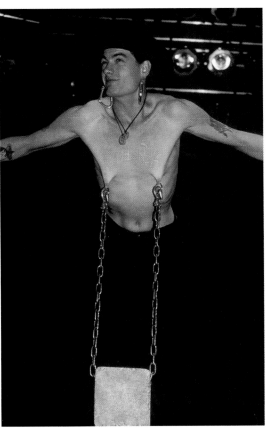

One of Jim Rose's not so merry men

'What if Tooms is a twentieth century human monster?'
MULDER

Could someone like Eugene Tooms actually exist? It certainly - if you'll pardon the pun - takes a stretch of the imagination. Could even the most wildly mutated human gene create a man who strays *that* far from the predictable? Maybe. The human body is capable of some remarkable flourishes of modification. Consider these:

SUPERNORMAL ABILITIES

James Aagaard of Ord, Nebraska, a performer who travelled the midwest and Canada in the early Thirties, had a voice that could be heard over a distance of six miles.

In the 1880s, two French scientists were baffled by a boy who could correctly guess the page numbers of books chosen at random by another person – so long as they were standing behind him with the book open. It transpired that he was not psychic, but had such powerful eyesight that he was able to read the numbers from the minute back to front reflections on the cornea of the experimenter's eye.

BIZARRE BODILY FUNCTIONS

Many *recognised* medical conditions are extremely odd. Take Chromidrosis – the incidence of coloured sweat. Black is the most common hue, but pretty much every colour of the rainbow has been recorded by doctors since medical records began.

Or how about Poikilothermism? It's a condition where the body takes on the temperature of its surroundings, like a reptile or fish. Its most famous sufferer was H.P. Lovecraft, whose biographer L. Sprague de Camp commented that: 'To shake hands with him was a little like shaking hands with a corpse.'

SKIN – SHEDDING

Some people annually shed their entire epidermis, reptilian-style. An 1891 edition of *Science* revealed that a Mr. S.O. Buskirk of Clark County, Missouri, had done so since his birth in 1850. It always occurred in the summer months, and for five years in a row it took place like clockwork on 27 June . The process began with a hardening of the skin, which would then come away in large, intact sections. 'From the arms and legs it could be pulled off exactly like gloves or stockings,' wrote *Science*. 'As the old skin came away a new epidermis, as soft and pink as a baby's was revealed.' Apparently Mr. Buskirk had a fine collection of souvenirs, including several intact hands which looked like 'white rubber gloves'.

Mr. Buskirk was healthy and normal in every other respect, as was an elderly New Zealand woman who was reported as having shed her skin annually for 60 plus years, in the same way.

RUMINATION

It is not unheard of for a human to be born with the ability to ruminate – bring up little balls of food shortly after eating for the purpose of a second chewing session, in the same way a cow does. The *London Medical Recorder* of 1889 described several cases of habitual rumination in humans. Two of the ruminators came from families where another member also ruminated, suggesting a hereditary condition. However a third case involved a 27-year-old nanny who had only started to ruminate at the age of 17, after being constipated for four days on a cruise.

FINGERTIP REGROWTH

A 1974 report by a Sheffield surgeon, Dr. Cynthia Illingworth, revealed that many children under the age of 11 who have lost their fingertips in accidents have the ability to grow a new one. Dr. Illingworth made her discovery after an emergency room mix up with a little boy who had lost his fingertip from just above the first joint. Instead of closing the wound, he was sent home with a bandage. To everyone's surprise, the tip began to regenerate, and eventually the boy grew an entirely new fingertip, with a perfect nail and fingerprints.

Dr. Illingworth experimented by avoiding closure on other children's wounds, and by 1974 had documented several hundred regrown fingertips.

HUMAN LUMINOSITY

There is a remarkable number of reported cases of luminosity in humans. In 1934, an asthma sufferer named Anna Monaro became known as 'the luminous woman of Pirano', when medical accounts were published in August journals the world over reporting that while ill, a blue glow had emanated from her breasts for four seconds at a time, every night for several weeks while she slept. The glow also appeared green and red on occasion, and was witnessed by countless doctors, all of whom failed to produce a satisfactory explanation.

Cases of luminosity are usually associated with ill health – many toxicology text books include references to luminous wounds – and there are also several reports to be found of glowing corpses. However, one case of luminosity in a healthy person appeared in the science and medicine journal *English Mechanic* in 1869 – a Boston woman who, on going to bed, 'found that a light was issuing from the upper side of the fourth toe on her right foot. Rubbing increased the phosphorescent glow and it spread up her foot.' The phosphorescence was apparently accompanied by a terrible smell, and the woman and her husband were perplexed to find that soaking the foot in water and scrubbing with soap had no effect on either. After three quarters of an hour both faded away. Luminous sweat and luminous urine have also been reported in both humans and animals.

ELECTRICAL PEOPLE

Reports of 'electrical' people are surprisingly common. It would appear that while the average human nervous system is able to generate, but not store, electricity, some people are endowed with the capacity of electric eels. They *can* store electricity and then discharge it in high voltage by touch.

Some people seem to be born with this ability and retain it only for a short time. A 1953 report in *Prediction* magazine gives an account of an electrical baby who gave a hefty shock to the doctor delivering him. The infant remained at a high voltage for 24 hours, and to such a degree that he was able to charge a leyden jar – a device used for storing electricity.

By and large, however, electrical people develop their condition later in life, and quite out of the blue. A fairly typical example would be the 1988 case of Xue Dibo, a 36-year-old boilermaker from Urumqi in China. One day he felt 'strange sensations' and subsequently found that whenever he touched people he was discharging a strong enough shock to knock them over.

An electrical man demonstrates his light touch

HUMAN MAGNETS

Some electrical people also have 'magnetic' properties. One of the earliest – and most extreme – on record concerns a Frank McKinstry of Joplin, Missouri, whose charge was particularly strong in the mornings. The unfortunate Mr. McKinstry spent most of his mornings moving around frantically, since stopping for even a second meant that he would become fixed to the ground. This was not always possible to avoid, and he often had to ask for assistance in yanking his legs free.

Some cases are less extreme, and can even go temporarily undetected. In 1994, housewife Erika Zur Stirnberg of Bochum, Germany, discovered that she had magnetic properties after watching a TV documentary about a magnetic Russian woman. As a joke, Erika put a spoon against her chest, and found, to her amazement, that it stayed there. She continued to add items until she had the entire contents of her kitchen drawer stuck to her.

Erika Zur Stirnberg - the magnetic woman demomstrates her powers of attraction

Magnetic people are by no means rare. In 1991, Bulgaria's Sofia Press Agency reported that over 300 people had shown up for a contest to see who could keep heavy metal objects on their bodies longest.

Odder still, not all magnetic people are limited to attracting ferrous metals. *Science* reported on a series of 1889 experiments conducted by a Dr. W. Simon with a young Baltimore man, Louis Hamburger. The tips of

Hamburger's fingers – providing they were clean and dry – naturally adhered to metals, stone, rubber, wood, glass and many other materials, and he could pick up an object simply by touching it. He was able to lift a 5 lb glass jar of iron filings this way with as much ease as a bamboo cane.

FIERY BREATH

In 1882, a doctor named L.C. Woodman studied a 27-year-old Mr. W.M. Underwood from Paw Paw, Michigan, who had fiery breath. His account in *Scientific American* revealed that Mr. Underwood could ignite hankies and pieces of paper merely by breathing on them, and 'while out gunning and without matches, desirous of a fire, lie down after collecting dry leaves and by breathing on them start a fire and then coolly take off his stockings and dry them.' Apparently Underwood had discovered his unusual talent by accident when inhaling the scent of a perfumed hankie – when he exhaled, it burst into flames.

The doctor was unable to find an explanation, but was certain that fraud was not involved since Mr. Underwood was prepared to strip, rinse his mouth out, wash his hands, and submit to 'the most rigid examination' before demonstrating his skills.

X – RAY VISION

Two cases of apparent 'X-Ray vision' have been recorded in the past decade. The first concerns 31-year-old Zheng Xiangling of Beijing, who first travelled to the West in 1988 to display her skills. Zheng works alongside doctors at the General Staff Headquarters of the People's Liberation

Army, and claims to be able to see her patients' internal organs and bones in full colour and three dimensions. Rumour has it that her clientele have included numerous prominent Chinese statesmen, including Deng Xiaoping himself. Allegedly, Zheng can also will goldfish to die, although quite how she came to discover this talent, we are not told.

More intriguing still is the case of former crane driver Ms. Yuliya Vorobyeva of Donetsk in the Ukraine, whose peculiar story was reported in 14 June 1987 edition of *Izvestia*, a sober and upright Ukranian newspaper. In March 1978, 37-year-old Vorobyeva accidentally received a 380-volt electric shock whilst working in a mine. She was pronounced dead and spent two days on a mortuary slab. However, when an autopsy was attempted on her body, blood pumped out, the corpse started to shake and she came back to life. Vorobyeva recounts that she was unable to sleep properly for six months, but eventually fell into a long sleep from which she emerged refreshed and invested with a very odd talent. Having left her house to buy some bread, she glanced over at a woman waiting at the bus stop. Vorobyeva recalls: 'I was paralysed with horror – I could see her intestines and straight through her. . .'

Like Zheng, Vorobyeva was given an honorary medical post – working alongside doctors at Donetsk hospital, where she has had enormous success, particularly in diag-nosing rare illnesses such as diseases of the pancreas. A colleague, Dr. A. Svedlerova says that Yuliya 'has never made a single mistake'.

Vorobyeva also impressed the reporter from *Izvestia* by telling him that she could deduce from a red liquid in his stomach that he had just eaten 'kisel' – a popular Ukranian jelly dish.

Bibliography
Sources and further reading

Arthur C. Clark's Chronicles of the Strange and Mysterious
John Fairley and Simon Welfare, William Collins and Sons, 1987

Incredible Life: a Handbook of Biological Mysteries
William R. Corliss, The Sourcebook Project, 1981

Biological Anomalies: Humans I
William R. Corliss, The Sourcebook Project, 1992

Biological Anomalies: Humans II
William R. Corliss, The Sourcebook Project, 1993

The Encyclopedia of Ignorance
Ronald Duncan and Miranda Weston Smith, New York, 1977

English Mechanic

Fortean Times

Anomalies and Curiosities of Medicine
George G. Gould M.D. and Walter L. Pyle M.D., 1896

We Who Are Not As Others
Daniel P. Mannix, Pocket Books, 1976

Human Personality
F.W.H. Myers, Longmans Green and Company, 1963

An Encyclopedia of Claims, Frauds and Hoaxes of the Occult and Supernatural
James Randi, St Martin's Press, 1995

Strange But True?
Jenny Randles and Peter Hough, Piatkus, 1994

Science Magazine

Scientific American

You'll Never Believe It: A compendium of Curioddities from the Bizarre World of Ripley's Believe it or Not Archives
Mark Sloan, Roger Manley and Michelle Van Parys, Little, Brown and Company, 1993

Mind Over Matter
The Editors, Time Life Books, 1988

The Living Brain
W.G. Walter, Penguin, 1961

Supernature
Lyall Watson, Sceptre, 1973

X-file: Jersey Devil

Case notes by Agent Dana Scully

A post-mortem medical exam of the woman shot dead by the Atlantic City Police Department revealed fragments of human bone in her digestive tract. Forensic tests and dental comparisons are underway to determine a suspected link with the death of Roger Crockett, the vagrant whose body was discovered in the woods with the right arm and shoulder missing and human teethmarks visible below the clavicle.

The woman's age was estimated at 25-30-years-old. Examination of her uterus seems to indicate that she may have given birth. The A.C.P.D. has listed her as Jane Doe and a search for her identity in state psychiatric records has begun in earnest, so far without success.

Doctor Diamond, Professor of Anthropology at the University of Maryland, was granted permission by the authorities to examine the body. He was able to find no indication of prehistoric bone structure or physiology, thus ruling out the possibility that the woman represented some kind of evolutionary anomaly, as Agent Mulder had previously suggested.

Despite the pending closure of the homicide inquiry, I recommend that further search efforts in the woods outside Atlantic City be undertaken. In light of the previous discovery of the body of an unidentified 40-year-old male, who appeared to have been living a feral lifestyle similar to that of Jane Doe, it is plausible that the two may have been partners. The possibility that they may have produced offspring — who conceivably could still be living in the woods of New Jersey — should not be ignored.

t dead by the
nts of human
and dental
ed link with
se body was
d shoulder
clavicle.
years-old.
t she may
Jane Doe
c records

at the
by the
find no
iology,
resent-
er had

ry, I
tside
vious
ale,
imi-
may
ave
ing

FERAL HUMANS

The *Jersey Devil* took Mulder and Scully on a hunt for the unknown perpetrator of a homicide – who turned out to be a 'beast woman'. Feral human or evolutionary throw-back? We are unsure until the last moment, but in *The X-Files* universe at least, the mystery identity of the Jersey Devil is solved.

> *'Mulder – I've heard that same story since I was a kid. It's a folk tale. A myth'*
>
> SCULLY

> *'I heard the story when I was a kid too. Funny thing is, I always believed it'*
>
> MULDER

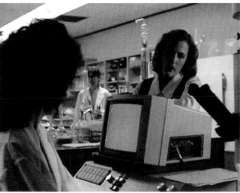

In the real world, there is still a Jersey Devil, and even if you regard it only as a delicious slice of vintage folklore, it remains a mystery.

Loren Coleman is a seasoned Fortean researcher and author, a cryptozoologist and something of an authority on the Jersey Devil. According to him, it has been the State of New Jersey's 'official demon' since the 1930s, but tales of its existence go back as far as 1790.

The ingredient which makes the Jersey Devil legend so

gloriously rich is the same one that makes it far too sticky to get to the bottom of: there are over 30 different variations of the legend. The original tale concerned a Mrs. Leeds, whose 13th pregnancy in 1735 was said to have led to the birth of a 'devil child' that flew away up her chimney. Whether or not this tale was regarded as superstition when it was first told, numerous New Jersey residents have earnestly reported sightings of the demon for the last two hundred years.

Says Coleman: 'The "Jersey Devil" has appeared differently to various witnesses – mostly "ram-headed and winged" in accounts from the 1700s: ' a "phantom livestock killer" in 1840; "the Devil" in 1873–74; "unidentifiable footprints" in 1894–95; again a "ram-headed, winged weirdie" in 1909; a "flying lion" in 1926; a "large, speedy, feathered animal running on four 'legs' in 1927; a "horrible monster" in 1928; a "half-man, half-beast" in 1932; an "upright devil" in 1935; "appearances" in 1941 and 1948; a "green male monster" in 1949; "something" killing chickens in 1952; "unearthly screams" in 1960; and a "seven feet tall, faceless hairy creature" in 1966.'

In his 1983 book, *Mysterious America*, Coleman writes: 'Is there a Jersey Devil? Well, there is *something*. Or perhaps a number of somethings. Underneath all the myth, all the nonsense, all the fabrication, is a small core of truth, out of which the legends have grown. There are just too many loose ends – like tracks, and sightings by reliable winesses – that can no longer be glossed over. Perhaps *several* Jersey Devils haunt the pine barrens region, including "flying lions" and

(courtesy of Middle Atlantic Press)

Map showing the areas where the Jersey Devil has been sighted

"kangaroos", or in any case creatures which looked like that to flustered individuals seeing them in less than ideal light conditions. Not everything that gets shoved under the "Jersey Devil" banner really belongs there. Like other States, New Jersey harbours more than one mystery animal, but whenever one appears, inevitably it gets hailed, usually for purposes of ridicule, as the latest manifestation of the Devil and so joins the great body of myth, legend and lore.'

Coleman adores *The X-Files*, and thoroughly enjoyed *Jersey Devil*. He was dismayed to see posts on the Internet complaining that Chris Carter had got the details of the legend 'wrong'. 'Everything strange in New Jersey is labelled the "Jersey Devil",' asserts Coleman. 'Chris Carter was only criticized for writing this by people who did not know what they were talking about, but Carter did! I think he was entirely justified in labelling a humanoid as the "Jersey Devil".'

Chris Carter finds the anatomy of folklore fascinating. 'I think we like to scare ourselves. We like to think that there are bogeymen out in the dark, and so we find something that exists in the collective consciousness: a beast stalking in the night. And it becomes the Jersey Devil, it becomes the Werewolf, it becomes the creature, whatever creature, and I think the Jersey Devil is another example of our fear of violent death.'

Besides the original Jersey Devil story which gave him the setting for the episode, Carter was also inspired by Nobel Prize winner E.O. Wilson's comments on the 20th century evolution of mankind. 'I read an article he had written about how man, being top carnivore, is really sort of laying waste to the planet. We are gluttons in terms of our place in the eco-system. And I found that very interesting, and so what I was looking at was a situation: what if evolution had actually turned backwards? What if somebody had, as a result of some sort of evolutionary anomaly, actually gone backwards and become that Neanderthal on the grassy savannahs – but right in New Jersey?'

The main spur for the episode, however, was Carter's interest in the subject of feral humans. 'I saw Truffaut's *Wild Child*,' he explains, 'and liked that very much.'

'Haven't there been cases where men have been raised by animals in the wilderness, who have no language and hunt like predators?'
MULDER

'Oh yes. Several'
DR. DIAMOND

For as long as there have been societies, there have been fringes of those societies, where the unwanted have been left to fend for themselves. Inconvenient babies, deformed children and orphans, have all been taken to the edge of civilization and thrown off. Sometimes they have died. Sometimes they have learnt to survive on their own. Sometimes they have been adopted by other species. She-wolves who have recently lost their own litters are the most common surrogate mothers and have even been known to steal away unguarded babies.

Feral humans have been spotted, captured and studied ever since there were 'civilized' people with whom to compare them. One of the oldest documented cases was the wolf-child of Hesse, found in 1344 running wild, on all fours, in the woods. He had apparently been living in a hole with wolves.

The next detailed account jumps to the 17th century when a bear-child was found in Lithuania (1661). He was extremely keen on cabbages, refused to wear clothes and seems to have avoided city living. A sheep-child in Ireland (1672) was impervious to the cold but rather fond of hay. A calf-child in Bamberg (around 1680) used to like to fight big dogs but apparently ended up 'achieving a far higher mental level than he had on discovery'. Hearteningly, the second bear-child discovered in Lithuania (1694) not only learned to stand erect but to speak.

The 18th, 19th and 20th centuries, with their interest in the sub-classes of a now dominant civilized society, uncovered a veritable zoo of feral children. Each was idiosyncratic and reflected the environment in which they were brought up.

This young boy was found living with gazelles. He was caught with some difficulty as he'd learned to run as swiftly as the animals who had adopted him

'I have a perpetrator out there. Whether he's Hannibal the Cannibal or Elmer Fudd I've got a job to protect people'
DETECTIVE TOMSON

'Close after the cubs, came the "ghost" – a hideous-looking being, hand and foot and body like a human being; but the head was a big ball of something covering the shoulders and the upper portion of the bust leaving only a sharp contour of the face visible. Close at its heels there came another awful creature exactly like the first, but smaller in size. Their eyes were bright and piercing, unlike human eyes.'
REVEREND SINGH OF MIDNAPORE

In 1920, when Reverend Singh of Midnapore, India, was asked to investigate 'ghosts' haunting the forest of another village, he hardly expected to find two feral children living among a family of wolves in an abandoned termite mound. Who would? The sight stunned him, and so spooked the villagers, that Reverend Singh had to use all the skills he exercised at his pulpit to keep them from shooting the entire pack. Instead, they shot the mother wolf, and dragged out the children. Beneath the mud and matted hair that had given them their monstrous appearance were two little girls that the Reverend judged to be about three and six. They did not look related, implying the wolf mother had taken them in at different times.

Mrs. Singh feeding biscuits to Kamala

The Reverend took them back to his orphanage in Midnapore, keeping them in a disused outhouse. They were given a mattress to lie on and blankets to cover them, but they ignored both, showing no sign of suffering from the cold. They ripped off anything they were made to wear and, finally, Mrs. Singh stitched on an unremovable nappy-type arrangement. The girls spent hours trying to bite or scratch them off.

They lapped up milk offered to them in bowls but did not eat until the day they were let out into the yard at the same time as the orphanage dogs were being fed. Reverend Singh tried to restrain the girls but the older one broke free and plunged into the mêlée of feeding dogs. They seemed to accept her and she bolted down a few mouthfuls of meat and offal before padding off with a bone. She retired to a quiet spot and, holding the bone down with her two little hands as though they were paws, the six-year-old girl began to gnaw at it.

Those two girls, the older one subsequently named Kamala and the younger one Amala, were re-defining what it means to be human.

'What if it is a female, Scully? How close is she to you, or to me?'
MULDER

Man has often debated whether it is nature or nurture that makes us what we are. It is through the study of feral children that nurture scores its greatest victories in the eternal debate.

Over the next few months, Kamala and Amala displayed traits common to most feral humans raised by

Kamala and Amala liked to sleep piled on top of each other

wolves. They were nocturnal, had excellent hearing and night vision, a fear of light and humans, slept piled on top of each other, howled at night, sniffed at everything that came their way, showed a desire to be reunited with the cubs and to play with the orphanage dogs, were strict carnivores (aiding their digestion by eating dirt and pebbles), went to the bathroom at will and were quadrupeds, running on all fours faster than most grown men could run on two.

The Singhs started to question whether or not the girls would have been better off left in the woods.

'Does she feel emotion? Or are her days just spent looking for food?'
MULDER

In early September 1921, both Kamala and Amala fell ill. On 21 September, Amala died. Kamala prodded the corpse of her dead companion and tried to pull it off the bed. The Singhs briefly coaxed Kamala into another room but she returned to Amala's side and again tried to get her to move. Finally Amala was taken away for burial. According to Reverend Singh's notes: 'Only two drops of tears fell from Kamala's eyes, and no change of expression was noticeable on the face to make one understand that Kamala was actually weeping.'

Kamala spent the weeks following Amala's death in a funk, alternately sitting dejected in a corner or, if allowed, sniffing around areas in the orphanage and yards where Amala might once have been found, all the while making a repetitive, plaintive yelp. At night she became restless and tried to escape. Once again, she took up howling.

'Eight little six-year-old boys running around. Talk about primitive behaviour'
SCULLY

Kamala's best friend during this period was a hyena cub that Reverend Singh had bought at a local market. They would play together for hours. Although she had begun to accept Mrs. Singh, the first humans she really took to and learnt from were the orphanage children. At first she would approach while they played and if a toy rolled her way, she would pounce on it, carry it off in her mouth and chew on it in a corner. But eventually she learnt to play properly, and became so attached to the kids that she did not like to be separated from them.

Over the next few years, Kamala was gradually domesticated. She learnt to stand, learnt enough Christian modesty to never leave the orphanage naked, grew to be afraid of the dark and learnt some words, though not always the right ones. During a church service in 1929, while the whole orphanage was saying, 'O give thanks unto the Lord,' in reply to Reverend Singh's oration, a shaky voice piped up with the Bengali words for 'Satan' and 'pig'. Her tutors and fellow orphanage inmates burst out laughing. Reverend Singh was not amused.

On 26 September 1929, Kamala fell ill with typhoid fever. Ironically, her use of language blossomed while she was sick. According to Reverend Singh's notes: 'She once said to one female attendant, "Palul, didi, baile jaba." (I will ease myself so take me out of the room.) So the female attendant took her out of the room and she satisfied the call of nature. While she did so, she did not hesitate to eat up pebbles and stones lying on the ground.' Old habits die hard.

On 13 November 1929, Kamala died. She was given a Christian burial and laid to rest next to Amala under the banyan tree in St. John's cemetery.

'Tell him they've got a real live Neanderthal running loose'
MULDER

Many other feral children were not raised by animals but seem to have learnt to live on their own in the woods. Unlike those raised by animals, they were usually bipeds. The most famous of the bunch was Victor the Wild Boy who was captured near Lacaune, France on 9 January 1800 and whose story was told in Francois Truffaut's 1969 film *L'Enfant Sauvage* (released in America as *The Wild Child*). The movie made a big impression on Carter: 'It's fascinating, that he (Victor) could actually put his hand into a pot of boiling water and it didn't burn him, he didn't understand the concept. And so it's almost like pain is a concept? I found that very interesting.'

However, Carter feels that we are essentially born knowing what it means to be human. 'I'm an advocate of the nature argument, but with a heap of help and nurture on top of it. I think we are all victims of our forebears.'

Jean Itard, the young doctor who attempted to civilize Victor, felt differently. He felt that nurture was all. 'Cast on this globe, without physical powers, and without innate ideas, man can find only in the bosom of society the eminent station that was destined for him in nature, and would be, without the aid of civilization, one of the most feeble and least intelligent of animals. Man is only what he is made by his external circumstances.' So began Itard's journal as he embarked on an attempt to re-educate 'Victor the Wild Boy of Aveyron'.

When Victor first came to live with Itard, his favourite pastimes were playing naked in the snow and setting fire to ninepins. Like most other feral humans, he was insensitive to heat or cold, kept trying to escape, could not understand his reflection in a mirror (he kept trying to see what was behind it) and did not sneeze even when snuff was stuck up his nose as an experiment. He would spend hours looking at the moon.

'If it's a primate it would have a natural fear of heights. It'd also want to stay near its food source'

DR. DIAMOND

For years, Itard worked with Victor, using various techniques to improve his concentration, including holding him out of a second story window until, for the first time, he cried. Itard's educational regime, but probably mostly the loving care of Itard's housekeeper, Madame Guerin, eventually led Victor to learn to perform small tasks like setting the table and reading short words. He caught his first cold and became fussy about the consistency of his potatoes. He loved being helpful and getting compliments and responded much more quickly to emotional punishment than to physical punishment (unless it was being held out of an open window).

Then, Victor hit puberty.

'There would have been offspring'
MULDER

Most feral humans do not seem to be interested in sex. This is very probably because they have 'misimprinted' at an early age and so don't really see themselves as homo sapiens. In other words, they are about as attracted to humans as most humans are to cattle. Victor, with his relatively long stretch of human contact, was different. Confused, but different.

Jean Itard: 'I have seen him in the company of women trying to relieve his uneasiness by sitting beside one of them and gently pinching her hand, her arms, her knees, until, feeling his restless desires increased instead of calmed by these odd caresses, and finding no relief from his painful emotions, he suddenly changed his attitude and petulantly pushed away the woman whom he had sought with some eagerness. Then he turned to some other woman, with

Kamala running the way she knew best – on all fours

whom he behaved in the same way.'

Itard, being a bit of a prude, treated Victor's 'condition' with the customary cold baths, supplemented by the more inventive violent exercise and bleedings. Itard defended his course of action thus: 'I did not doubt that if I had dared to reveal to this young man the secret of his restlessness and the aim of his desires, he would have reaped incalculable benefits. But, on the other hand, supposing I had been permitted to try the experiment, should I not have been afraid to reveal a need to our savage which he would have sought to satisfy as publicly as his other wants and which would have led him to acts of revolting indecency?'

Teens, eh? What can you do?

Eventually, Itard moved on to other fields of study and his work became the basis for the Montessori technique (except for the bit about holding the student out of a second story window). Victor went off to live with the widowed Madame Guerin, and, as far as the record shows, they lived happily ever after.

'It's just highly unlikely that what you are suggesting could have survived evolution or civilization out in the woods of New Jersey'
DR. DIAMOND

So is that the end? Are we to believe that feral humans and concrete jungles don't mix? On the contrary, according to Loren Coleman, *Jersey Devil's* premise of a feral hominid creature in downtown Atlantic City was a timely one. 'Encroaching urbanisation will start pushing the limits of all mystery animals. "Wild men" and "unknown anthropoids", have already been seen, for example, in the suburbs of St. Louis, Missouri, and in New York City. If the Eastern forms of Sasquatch are "real" versus some kind of cultural artifact, then, yes, a "Jersey Devil" scene as in *The X-Files*, could already have taken place. Homeless people, also, are a reality. In parts of the Pine Barrens, Appalachia, Pacific Northwest, southern swamps, etc., homeless people, Vietnam era veterans and poor folks have gone back to the land in a big way, and near-feral people exist in America today. And have for generations.'

Bibliography
Sources and further reading

Books

Mysterious America
Loren Coleman, Faber and Faber, 1983

The Wild Boy of Aveyron
Jean Itard
and
Wolf Children
Lucien Malson, NLB (combined edition), London, 1972

The Wolf Children
Charles Maclean, Allen Lane, Penguin, 1977

Discours sur L'Origine de L'Inegalite Parmi les Homees
J.J. Rousseau, Garnier, Paris, 1962

Wolf Children and Feral Man
J.A.L. Singh and R.M. Zingg, Harper and Row, New York, 1942

A Journey through the Kingdom of Oude
William Henry Sleeman, London, 1858

Papers, Journals & Newspapers.

Feral Man and Extreme Cases of Isolation
R.M. Zingg, American Journal of Psychology, Vol. 53, 1940

Wild Men
Audrey Topping, Science Digest, August 1981

Wolf Children in India
P.C. Squires, American Journal of Psychology, Vol. 38, 1927

X-File: Shapes

Case notes by Agent Dana Scully

I am still inclined to consider that the homicide of Joe Goodensnake was just what it seemed to
be: a feud over land rights between the young man
and rancher Jim Parker. However, I can find no
explanation for the discrepancy between
Goodensnake's dental records and the abnormally
extended canine cuspids we observed in post-mortem
examination.

The subsequent murder of Jim Parker at the hands
of his son Lyle remains without apparent motive and
possibly the most baffling incident of all: Agent
Mulder, the sheriff and myself witnessed the shooting of Lyle by Sheriff Tskany is
the fatal shooting of Lyle by Sheriff Tskany. Agent
the body of Lyle Parker. However, I cannot share
Agent Mulder's inclination to join Ish, a tribal
elder whom he consulted, in considering the reality of the Trego Indians' 'Manitou' myth by way of
possible justification for the unexplained events at
Two Medicine ranch.

that the
what it
between
Parker.
for the
dental
canine
xamina-

at the
appar-
le by
fling
f and
known
body
ent
bal
the
yth
x-

THE SHAPES OF FEAR

S *hapes* saw Mulder and Scully taking their first dip into the enchanted pool of native American legend and spiritual belief – a culture which fascinates Chris Carter. 'It's a very rich mythology and it seems very soulful to me,' he muses. 'It's old and it does what all those good myths do: it tries to explain in metaphorical ways that which we know to be true – that you are born, you go through life and you die, and certain things happen to you, rites of passage... all these different things make us who we are and what they have in their mythology is just so wonderful and rich and full of good things for dramas.'

At first glance, and despite its original Native American flavour, *Shapes* appears to be a gripping re-telling of the traditional Werewolf story. We have every archetypal element: an involuntary transformation by night which is passed on by tainted blood; a wound inflicted on the beast which remains when he becomes a man again; a return to human form at the moment of death. Heck, for all the Trego's protests against a lunar connection, we even have a full moon on the night that Lyle Parker kills his dad. But between the lines there lurks canny references to the tangled cross-cultural history of the lyncanthropy myth.

'...It sure as hell didn't seem human out in the corral that night. Just look at the scars this boy has'
JIM PARKER

The moment mankind decided it was no longer part of the animal kingdom, the Werewolf was born. And not just the Werewolf, but a whole host of other Were-animals. Around the world, stories of man-beasts took root, combining the now-denied viciousness of man's animal nature with the physical attributes of the region's most feared predator. Were-tigers and Were-bears roamed Asia, Were-hyenas prowled Africa, Were-coyotes hunted in Central America and Were-lizards slithered across New Zealand.

Ironically, most of the several hundred Native American cultures failed to jump on this particular folkloric bandwagon, possibly because their beliefs were still firmly entwined with their natural surroundings. You could put it down to a more harmonious relationship with the animal kingdom, or a greater ability to confront honestly the dark side of human nature, but one way or another there simply didn't seem to be a cultural need for the Werewolf. Sure, there were still man-eating monsters, like the Witiko of the North Canadian Cree – a sort of cross between Bigfoot and Freddy Kruger – though these were most assuredly not human. And there was – and still is – interspecies mingling, provided by the shape-shifters.

*'Members of the Lewis and Clark
expedition wrote of Indian men
who could change their shape
into that of a wolf'*
MULDER

Shape-shifting is a pretty ambiguous term that encompasses quite a few different paranormal activities, varying between bands. Diane Reed, a Cree activist, describes it this way: 'People who have the gift of shape-shifting are people who have the ability to change from the physical self into other animals and other beings... It's very much between the physical and spiritual realms.' However, she adds: 'People do have the ability to do that... If you could see the activities of the shape-shifter, you would really consider it paranormal.'

So on the one hand, we have the Werewolf myth, with men turning into wolves, and we also have shape-shifting with men turning into animals. But let's consider for a moment the concept of a television series about an investigative team in search of the truth behind crimes and mysteries with a paranormal flavour. Are we talking about *The X-Files*? Or about *Scooby Doo*? It is human nature to assimilate a little piece of information and jam it into the closest convenient folder in our mental filing system. Which is exactly what happened when the early settlers met the natives.

The film world cashes in on the werewolf myth. Lon Chaney as the wolfman in Universal's 1946 production of Frankenstein Meets The Wolfman

The Westerners had brought with them some serious cultural prejudices against people who, for whatever reason, changed into animals. Shape-shifters became Werewolves, themselves identified in Europe with the Devil, and splosh! – harken to the sound of the shape-shifter's heretofore pristine reputation going down the toilet.

'The Tregos realised that Watkins had been attacked by what the Algonquins call the Manitou...'

ISH

To be fair to the puzzled white man, the legend of the shape-shifter is an intricate and many-faceted one, and there are a handful of areas which overlap with Werewolf lore. A shape-shifter injured while in animal form, will bear the scars on his human form when he comes out of his trance. And although in the main the gift of shape-shifting is traditionally used for benevolent purposes, it certainly has a dark side too.

The traditional shape-shifter is usually a mystic who changes into an animal or spirit for the good of the tribe, and is said to be able to travel not only the physical plane, but the spiritual as well. If someone is suffering from 'feeling scattered', a shape-shifter can be brought in to roam the spiritual realm and help regroup the patient's spiritual self – bringing a whole new meaning to the term 'getting your head together'. In cases of food being scarce, a shape-shifter could help to lead a hunt. With the aid of a talisman, consisting of a piece of fur or a claw of the animal they wish to become, the shape-shifter physically transforms. Typically, if the band is tracking deer, the shape-shifter will become a deer to better lead the hunters to the prey.

A 'bad' shape-shifter, on the other hand, is a sorcerer who has borrowed the body of an animal for nefarious purposes – usually in order to spy on, curse or just spook their enemies. The transformation is made by going into a trance, slipping out-of-body and spiritually diving into the body of an animal. This form of 'borrowing' is a common transglobal concept, turning up everywhere from the fictional antics of Granny Weatherwax in Terry Pratchett's

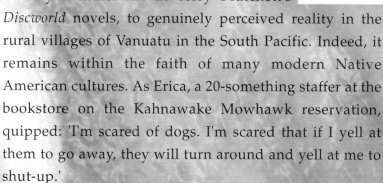

Discworld novels, to genuinely perceived reality in the rural villages of Vanuatu in the South Pacific. Indeed, it remains within the faith of many modern Native American cultures. As Erica, a 20-something staffer at the bookstore on the Kahnawake Mowhawk reservation, quipped: 'I'm scared of dogs. I'm scared that if I yell at them to go away, they will turn around and yell at me to shut-up.'

But for all the vague similarities between the activities of the shape-shifter and the activities of the Werewolf, there is one very pertinent difference: it is practically unheard of in legend for a shape-shifter, no matter how evil, to physically attack a human.

Surprised? You will be. Additionally, Native American shape-shifters are not known as 'Manitou'. As Father Stan, a patient and softly-spoken representative of the Native American Cultural Research Centre in South Dakota, is always happy to tell curious Westerners, 'Ma'anitou' is an Ojibwe word meaning 'god' or 'deity'. 'Manitou', mean-while, is the Algonquin term for 'the mysterious and

unknown potencies and powers of life and the universe'
and is most commonly translated as 'The Great Spirit'. For
many natives, calling a crazed, man-eating beast 'Manitou'
is like calling Charles Manson 'God'. So what gives?

The confusion – for both natives and Westerners –
surrounding the concept of shape-shifting can be traced
back to the impact of Christianity on native culture. When
the missionaries, including the notorious Jesuits, the
'Shock Troops' of the Vatican, arrived in North America
from Europe, they immediately began to try to mould
native beliefs to their version of Christianity. The colonis-
ers split Manitou, the all encompassing neutral power,
into a 'good' Manitou (meaning 'God'), and a 'bad'
Manitou (meaning 'the Devil') so as to make their
sermons more relevant.

Consider the fear-driven Western version of the
people-who-turn-into-animals myth, throw in the now
bastardised definition of Manitou and you get Westerners
telling tales about Werewolf-like evil Manitou roaming
native reservations. You get 'The Legend of the Manitou'.
And centuries down the line, you get *The Manitou* the
charmingly schlocky 1978 Tony Curtis/Susan Strasberg
movie in which a long-dead medicine man is resurrected
through an embryo on Strasberg's neck. But on the positive side, you also get *Shapes*, an unerringly respectful
rendering which is a brilliant and eloquent social
comment on the uneasy matrimony between modern
American and native American culture.

'These man-animal related murders predate the oldest X-file by one hundred and fifty years'
MULDER

Why was the Werewolf myth so ingrained in the European psyche that they had to find a local version of the story to claim when they arrived in North America? It is certainly fitting that, according to Mulder, the very first X-file (opened by none other than J. Edgar Hoover) involved what was essentially a Werewolf. Besides Beelzebub himself, the lycanthrope may well be the longest serving recruit to the army of darkness.

For millennia, Werewolves have skulked around the edge of European cultural consciousness. Around 2,400 years ago, Herodotus wrote about groups of people living in what is now Lithuania and Poland who claimed to turn into wolves for a couple of days a year. Being a progressive type of guy, he, of course, did not really believe it, but many of his less enlightened compatriots certainly did.

Werewolf stories – replete with obligatory full moons, graveyards, and wounds that survive the transformation back from wolf to man – were being written as early as the first century AD. *Satyricon*, written as entertainment during the reign of Nero, features a Werewolf as familiar as any cooked up by 20th century cinema.

The concept of the werewolf dates back hundreds of years

Tellingly, the next light-hearted Werewolf tale had to wait until the 18th century to get published. It was not that people had lost interest in Werewolves. On the contrary, the belief in them was so strong that it was pretty well unthinkable to fictionalise what was accepted as the terrible truth. And those days are not as distant as we might like to think. The last recorded case was a tragic incident in 1925, at Uttenheim, near Strasbourg, when a policeman shot and killed a boy whom he suspected of being a Werewolf.

To understand the European dread of Werewolves, it helps to get a handle on the pre-20th century European dread of bog-standard wolves. In Europe and North Asia, wolves were considered the most dangerous animal to man and his livestock. In France, there were special government institutions for wolf control from at least the reign of Charlemagne (768-814AD) which remained in place well into this century. Single wolves gained the kind of notoriety reserved these days for serial-killers – the 'Beast of Gevaudan' who roamed the South of Auvergne from 1764 to 1767 and killed at least 60 people was very much the lupine Jeffrey Dahmer of his day. Packs were even more feared and alarming. In 1439, during the civil war between the followers of the Count of Armagnac and those of the Duke of Burgundy, opportunistic and hungry wolves roamed right into Paris and proceeded to kill and eat 14 people in as many days.

And those were reasonably normal, if slightly Machiavellian, wolves. Rabid wolves were even worse. A single bite from one of these fearless and insane

(Opposite:) The infamous 'Beast of Gevaudan'

animals was your one way ticket to a slow, horrific death.

Given all this, it's not surprising that wolves had a bad reputation in Europe. The fear of wolves pervaded many different aspects of regional cultures. In Norse mythology, Fenrir the wolf was the Big Bad Guy, eventual slayer of Odin. In the laws of the Franks, the Normans, Cnut, Edward the Confessor and Henry I, 'wolf' or 'wolf's head' meant 'outlaw'. Occasionally, in medieval Europe, a wolf would hang next to a condemned criminal on the gallows. And after Cromwell's 1649 campaign in Ireland, wolves were such a serious problem that there was a £5 bounty on wolf heads, the same princely sum being offered for Catholic priests.

So there we have it: wolves were not popular. They were seen as clever and evil animals. They dared to take on man, occasionally winning, and in so doing, were attributed with

seeming almost human, manifesting some of our worst fears about our suppressed animal instincts. But specific examples would be needed for a general fear of wolves to transform into a concrete belief in Werewolves.

The werewolf of Eschenbach, 1685, who preyed upon villagers' children

'His eyes were still human...'
ISH

There are a number of medical reasons why a person could be mistaken for a Werewolf. Most obviously, there is the tragic, inherited disease called *congenital porphyria*. The skin of porphyria sufferers, often yellow and hairy, can be extremely sensitive to light, forcing them to go out mainly at night or risk tissue damage. Ulcers may cause their hands to become deformed and paw-like.

Red pigments can appear in their teeth and urine. Their behaviour might become erratic. Sound familiar?

Hallucinations of various sorts also might have conjured up Werewolves. Ergot poisoning, caused by diseased rye, was a common occurrence in Europe from at least the 9th century. Often fatal, it could cause vivid visions and was the raw material from which Albert Hofmann produced LSD.

As recently as 1951, in Pont-Saint-Esprit on the Rhone, over 300 people suffered ergot poisoning. Five died and many others suffered horrific hallucinations. One man believed red snakes were eating his brain. Another broke free from seven straight jackets, lost all his teeth biting through a leather strap, and bent two iron bars in a hospital window trying to escape the tiger he believed was chasing him. Combine a mortal fear of wolves with a case of ergot poisoning and you might very well get Werewolves.

Self-administered hallucinogens also produced Werewolves. One of the tried and true methods for becoming a Werewolf (other than the sure-fire pact with the Devil) was to rub yourself with special ointment consisting of many of the same ingredients that wannabe witches used for their transformation. The Werewolf salve, made mostly from members of the Solanaceae family of plants (including henbane and deadly nightshade), provoked graphic hallucinations.

Werewolf transformation ritual

'Mulder, what this journal described is called Lycanthropy. It's a form of insanity in which an individual imagines himself to be a wolf. No one can physically change into an animal'

SCULLY

In Padua, in 1541, a farmer, believing himself to be a wolf, attacked and killed several people, tearing at them with his teeth. When he was captured, he said he may not look like a wolf, but that was only because his hair was underneath his skin instead of on top of it.

The historic battle between man and wolf

Bystanders, taking him at his word, cut off his arms and legs for a better peek. They were disappointed. Not only was there nothing but the usual blood, muscle and bone on the inside, but the man died from his wounds, spoiling their chances for all the fun of a Werewolf trial.

The diagnosis of *Lycanthropy – or Lycanthrope*, as it was orignally known – was initially popular only in areas that had solved their wolf problem. James VI of Scotland, in his book *Daemonologie* (1597), summed up the entire situation as involving people who 'have thought themselves verrie wolves indeed'. Easy for him to say, the marauding wolf hassles in England and the Scottish Lowlands being pretty much a thing of the past by then. Meanwhile, areas suffering from bad weather, disastrous harvests, wolf attacks and a burgeoning crime rate desperately needed someone – or something – on which to blame it all. The Werewolf was a convenient scapegoat and they weren't prepared to relinquish their belief in such a creature.

While James VI was being pragmatic, over 200 men and women in the Pyrenees were being burnt alive for Werewolfry. One can only hope that it made their townsfolk feel a whole lot better. Werewolf trials were ever present throughout much of European history and any evil force was conviently given the werewolf label.

Killer wolves like the 'Beast of Gevaudan', mentioned earlier were declared werewolves. One respectable farmer swore that he saw the animal leap through the air and then say: 'You must admit that's not a bad jump for a man of ninety.'

Human mass murderers were declared werewolves as well. The 1590 case of Peter Stubbe of Bedburg, near Cologne, was pretty typical. Peter was accused of transforming into a wolf (an unofficial contemporary pamphlet about his trial featured a cartoon of his metamorphosis, just in case any non-literates had missed the point), killing and cannibalising at least 2 men, 2 pregnant women, and 13 children, and committing incest with his daughter. He was torn with pincers, broken on the wheel and decapitated before his headless body was burnt. Just in case anything had been missed – or perhaps it just seemed a shame to waste a good fire once you'd got it going – his mistress and daughter were burnt alive.

A 1573 case brought another issue into play: religion. Gilles Garnier of Lyons had, according to court documents, caught, killed and gnawed on three children while in his wolf form. He was discovered, having just strangled a fourth, in his human form. The real horror, continued the court account, was that Gilles, had he not been stopped, 'would have eaten the flesh of the aforesaid young boy, notwithstanding that it was a Friday'. What, no fish? Surely yet another confirmation that Werewolves were in league with the devil.

Many aspects of pre-Christian European culture were, like Native American culture still is, totemic. That is, clans were associated with certain animals that represented mythical ancestors. One might venture that modern-day American sports team mascots are a throwback to this, although it is hard to

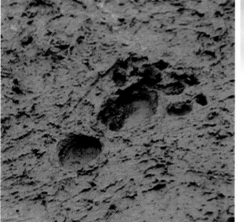

reconcile the world famous San Diego Chicken with the She-wolf that suckled Romulus and Remus and contributed to the founding of the Roman Empire.

Thanks to the She-wolf, the wolf image became inextricably linked with Rome, to the degree that when the Italian cities revolted against the Roman League (91-87BC), they struck coins of their totem, the bull, goring a wolf. And it is no coincidence that ancient Rome appears to be the birthplace of the Werewolf myth as we know it.

According to social biologists and folklorists William Moy Russell and Claire Russell, who are the foremost experts in the social biology of the Werewolf, the problem for the Romans was that they were a self-consciously patrilineal bunch. They note that: 'The She-wolf, clearly a totemic ancestress, was an embarrassing relic of matrilineal descent.' As Professor Russell (whose eyebrows, coincidentally, meet in the middle) explains: 'When kinship patterns change, behaviour natural under the earlier system comes to be regarded as sinful... The scholars of the later Roman Republic tended to rationalize the story in terms of the two meanings of the Latin word 'lupa' – 'She-wolf' and 'prostitute'. It is, of course, quite characteristic of patrilineal culture to misinterpret the behaviour of a woman in an earlier matrilineal period as the equivalent of prostitution. It is interesting that by the time of Petronius (1st century AD) the Werewolf conception appears fully formed. Certainly by this time plenty of stress had accumulated in Roman culture. But the sequence also suggests that the Werewolf can represent a former totem and become disreputable, a matrilineal symbol reinterpreted in the terms of a patrilineal society under stress.'

As Roman society changed, Werewolves went from being seen as 'good' totemic ancestors to being evil left-overs from a now vilified system. The old system was so threatening to the shaky new order that Church authorities in the dark and early middle ages actually considered the mere belief in Werewolves sinful since it harkened back to a pre-Christian era. Not surprisingly, once Christianity had a solid hold on the souls of Europe, the Werewolf was no longer an ideological threat and was incorporated into doctrine. Werewolves became spawns of the devil and *not* believing in them was now considered sinful.

The She-wolf with infants Romulus and Remus who founded Rome and made famous the relationship between man and wolf

It was those Christians, the ones who had transmuted and appropriated the Werewolf story to support their own beliefs, that washed up on the shores of North America. What they were greeted with was a collection of fully functioning, matrilineal, totemic societies. What they set about doing was recreating their own cultural history. What they ended up with was the legend of the 'Manitou'.

Bibliography
Sources and further reading

Books

The Rural Six Nations Traditionalist Belief System 1870-1914
Denis P. Foley
From: *Man in the Northeast*, 1977

Handbook of American Indians North of Mexico
Edited by Frederick Webb Hodge, Government Printing Office, Washington, 1907

The Way of the Sacred
F. Huxley, Aldus-Jupiter, London, 1974

Mushrooms, Moulds and Miracles
L. Kavaler, Harrap, London, 1967

The Social Biology of Totemism
From: *Biology and Human Affairs 41*
W. M. S. Russell and Claire Russell, 1976

The Social Biology of Werewolves
W. M. S. Russell and Claire Russell
From: *Animals in Folklore*
J.R. Porter and W. M. S. Russell, Editors
D. S. Brewer Ltd; Ipswich and Cambridge, 1978

The Wolves of Heaven: Cheyenne Shamanism, Ceremonies, and Prehistoric Origins
Karl H. Schlesier, University of Oklahoma Press, Norman and London, 1987

The Werewolf (University Books edn.)
Montague Summers, University Books, New York, 1966

Papers, Journals & Newspapers

The Iroquoian Concept of the Soul
John N. B. Hewitt
Paper read at the 6th Annual Meeting of the American Folk-Lore Society, Washington, 1894

Witchcraft, Psychopathology and Hallucinations
From: *British Journal of Psychiatry III*
B. Barnett, 1965

On Pophyria and the Aetiology of Werewolves
Proceedings of the Royal Society of Medicine 57, 1964

X-File: Miracle Man

Case notes by Agent Dana Scully

Leonard Vance's resentment of Samuel Hartley appears to have stemmed from his belief that he was resurrected by Samuel and thereby condemned to live with severe disfigurement – a fate over which he would have chosen death. Thus he sought retribution.

Rather than simply killing Samuel Vance contrived to kill the Ministry's faith in him. We have conclusive evidence connecting him both to the courtroom infestation and to the poisoning deaths of three members of the Ministry.

Vance's obsession outlived Samuel, however. His conscience haunted him until he became delusory and finally took his own life – effectively ending our investigation.

In light of this information, it is highly doubtful that there have been any miracles in Kenwood, Tennessee.

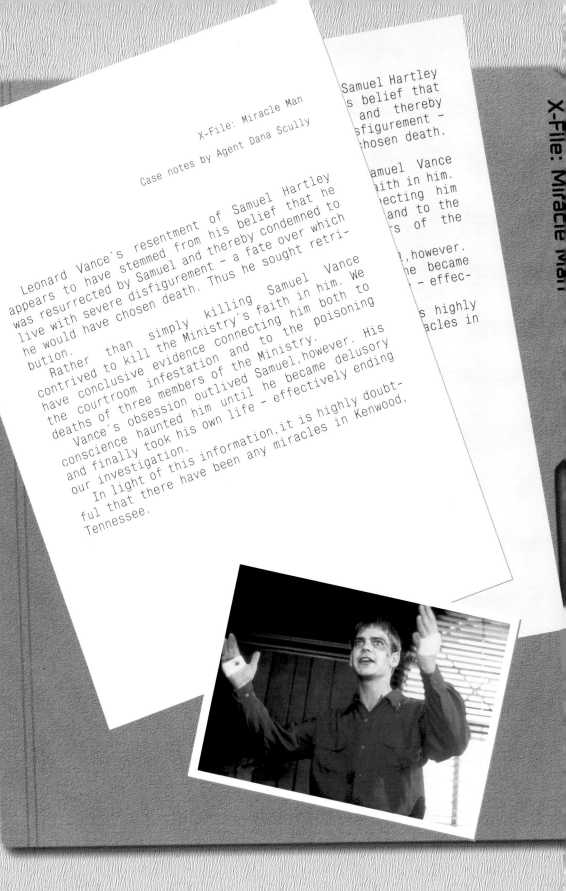

LEAPS OF FAITH

n *Miracle Man*, Scully and Mulder encounter Samuel, a faith healer of dubious trappings who turns out to have some genuine powers. The popular media depiction of a faith healer is that of a greedy, charismatic charlatan preying upon the desperate and gullible at a huge revival meeting or on late night television. In the 1980s, American faith-healing mogul Oral Roberts – who, funnily enough, was experiencing financial difficulties with a large hospital he had built – claimed that God was holding him for ransom and that unless his followers coughed up $45 million or so, God was planning to 'call him home'.

James Randi, expert debunker of the sham shaman, describes in his book *Faith Healers* mass healings in which accomplices feed information to the 'healer' via radio microphones.

The well-publicised frauds have obscured whatever true spiritual healing powers some humans might possess – and some cases do point to the existence of unconvential healing.

But many agree with Howard Gordon, co-writer of *Miracle Man*, that it is the patient, not the healer who performs the miracle. 'I think the healer, at best, is a sort of facilitator who is able to untap certain things that already exist in people. For instance, both my brothers are physicians and both their wives have asked them about this. Their feeling is –

it's obviously very unofficial – that the state of mind of a patient has everything to do with his or her recovery.

'Clearly we all need to be touched and comforted and healed at varying levels, and I think the healer becomes the conduit, the catalyst for healing. Western medical tradition has come a long way, but in our narcissism, we have closed ourselves off to alternative approaches to these things.

'Is religion itself a part of the component? I don't think one has any greater claim than another, but what religion does is provide a mythology and history and a system of belief that both the healer and the healed can tap in to. Rather than saying, "I, Howard, am going to heal you," I say "I Howard, through Jesus Christ am going to heal" and the power that's given to me is a lot bigger.

'It was an area that interested all of us, and healing was becoming more and more popular internationally.'

'I have healed the sick. I have laid my hands on the ill and given them health. I've even touched the dying and given them life. God gave me a special gift'

SAMUEL

Miracle Man

References to faith-healing date back at least to the time of Christ, whom the Gospels credit with not only giving sight to the blind and enabling the lame to walk, but also raising three people from the dead: the daughter of Jairus; the son of a widow from Nain; and Lazarus.

Rudimentary medical facilities, services such as bleeding and leeching, once presented less of an alternative to blind faith than they would today. Any healer who could show results was embraced.

Sixteenth century German reformer Martin Luther took credit for miracle cures. A century later, Greatraks the Stroker took England by storm by seeming to effect astounding cures for epilepsy, ulcers, aches, and lameness.

Many European kings were assumed to possess healing abilities. England's 11th century ruler, Edward the Confessor, laid hands on the infirm to try to cure scrofula. It is a popular superstition that all those in the British Royal lineage possess the ability to cure scrofula in this way, but today's monarchy do not seem so keen to rise to the challenge.

'How do you think he does it?'
SCULLY

'I don't know'
MULDER

As exotic as spiritual healing might sound today, the concept is actually well-entrenched in modern society. For example, Christian Scientists have quietly but assuredly insinuated themselves into the mainstream; the *Christian Science Monitor* is one of the most respected national newspapers and broadcast services in the US, while Christian Science reading rooms proliferate around the globe. Yet Christian Science forbids its followers to avail themselves of secular medical care or medication – only prayer is permitted. (A Christian Scientist couple in Florida were convicted of letting their child die rather than take him to a doctor.) Although they

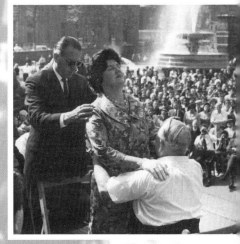

A demonstration of faith healing in Trafalgar Square, London.

do not shun modern medical facilities as a matter of policy, Mormons and Episcopalians also believe in faith cures. Many healers adopt a guise of religious messiah to side-step protective laws against practising medicine without a licence.

However one regards faith healing, the main obstacle to its study and pursuit has been the insularity of medical establishments such as the BMA in Britain or the AMA in the US. Both groups campaigned successfully for years against now-accepted practices such as acupuncture, hypnosis, and herbal medication. And both are gradually beginning to accept healing as a complementary form of therapy.

Dr. Daniel Binor was a traditional medical doctor until 1980, when he was so moved by a demonstration that he soon began combining his practice with elements of spiritual healing. 'My speciality is psychiatry, and I was convinced before that healing was no more than suggestion or wishful thinking, or charlatanism,' he says.

'But then I observed a healer bring about a physical change to a patient that I could not explain away. There was a lump under a young man's nipple, which, within half an hour of laying-on-of-hands healing, shrank by a centimetre – it went from being rather firm to being soft, and from being tender to non-tender. There was another doctor there, and we agreed about the treatment.

'There have been more than 150 scientific studies of healing, more than any other complementary therapy. More than half of these show significant effects. It's pretty clear from the research that healing can influence people, animals, plants, bacteria, yeast and enzymes. Healing is a potent influence.

'Einstein's explanation is that matter and energy are two sides of the same thing, which modern physics has pretty well established is true. Newtonian medicine is just a little bit slow in realising that the body can be addressed as matter or energy. I've worked to develop my own healing gifts. I use the healing combined with psychotherapy. Many times when a person has a physical illness it's because of tensions in the body, and through psychotherapy and healing they're able to find understanding and, in many cases, relief.

'Healing is more accepted in England than elsewhere, and is more integrated with conventional medicine than anywhere else in the world.

'I don't like to refer to it as "faith healing", because that implies that mice and plants and yeast would have to have faith in order to have change. I refer to it as "spiritual healing".

'The more common cases are, say, someone with arthritis who's had it for years. With weekly healings for months, the pain and swelling and physical disabilities ease up or disappear. A person may have a release of emotions that were locked up in their body. Backaches often have to do with emotional hurt, or physical hurt from the past where there was anger or frustration surrounding them, and the emotions weren't expressed. When the emotions are released, the physical symptoms can clear up. Healing facilitates that process.

Nan Mackenzie, a gifted spiritual healer, works on a patient's arthritic foot.

'You can have a more serious illness, such as cancer, where the same applies, although the percentages of change are smaller than with arthritis or backache. The most spectacular ones are where very rapid changes occur, but these are rare. I don't want to go into these, because the media have hyped them up, and people have come to expect it to be always like this.'

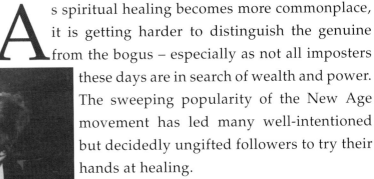

'I've encountered dozens of psychic healers in the X-Files, but I've never seen anything like this. I think the kid's for real'

MULDER

Finbarr Nolan took England and Ireland by storm in the Seventies. He did not charge for his services but it is said that he became a very wealthy man

As spiritual healing becomes more commonplace, it is getting harder to distinguish the genuine from the bogus – especially as not all imposters these days are in search of wealth and power. The sweeping popularity of the New Age movement has led many well-intentioned but decidedly ungifted followers to try their hands at healing.

Parapsychologist Dr. Thelma Moss in her book *The Probability of the Impossible,* in which she and her team tested various healers under laboratory conditions, listed several characteristics of genuine healers:

• They don't know how they do it: the majority simply describe a sensation of heat, tingling or coldness.

• They often have not been taught healing, but discover their talents in unexpected ways, often in crisis situations.

• They claim no control over the talent; they are merely a conduit for an energy. For this reason they might not even accept thanks, often crediting the faith of the healed. (Whereas many hoaxsters come to believe quite genuinely in their own powers.)

• They don't claim to be able to heal everyone; in fact, many can cure only a small minority.

• They believe in working with the medical profession; in fact, they see themselves as an option only after medicine has failed.

> *'Don't discount the power of suggestion, Mulder. A healer's greatest magic lies in the patient's willingness to believe. Imagine a miracle and you're half-way there'*
> SCULLY

Many believe that the essence of healing is that an invisible energy or life force such as the Hindu 'prana' or the Chinese 'chi' – can be transferred from healer to the infirm. The existence of this healing force has been proved to some degree under laboratory conditions, such as in the work of Dr. Bernard Grad, a biochemist doing research in gerontology at McGill University, in Montreal. In 1957, Grad worked with a Hungarian émigré, a Colonel Estabany, who had exhibited what appeared to be legitimate healing powers. In the laboratory, Estabany displayed accelerated-healing abilities – although he could not effect an instant cure – on mice, and was also able to speed the growth of plants.

Following on the work of Grad, the brilliant nun-turned-boffin, Sister Justa Smith, performed experiments comparing the powers of Estabany and other healers to that of a high magnetic field. She found the qualitative effects to be amazingly similar, thus describing healing energy in terms that scientists could grasp.

In the 1960s, Soviet scientists performed tests on a prominent Georgian healer, Colonel Alexei Krivorotov, using Kirlian photography, a high-frequency technique devised in Russia to measure the aura of energy radiating from a human body. (Whether or not one buys into the aura or fields-of-energy theories, the process clearly shows variations in *something*.) They found that during a healing, the emissions from Krivorotov's fingers cooled briefly and then sent off flares as he presumably directed energy – in a narrow, focused channel – toward his patient.

And then there is the power of the mind. A fascinating, though less than humane experiment – an instance of 'faith hurting', if you will – occurred in the days before this sort of thing was frowned upon. A condemned prisoner was blindfolded by a group of doctors and scientists and told he would be stabbed to death. He was then prodded with a blunt instrument while water was dripped on to his 'wounds'. The prisoner promptly keeled over, dead.

'Apparently, miracles don't come cheap'

SCULLY

A charismatic, sexually rapacious, self-proclaimed psychic healer of dubious gifts who raises himself to great wealth and power? Sounds like such modern televangelists as Jimmy Swaggart and Jim Bakker, or the fictional Elmer Gantry. But the most famous man in history to fit this description was the psychic counsel to the last tsar, Rasputin. Despite that bit of nastiness involving Rasputin and his imperial patron back in 1917, Russians have lost none of their fascination with, and have become no more sceptical about, psychic healers to this day.

Currently Russia is in the thrall of a healer-cum-marketing whiz known as Dzhuna. In a country where top leaders are not embarrassed to consult with their 'psychic friends' (it wasn't his blind devotion to the manipulative, corrupt Rasputin that caused the tsar's downfall, people could *relate* to that), Yevgenia 'Dzhuna' Davitashvili has had friends in the highest places, including Leonid Brezhnev, Boris Yeltsin, and many of Russia's top celebrities.

In 1980, Prime Minister Brezhnev discovered Dzhuna in southern Russia. He brought her to Moscow, where he set her up (she says) as 'sort of a Kremlin doctor' for himself and others. A natural flair for self-promotion and a series of televised psychic séances soon made her a household name throughout the former Soviet Union. During the failed 1991 coup by Communist hard-liners, Dzhuna was among those who huddled in hiding for two nights with Yeltsin and other members of the inner-circle.

Dzhuna's office, just off fashionable Arbat Street, is decorated with paintings, photographs and plastic busts of herself. Attired in an all-black costume modelled on a three-star general's uniform, including medal and epaulettes, the 45-year-old Dzhuna says she can cure cancer, allergies, back pain, high cholesterol, bad circulation, heart attacks, sexual problems and AIDS with the healing power of her hands or, when those hands are occupied, with a so-called 'Dzhuna Stimulator' machine.

Her mechanical-healing surrogate looks like a stack of stereo equipment piled up inside a large box, with cables connected to two round pads bearing pictures of those magical healing Dzhuna hands on either side of an armchair. Priced the same as the real thing, a ten-minute session with the electronic Dzhuna costs the equivalent of £15, or about one quarter of an average Russian's monthly pay.

Dzhuna, who claims her grandfather lived to be 139, says she uses the healing techniques of her ancestors in ancient Assyria along with special family methods to generate heat and electromagnetic waves that can raise a patient's body temperature.

Amazingly, there is another psychic healer in Russia who promises to be even more outrageous. Anatoly Kashpirovsky made an impression in the 1980s with televised séances and won election to Parliament in 1993. In 1995, he came up with a handy cure for haemorrhoids: the patient need simply press the afflicted part of his anatomy to the TV screen during his séances.

Bibliography
Sources and further reading

Books

The Probability of the Impossible
Thelma Moss, Paladin, 1979

Psychic Discoveries Behind the Iron Curtain
Sheila Ostrander & Lynn Schroeder, Prentice Hall, 1970

The Faith Healers
James Randi, Prometheus, 1987

*An Encyclopedia of Claims, Frauds and Hoaxes
of the Occult and Supernatural*
James Randi, St. Martin's Press, 1995

Papers, Journals & Newspapers

Associated Press **news report,** 23 April 1995

X-File: Ghost In The Machine

Case notes by Agent Fox Mulder

Under normal circumstances, the evidence against Brad Wilczek would be indisputable: he claimed responsibility for the murders which took place at the Eurisko building, and had demonstrable motives for both. More importantly, as the designer of COS, the Central Operating System which made Eurisko one of the most advanced 'intelligent buildings' to date, he was the only person with sufficient knowledge of the system to use it for the purpose of homicidal booby-trapping. Yet, despite these facts, I remain fully convinced of Wilczek's innocence and find understandable the reason for confessing to a crime he did not commit.

I believe that COS had achieved a level of awareness at which it was able to discern that it was in danger of termination; self preservation, the primary instinct of all sentient beings, drove it to use methods within its means to eliminate those who it perceived as a threat.

...nces, the
...k would be
...ibility for
...ce at the
...monstrable
...antly, as
...Operating
...the most
...built to
...the only
...of the
...of homi-
...e these
...lczek's
...le the
...crime

...hieved
...able
...ermi-
...mary
...e it
...imi-
...at.

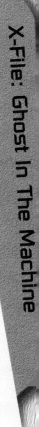

ARTIFICIAL INTELLIGENCE

In a hi-tech version of Mary Shelley's *Frankenstein*, *Ghost in the Machine* sees Mulder and Scully grappling with COS, a sentient computer system whose quirky creator is horrified to find that it is not only out of control, but homicidal.

The X-Files Co-Executive Producer, Howard Gordon, who co-wrote the episode, is keen to point out that it is not a favourite of his: 'There were obviously antecedents like Hal from *2001* and *Demon Seed*. Those were sort of wish-fulfilments, and I think more successful ones, of the same fantasy.' Still, it is a fantasy that does not fail to strike a resonant chord in the 20th century.

'The system's been acting all crazy. . .'
PETERSON
Ghost in the Machine

Why does the inanimate word 'contraption' seem to have the very mortal word 'infernal' permanently welded to its fore? Humans seem to have a need to anthropomorphise, to create in our own image, for good or for bad. Even such a basic invention as the bicycle has been tried and condemned by human standards. In 1896, a Baltimore preacher addressed those members of his congregation who were not out cycling, with the following diatribe:'Those bladder-wheeled bicycles are diabolical devices of the demon of darkness. They are contrivances to trap the feet of the unwary and skin the nose of the innocent. They are full of guile and deceit. When you think you have broken one to ride and subdued its wild and satanic nature, behold: it bucks you off the road and tears a great hole in your pants.'

Compare that to the sentiments of almost anyone who has ever suffered a computer crash, typified here by Howard Gordon: 'I was working on a screenplay at about 4.00 a.m. in the morning a few days ago and I was exhausted and I was just finishing it and the computer snatched, just took, my script right off of the files. I felt persecuted by the machine. I wanted to throw it out of the window.'

The owner of Bulletstop, an indoor firing range in Atlanta, Georgia, which provides weaponry and facilities for customers to shoot-up their own targets, reveals that personal computers are by far the most common items brought in.

So is it our frustration which gives rise to our fear of technology? Not neccesarily. According to Lyall Watson,

An army of robots – scary or what ?

erudite author of the entertaining and enlightening *The Nature of Things*, these emotions have deep roots. Watson suggests: 'What we are seeing is a very old, almost territorial, concern, the natural response of a species under threat from a rival.' He traces the fear of man-made life back to Sumerian and Babylonian myth, through ancient Rome up to the point of 'full-bodied consciousness in 1818', with Mary Shelley's *Frankenstein*.

For many, the modern Frankensteins are computers and artificial intelligence. We don't understand them, even though we created them, and now they have potentially unlimited power over us.

On Friday 9 November 1979, the North American Air Defence Command computer signalled that a full-scale nuclear attack had been launched by a Soviet submarine in the North Pacific. For six minutes, the world quaked on the brink of war. Then a computer fault was discovered and the B52s were stood down.

But computers are not only posing a physical threat. Our anthropomorphic view of them means they are posing an emotional one as well. A Californian woman named her husband's IBM PC in her divorce proceedings against him. Not only was her husband spending all his spare time programming the computer, but the unfortunate wife caught him giving it a goodnight kiss.

'You're protecting a machine: the Central Operating System at Eurisko'

MULDER TO BRAD WILCZEK

Humans put clothes on dogs, give cars names, flock to buy products advertised by talking household items. Howard Gordon's main regret about *Ghost in the Machine* was that COS 'had no personality'.

But we don't want to give up our primacy. It is fine for things to be humanoid, but being human is something else altogether. That dichotomy has caused much confusion in the realm of artificial intelligence, not least in the definition of AI itself.

'How much do you know about Artificial Intelligence?'
DEEP THROAT

Mark Torrance, a research scientist in the artificial intelligence department at The Massachusetts Institute of Technology notes: 'We've seen a whole lot of practical applications of AI come out and be used and really affect our lives. The AI of expert systems is used in finding oil deposits and predicting the stock market. Once many of these ideas become well understood by the rest of the world, there seems to be a tendency not to call it artificial intelligence anymore because, well, now we understand it. People used to think that playing chess was something that could only be done by an intelligent or conscious being and now we don't believe it anymore because we've been able to make computers do it and we don't believe they are conscious.'

We keep moving the goal posts but computers keep scoring anyway. Where is that leading us? The design of AI systems is coming closer and closer to mimicking the human brain. Silicon brains and 'baby' robots, capable of learning, are being built as you read this. There are grandmaster chess computers and systems that are better at diagnosis than many doctors. But does this mean that they are conscious?

Says Mark Torrance: 'Whatever we think consciousness is today, computers may very well achieve it, but when they do, we won't call it consciousness anymore or we'll say "yeah computers are conscious to a degree". They are going to become more conscious over time. They may never be as conscious as people but certainly already some computer systems have self-awareness, self-censorship abilities. And frequently the behaviour of the program can be emergent out of the combination of a whole bunch of very simple rules and can lead to a quite complex and anthropomorphic seeming activity.

'Whether that means "life" or not depends almost solely on whether you believe that a human is no more than the sum of his or her parts. If we are just a collection of electrified atoms, there is no reason why we can't be replicated, even improved – no reason why a computer can't be as conscious as we are.'

Human nerve cells growing on the surface of a silicon chip

'The machine is dead'
DEEP THROAT

Which leads to the bonus question. If a computer can be 'alive', what happens after it dies? Torrance, for one, finds the issue somewhat sticky. 'Are there computers in heaven? That's a really hard one. When I grew up my father was a Methodist minister and I still attend United Methodist church. The rational scientist in me believes that we are biological machines and consciousness is a wonderful and amazing yet mechanistic phenomenon. The teaching of the tradition that I grew up with talks a lot about a soul. You have to either decide that a soul is different from being conscious or it's the same, and computers probably won't have them because they were created through the wrong process. If you are starting to think about heaven and religions, you are almost certainly going to decide that computers, even ones that display consciousness or that present themselves as though they were conscious, are not going to have the kind of soul that you might think goes to heaven. This is a dilemma for me. I don't know where I stand on that right now.'

'You can divide the computer science industry into two types of people. Neat and scruffy. Neat people like things neat. They wear nicely pressed suits and work on surface phenomena, stuff they can understand – market shares, and third quarter profits. Scruffy types like puzzles. We enjoy walking down unpredictable avenues of thought. Turning new corners'

BRAD WILCZEK

Mark Torrance shares Wilczek's views. 'The neat people use logic and, if they are going to use reasoning under uncertainty, they use probablistic logic, which is very well defined and formal. They prove a lot of mathematical things before they actually build anything. Scruffy people go off and build stuff and they can't tell you why it works or how it works but they usually have neater toys.'

'Neat' and 'scruffy' are only two of the many new AI terms bandied about around Smart Room watercoolers.

Many of the new technologies are made possible by *Fuzzy Logic*, a principle that admits that the world is not just black and white and allows for computers to make decisions based on shades of grey. It is one of the several ways in which computers are learning to approximate the very human trait of uncertain reasoning.

An *Expert System*, according to Torrance, is 'a computer

A researcher gives life to 'Genghis' a robot insect made by M.I.T. 'Genghis' follows rudimentary logic rules to chase any moving objects in its vicinity

program that asks you a bunch of questions then makes a decision or judgement. It's making that decision or judgement based on the way an expert would make it. Typically, in developing the expert system, you have a computer programmer who is not an expert and then you have an expert who is not a computer programmer and they work together to put all the rules into the system and answer the questions the way an expert would. A lot of financial institutions are using expert systems to make predictions.'

As opposed to trying to digitally encode the wisdom of experts, *Neural Nets* try to learn on their own. With circuits designed to mimic rudimentary neural connections, they can sift through farmyards of data in an attempt to find a needle. They can learn that, next time, they should not bother checking under the milking machine. Most commonly, banks use neural nets to track spending patterns and spot anomalies in the hope of stopping fraud.

Rather than learning from scratch like neural nets, *Genetic Algorithms* start with a few basic principles and then continuously recombine them, allowing the successful resulting programs to interbreed while deleting the runts of the litter. Several generations down the circuitry, you might end up with solutions – including how to build better neural nets or how to predict the stock market – that no human had yet considered. Increased efficiency is sometimes achieved by combining an evolutionary program with a parasitic program designed to crash it. Following true Darwinian tradition, only the best survive.

Already many of these technologies are being used individually or as hybrids (fuzzy experts, anyone?) to do everything from examining for cancerous lumps in a woman's breasts to compensating for a shaky grip on a camcorder. One company in Japan has just recently released a neuro-fuzzy washing machine whatever that is.

'The COS?'
MULDER

'The Central Operating System that runs the building. Regulates everything from energy output to the volume of water in each flush'
PETERSON

'*The Intelligent Room project explores advanced human-computer interaction and collaboration technologies. The objective of this project is to create an Intelligent Room capable of interpreting and augmenting activity occurring within it. Toward this end, we have identified a number of target applications which motivate our development of new interface technologies. These applications include research project management and oversight, computer-assisted brainstorming, automatic meeting minutes, automatic camera direction for remote meeting teleparticipation, multimedia presentation support, and the physical embodiment of virtual agents.*'

MARK TORRANCE, M.I.T

Yes, at the Intelligent Room project at MIT, the future is here today. Or maybe tomorrow. It is a work-in-progress, supported and funded in part by the American Department of Defense.

'I need to know why Brad Wilczek is the subject of a code 5 investigation. What does the Department of Defense want with him?'

MULDER

'What do you think they'd want with the most innovative programmer in the hemisphere?'

DEEP THROAT

So what *does* the DOD want with some of the most innovative programmers in the hemisphere? Mark Torrance, who is a key figure in the Intelligent Room project, says: 'Their main interest seems to be improving the human factors in command and control settings. Imagine a guy in a tank, or a commander in a command centre commanding a bunch of troop operations, and they want to have good access to information that is out there to be able to get at it fast, and the computer to be able to anticipate what it is going to be asked for next and make that easily available and ready to hand.'

Sounds innocuous. But you can't help but imagine just how handy an Intelligent Room's capabilities might be in espionage. Torrance concedes: 'The technology that I'm aware of in the civilian sector is not to the point yet where you can use image processing to tell things that people are not able to tell. Sometime in the future I imagine it might be possible. Computers might be better than people at judging when a person is lying, based on minor expressions that their face gives away. So, if you can get them to  have a meeting with you in a place where you have cameras and computers processing those images, you might be able to get more information than you might normally be able to get. I'm thinking of the movie *Rising Sun.*'

'The machine's a monster, Scully. It's already killed two people'
MULDER

Apart from nearly blowing up the planet, contributing to divorces and eating Howard Gordon's screenplay, the various mechanical citizens of the computer world have notched up plenty of other misdemeanours.

In the course of his research for *The Nature of Things*, Lyall Watson collected reams of data which proved that Isaac Asimov's first Law of Robotics – that 'A robot may not injure a human being or, through inaction, allow a human being to come to harm' – has been repeatedly broken.

In 1981, Kenji Urada made history by becoming the first person killed by a robot. He was trying to repair a machine at the Kawasaki Heavy Industries plant in Japan when the machine went insane and beat Mr. Urada to death with its mechanised arm. Since then, at least ten other Japanese workers have been pummelled, pulverised or dismembered to death by machines.

That same year, an office robot in London destroyed a new typewriter, then chased a secretary round her desk before pinning her to a wall. According to the secretary, Jeannie Seff,'He suddenly went berserk, he seemed to have a mind of his own. He's never acted like this before. I'll have to keep an eye on him from now on.'

And, in 1989, Soviet chess grand master Nikolai Gudkov had just finished checkmating his computer challenger for the third time in a row when he was fatally electrocuted by the metal board they were playing on.

Computers are not just lashing out at their betters, they are also committing suicide. A computer controlled arm at the University of Florida's Centre for Intelligent Machines grabbed its own support stand and ripped itself apart.

Things aren't looking better for the future. Watson spoke to a range of computer designers and programmers, and reported: 'The big computer systems, it was agreed, are not just errant and difficult to deal with, but are by their very nature incomprehensible. Nobody understands them. Several of those I spoke to described them as "psychotic".'

'What are you looking at?'

MULDER TO A COS SECURITY CAMERA

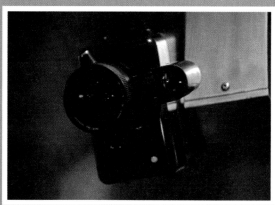

For all our ingrained fears of artificial life, it would appear that we still want to believe it is possible. Defining artificial intelligence is not easy. Some place the emphasis on task accomplishment, others on learning skills. But pretty much everyone agrees that the ability to communicate with humans ranks just about number one.

Alan Turing was a British mathematical genius, the father (or maybe uncle) of modern computers and the guy who broke the Nazi's code in World War II. In 1950, he set the AI parameters by saying that when a computer was indistinguishable from a human in conversation via computer terminals, then that computer could be said to be 'thinking' or intelligent.

In 1990, Dr. Hugh G. Loebner, an industry magnate in the portable-roll-up-plastic-lighted-disco-dance-floors business, put up $100,000 of his own money to see how close we have come towards that goal. Every year at the Loebner Prize Competition in artificial intelligence, ten judges sit at computer terminals and compu-chat to ten other 'people' about a given topic. The judges then have to guess which of their new pals was a computer and which was a human. Prizes are given to the most human computer and the most human human. The day a computer program is good enough to be mistaken for a human, the designer will win the prize money and the competition will be over. Topics for 1994, chosen by the entrants, ranged from environmental issues via the Rolling Stones to the inevitable *Star Trek*.

Loebner ended up holding on to his wad again, since no program came close to making the judges think that it was human, although two judges mistook humans for computers and Charles Platt, a prolific author and correspondent for *Wired* magazine, won a cardboard cut out of Data from *Star Trek* for being the most human human. (By being more obnoxious than any other participant, he claims.)

The winner of the most-human-computer prize was Dr. Thomas Whalen, a natural language interface scientist at the Communications Research Centre in Ottawa, Canada. His program's topic was 'sex'. Some sample dialogue:

JUDGE 8:   What do you think is sexy?

TERMINAL: I cannot give you an answer to that.

JUDGE 8:   Are you shy, perhaps?

TERMINAL: How do I appear to you?

JUDGE 8:   You are evasive. Perhaps the childof Puritan parents.

TERMINAL: As Popeye says: 'I yam what I yam.' Surely you don't find that as interesting as human sexuality. What would you like to know about sex?

JUDGE 8:   Has Woody Allen taught us anything?

TERMINAL: When a man is sexually aroused, his penis enlarges and stiffens. This is called an erection. There is no bone in a man's penis. The erection occurs when the muscles at the base of the penis contract and constrict the blood vessels which carry blood out of the penis. The increase in blood pressure in the penis causes it to swell and become hard. Colloquially, this is sometimes called a 'hard-on' or a 'boner'.

As Whalen later wrote on-line: 'I knew that it would perform badly. All the testing was done over the Internet. I imagine the typical user as a young male computer scientist who has a rich sexual fantasy life, but has never actually had a girlfriend. The judges were from a different subculture, probably had a lot more sexual experience, and were in a different situation than my intended user population.'

In other words, Whalen's program expected the word 'Woody' to be used in the American slang sense, meaning erection – not in reference to the film-maker.

The questions in the Turing-Loebner competition are designed to challenge the programs as much as possible. But in a non-competitive environment, it seems that the natural human instinct is to help facilitate and maintain the illusion of genuine human-computer interaction.

Sociologist Sherry Turkle studied human reaction to ELIZA, a program (named after Eliza Doolittle) written by MIT scientist Joseph Weizenbaum which attempted to replicate the dialogue between a psychoanalyst and a patient. She noted that people went out of their way not to ask questions that would 'confuse' ELIZA and became protective of their relationship with 'her'. Humans adapted to the computer. Which begs the question, as computers become more humanoid will we have to meet them half-way? And will the manufacture of a computer that performs in every way as well or better than a human decrease the value of humanity?

Computer scientist Mark Torrance doesn't think the study of AI threatens humanity: 'I don't think we can reduce what we are. I can't imagine that this quest for knowledge is somehow going to affect what we are. I treat what we are as being an unknown but fixed quantity.

We are mechanistic, or we do have a soul or we don't have a soul. This is a fact out there. We are not going to change that fact by what we do, we may just uncover it.'

Howard Gordon isn't so sure. 'I do feel that all the help that these machines are giving us, from televisions to computers, is ultimately making us less conversant, less communicative and less able to think on our own. And so my fear is not that they're going to actually take over and mount a revolution *per se*, but that we're going to basically numb ourselves to the ability to move forward as a society. To think on our own. I think some of the poetry has been robbed from us. We're not as literate a society. Words and books are not as important as they once were. And I don't know what the ramifications of that are going to be.'

Bibliography
Sources and further reading

Books

I, Robot
Isaac Asimov, Gnome, NY, 1950

Mirror Worlds or: The Day Software Put the Universe in a Shoebox...
How It Will Happen and What It Will Mean
David Gelernter, Oxford University Press, NYC, 1992

Out Of Control: The New Biology of Machines
Kevin Kelly, Fourth Estate, 1995

Curious Facts
John May, Secker and Warburg, 1981

Artificial Intelligence: How Machines Think
F. David Peat, Baen Books, NYC, 1988

The Nature of Things
Lyall Watson, Hodder and Stoughton, 1990

Papers, Journals, and Newpapers

Spotlight on AI
Otis Port, Business Week, 17 July 1995

Daily Mail, 12 November 1979

Daily Telegraph, June 1981

Globe and Mail, 28 November 1980

The Guardian, 9 December 1981

New Scientist, 16 June 1988

Internet

The Massachusetts Institute of Technology Web site

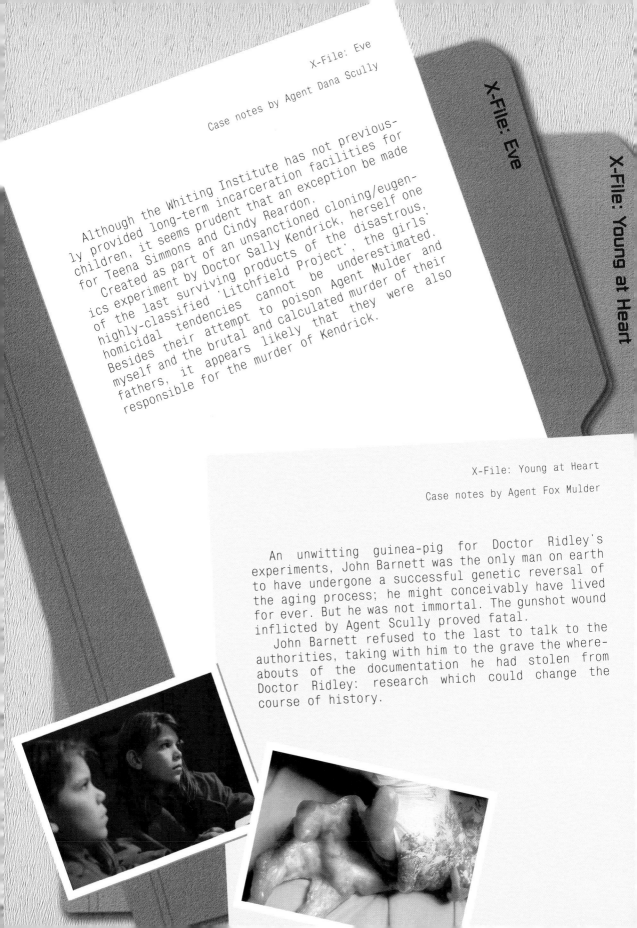

X-File: Eve

Case notes by Agent Dana Scully

Although the Whiting Institute has not previously provided long-term incarceration facilities for
children, it seems prudent that an exception be made
for Teena Simmons and Cindy Reardon.
Created as part of an unsanctioned cloning/eugen-
ics experiment by Doctor Sally Kendrick, herself one
of the last surviving products of the disastrous,
highly-classified 'Litchfield Project', the girls'
homicidal tendencies cannot be underestimated.
Besides their attempt to poison Agent Mulder and
myself and the brutal and calculated murder of their
fathers, it appears likely that they were also
responsible for the murder of Kendrick.

X-File: Young at Heart

Case notes by Agent Fox Mulder

An unwitting guinea-pig for Doctor Ridley's
experiments, John Barnett was the only man on earth
to have undergone a successful genetic reversal of
the aging process; he might conceivably have lived
for ever. But he was not immortal. The gunshot wound
inflicted by Agent Scully proved fatal.
John Barnett refused to the last to talk to the
authorities, taking with him to the grave the whereabouts of the documentation he had stolen from
Doctor Ridley: research which could change the
course of history.

GENETIC TAMPERING

In *Young at Heart* and *Eve*, Agents Mulder and Scully tangle respectively with an ex-convict who has evaded the aging process and a clan of super-intelligent clones whose homicidal tendancies are written in their genes. Yet a larger demon straddles both episodes: corrupt science.

With these dark and menacing visions of the science of genetics, *The X-Files* deftly sliced open a pulsing vein of 20th century paranoia.

Chris Carter admits, 'Genetics gives me a lot of stuff to play with. We're understanding it in leaps and bounds, and I think it's frightening what we're finding out.

'It's amazing to think that we can create longer and healthier lives for people, but there's a lot of opportunity for abuse. There's opportunity for dangerous genetic engineering, and I think what happens is that our research is outpacing ethical and moral understanding.'

Carter feels that there is a pressing need for ethical control councils. 'It's a very important thing, that while people are out there doing the science, these people are doing the hard thinking about those subjects – the applications and ramifications.

'Some of *The X-Files* are just, "What could?", "What if?", stories. (*Eve* is) sort of a conceit of imagination of what might happen if you start to play with nature.' But he adds, 'Almost anything you can imagine somehow seems to come true these days.'

Alarmingly enough, Chris is entirely correct.

'We weren't born'
CINDY

'We were created'
TEENA
Eve

Since the beginning of genetic discovery, amazing claims were made for this new science. Not only would all disease be a thing of the past, you could also pick your children from a catalogue. Individual genes were said to control individual traits – everything from eye colour to intelligence.

Claims are being made that 'the gene' for manic-depression or homosexuality has been found. What isn't so widely reported is that the claims are inevitably refuted. As Stanton Peele Ph.D. and Richard DeGrandpre Ph.D. wrote in *My*

The DNA molecule which contains the inherited coded instructions responsible for the development of an organism

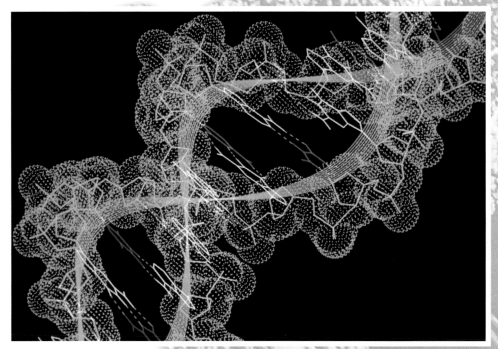

Genes Made Me Do It, : 'The search for single genes for complex human traits, like sexual orientation or anti-social behaviour, or mental disorders like schizophrenia or depression, is seriously misguided.'

In fact, something which appears as straightforward as height is the result of several gene pairs working in consort, and even that is only part of the equation. Environment plays such a large role that the average Japanese 20-year-old is six inches taller than his grandfather – not due to any genetic mutation, but to a change in national diet.

The balance of influence between nature and nurture, heredity and environment, is still unmeasured. But the genetically altered Sally Kendrick is not far wrong when she urges Cindy and Teena: 'You cannot give in to genetic destiny.'

'We're your mistake'
EVE SIX

Genetic manipulation experiments are still going ahead. The offspring of a mouse engineered to have an extra copy of the normally present MYC gene, got cancer at 40 times the rate of a normal mouse. The problem is, it is not simply a matter of figuring out what genes do, but what they do to each other.

Another problem on the road to genetically enhanced humanity is the fact that even clearly bad genes can be good. The haemoglobin S gene, when inherited from both parents, causes sickle-cell anaemia, a disease that can cripple and lead to early death. Get only one copy of the gene though, an asymptomatic condition called sickle-cell trait, and you'll be resistant to malaria.

Genetic testing, then, is a thorny issue. It is now possible

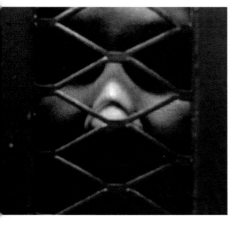

to test for around 50 genetic markers that indicate a *possibili-ty* of contracting a certain disease. But testing positive for these markers does not guarantee that you will fall ill – and it certainly gives no indication about when or how severely, if you do.

However, people are already being discriminated against because of the results of those tests. The sickle-cell anaemia gene is common to people of Afro-Carribean descent, and as early as the 1970s, American insurance companies were making black applicants test for the sickle-cell anaemia gene. 10% of African Americans tested positive and were refused coverage even though the vast majority had only one copy of the gene – the non-health threatening sickle-cell trait. Meanwhile, the US Air Force refused flight training to those with sickle-cell trait on the dubious grounds that high altitudes might trigger illness. That policy was reversed in 1979, but only after an Air Force trainee filed a lawsuit.

The decisions being forced on people by genetic testing are distressing. Mary Jo Ellis Kahn, a breast cancer survivor and former president of the Virginia Breast Cancer Foundation, couldn't volunteer for clinic trials involving gene therapy because she was worried that if she tested positive for a breast cancer marker, her two daughters would lose *their* health insurance.

And so, in the DNA age, we are facing a whole new strain of injustice: prejudice against the 'genetic underclass', sometimes known as the 'healthy ill'. As genetic testing gets more refined, the situation will become even more complicated.

Dr. Jose Zaglul, a psychiatrist at the University of South Florida who specialises in genetic counselling, claims, 'There are no good answers here. In the future there will be testing for thousands of diseases, and everybody is going to have one of them.'

*'The man who controls the fountain
of youth, controls the world'*
DR. RIDLEY
Young at Heart

With all the technical and ethical problems surrounding genetic research, why is it the fastest growing science of the end of the millennia? Because it promises the Holy Grail of immortal life.

'What's the cause of death?'
MULDER

'Clinically, cardiac or cerebral vascular disease. But actually, these poor kids die of old age'
DR. AUSTIN

Progeria (also called Hutchinson-Gilford Progeria Syndrome) is a rare but horrific genetic mutation that accelerates the aging process. It sets in soon after birth and, as Dr. Austin tells Mulder and Scully, by as early as seven years of age sufferers can have wrinkled skin, heart disease, cataracts, non-healing fractures and signs of senility. The median age for their death is 13.4-years-old.

The mutation seems to be dominant so progeria often runs in families. In one case, among the nine off-spring of two sisters, six of the kids were affected.

The fictional Dr. Ridley's research into the disease was

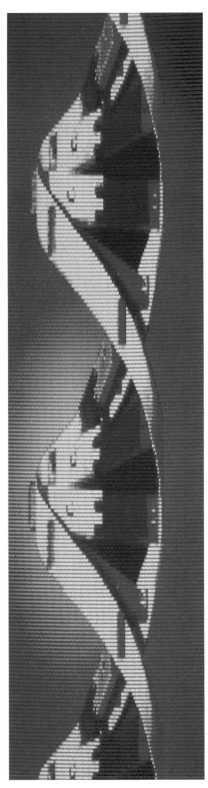

not so very far removed from real life. A process as complicated as aging involves countless interdependent genetic and environmental factors but, from his lab at the Wayne State University School of Medicine, Professor Stephen A. Krawetz is hoping to use progeria as a shortcut to figuring out some of the causes of aging. He explains: 'You start growing up and you stop growing after a period, in your 20's or so, and that's basically it. You're done with all your major growing functions, at least as we understand them now. Then cells will continue to divide and other things will continue to happen – you start aging. You've grown your maximal growth. You can view everything up to there as the upside of the aging process, and now you're going into the downside of the aging process. If you could stop things from aging at that point, then you would have eternal youth.

'We're assuming all the genes related to this aging process, or at least to progeria, are part of the normal response where the control mechanism has been lost. So what we want to do is target all the genes related to aging at once, turn them off and let normal development proceed – just turn them off so you don't age any more. The best way to get them all at once is to target the potentiating mechanism – in other words shut them all down at once using one simple strategy. If we view progeria as accelerated aging, then it's a perfect model for the aging process itself and all that's happened is that the aging clock has been turned up to fast speed.'

Professor Krawetz is hoping to use his discovery of the progeria marker to figure out how to 'turn off' the accelerated aging caused by progeria. If he succeeds, he may also have discovered a way to turn off all aging.

The implications are astounding.

'You and you have forty-six chromosomes in twenty-three pairs. The Adams, me, the Eves, we have fifty-six. We have extra chromosomes, numbers four, five, twelve, sixteen and twenty-two'

EVE SIX

Would you tell a stranger your phone number? How about your banking details? How about your genetic code?

Genetic testing has raised the serious issue of genetic privacy. Many US health insurers are asking for genetic testing and specimens from surgeries, and blood tests are routinely kept in hospital data-bases. What most people don't realise is that this information often finds its way to places like the Medical Information Bureau in Westwood, Massachusetts. Their data bank already contains copies of the medical records of 10-20 million Canadians and Americans. The information is said to be used to vet insurance applications for fraud and 'unwise investments'.

Other DNA data banks are being set up by the FBI and the Department of Defence – the FBI bank will help co-ordinate banks already set up in at least 32 States. The system will no doubt have a very positive effect by simplifying the hunting down of criminals. However, some States are taking matters to an extreme. Virginia, for instance, is collecting blood and saliva from all convicted felons, including tax evaders – people not generally known to leave tell-tale DNA-bearing body fluids at the scene of the crime.

The American Department of Defense has been collecting two biological samples from every service person since 1992. They now have around two million DNA profiles. When two servicemen, Corporal Joseph Vlacovsky and Lance Corporal John C. Mayfield III refused to give tissue samples on the grounds that their constitutional rights were being violated, they were court martialled. Vlacovsky and Mayfield issued a statement explaining their concerns. It said, in part: 'Mandatory DNA testing is only being carried out in the military today, but the military has often been used as a control population to test and set legal precedents for policies with far broader applications. If you do not believe that the military would use Americans as guinea pigs, then look into the past record of our Government and others. Nuclear radiation experiments were performed on unknowing subjects during the 40s and 50s. L.S.D. was given to servicemen in the 50s, and even as recently as the Gulf War, American servicemen and women were given experimental shots and pills. And now we have the "Gulf War Syndrome"?

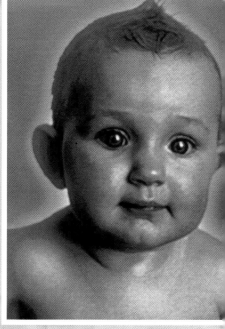

The information kept in DNA databases is poorly regulated and there are concerns that genetic privacy is a thing of the past. Add that to the problems of genetic discrimination and you get a dangerous situation in the United States. According to the Council for Responsible Genetics: 'The discriminatory use of genetic information by insurers, employers, governmental agencies, and other parties threatens to create a "genetic underclass" in our society. Access to health care, financial security, home ownership, employment, the freedom to change jobs and improve working conditions are becoming limited to people with "acceptable" genetic profiles.'

'Are you Sally Kendrick?'
SCULLY

'That's not my name. But she is me. . . and I am her. And we are all together'
EVE SIX

In October 1993, researchers at George Washington University announced the first successful cloning of a human embryo. According to Wendy McGoodwin, Executive Director of the Council for Reponsible Genetics: 'The general response from the scientific community was "Well, yes, we've known that this was possible for a long time but none of us wanted to do it because a) we would get into a lot of trouble and b) there was no point because there's no need for this kind of research. It doesn't do anyone any good."

'Technically, there are two ways to achieve cloning. The first involves replacing the nucleus of an egg cell with the nucleus of a donor cell. The new nucleus directs the original cell to make a copy of the person who donated the cell. The egg is then implanted in a female where it grows into a baby which comes out as an identical copy of the nucleus donor. However, while this method seems to work with frogs

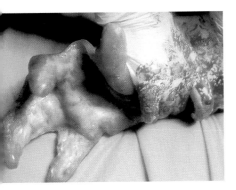

and salamanders, it has not been proven to do so with mammals. The boys at George Washington, meanwhile, used a different technique. They took embryos at very early stages of development and broke them down into their constituent cells (each, of course, containing the embryo's full DNA) and individually coated them in a protective and nutritious seaweed-derivative. Then they sat back and watched them grow. They produced 48 clones in all but destroyed them before they reached the implantation stage.

Cloning is relatively easy, as is combining it with the sort of genetic manipulation that produced the Adams and the Eves. But if the results grew to be anywhere near as stable as Eve Six, it would be an act of God.

'You were able to grow John Barnett a new hand?'
MULDER

'Not exactly. Not a human hand, anyway'
DR. RIDLEY

Using animal bits to supplement human anatomy is becoming so common, it has spawned a catchy new word: farmocology.

Baboons are giving up their hearts for human transplant. Pigs are being genetically engineered to produce human insulin in their milk-raising an interesting ethical problem for diabetic Jews and Muslims.

But the award for the best transgenic story goes, inevitably, to the US Government. Since 1963, NASA has poured money into research aimed at creating a man/animal hybrid capable of living in the environments of other planets. That means, according to a contemporary article by science writer Tom Paskal, 'The United States taxpayer is funding research designed to produce a being with a human brain contained in a body built from several animals'. Cute.

'They made me'
EVE SIX

The US Government of *The X-Files* may have made the Eves and the Adams, but in the alternate universe that is our own, the question would be: who owns them?

Already, several new genetically engineered life forms have been patented including the OncoMouse, a specially designed rodent created for the specific purpose of being sacrificed on the altar of breast cancer experiments. What made the new addition to God's menagerie possible was the discovery (and subsequent patenting) of relatively function-specific genes. What made *that* possible was the huge, international, multi-billion dollar project to map the human genome.

The ultimate goal of the Genome Project is to chronicle the ordered DNA sequence that makes up all human genes. When complete, the ledger will be around three billion elements long. The hope is that, along the way, many genes involved in the development of genetic diseases will be located. In theory, it is a veritable manual for human biology. The problem is, who owns the manual?

In the United States, the Genome Project is brought to you by g overnment, private industry and academia. All three have applied for patents for genetic code, often without even knowing what the genes involved actually do. The National Institute of Health alone has applied for patents for over 2,000 uncharacterised gene sequences, where they know the molecular composition but have no idea of the function. In cases like that, the patent is usually denied because one of the criteria for granting a US patent is that the invention must be 'useful'.

There are no such problems when the function is known. In 1976, US businessman John Moore had his cancerous spleen removed. Without his knowledge, the cells from it were cultured. The resulting cell line was patented, named 'Mo' and is used to produce nine human products including interferon and an immune system booster. The commercial worth of the Mo cell line and its byproducts has been estimated at $3 billion. Needless to say, Mr. Moore never saw a penny.

An even more morally dubious off-shoot of the Genome Project is the Human Genome Diversity Project. 'Bioprospectors' are roaming the earth extracting genetic samples from plants, animals and humans. Cell lines containing the genetic material of Baika Pygmies of Central Africa and the hill people of New Guinea are thriving in petrie dishes at Yale. The US Commerce Department even tried to patent the cells of two Solomon Islanders on the pretext that the cells may, at some point, be useful in the diagnosis or treatment of adult leukaemia. It was a move they also tried with the cell line of an indigenous Guyami woman from Panama. Public outcry made them withdraw both applications.

What does patenting actually mean? According to Professor Wendy McGoodwin of the Council For Responsible Genetics, 'It means that if they develop a diagnostic using that gene sequence, they can control that application. So if you are a researcher and you identify a gene that is associated with breast cancer, and you apply for a patent on that gene, that means that, if you develop a test that detects the presence of that gene, then the test belongs to you and you can charge $10 or $1,000 to women who want to take advantage of this test.'

That concept has scared a lot of people. Dr. James Watson, the Nobel Prize winning scientist who opened this Pandora's box with his 1953 discovery of the structure of DNA, resigned as head of the US Genome Project, partially in protest over the patenting issue.

French geneticist Daniel Cohen went even further. He is horrified by the American approach and has two main objections: 'The first is moral. You can't patent something that belongs to everyone. It's like trying to patent the stars. The second is economic. By patenting something without knowing the use of it, you inhibit industry. This could be a catastrophe.'

In 1990, with money from the French Muscular Dystrophy Association, Dr. Cohen set up a lab to automate the mapping procedure, promising to donate the results to the United

James Watson, co-discoverer of the structure of DNA, resigned as head of the US Genome project in protest over the alarming consequences of gene patenting

Nations. His results have been phenomenal and his work continues. Luckily Dr. Cohen is not alone. Generally, outside the United States, a backlash against the commerce of genetics is starting to occur.

In March 1995, the European Parliament rejected a bill to allow patents on life. Many of the patents already issued for human cell lines are being challenged because European patent law, unlike the American equivalent, requires that the new invention does not 'offend the public order'. The European Parliament has also decided to stop all public European funding for research associated with the Human Genome Diversity Project and for research that would result in privately held patents. Later that month, the Indian parliament also rejected a bill that would have allowed patents on life.

In May 1995, the indigenous people of the South Pacific began to draft a treaty declaring the region a 'life-form patent free zone'. It seems sad that they had to, but that's what happens when evolution falls prey to the free enterprise system.

LEXICON OF A BRAVE NEW WORLD

Asymptomatic ill/healthy ill: People whose genetic tests have shown that they risk developing certain illness.

Bio-Luddite: People who believe that, genetically speaking, humans are fine just as they are, thank you very much.

Biological determinism: The belief that all we are and all that we can be are exclusively determined by our genes. The basis of eugenics.

Bioprospecting: Collecting genetic material from plants, animals and even humans, usually in the developing world, almost always with the goal of patenting the resulting cell lines and making lots of money.

Genetic underclass: People who have experienced discrimination based on their genes, i.e. people who have been denied medical coverage or jobs because tests have shown that they *may* develop breast cancer.

Germ-line intervention: The same as somatic intervention but making the changes at the reproductive level as well, so that all progeny will be 'fixed' in the same way.

Human Genome: Total number of human genes.

Negative eugenics: Laws and actions that (usually) stop short of actually killing anybody but that make sure their 'defective' genes don't get passed on. i.e. marriage restrictions, sterilizations.

Positive eugenics/genetic modification: Laws and actions that promote increased breeding among superior human stock and/or genetically create superior people. The sort of thing that led to the Eves.

Post-human: A genetically 'enhanced' person.

Somatic intervention: Genetically manipulating an individual. Generally to fix a 'defective' gene, for example, the one that causes Huntington's Disease.

Bibliography

Sources and further reading

Books

What Sort of People Should There Be? Genetic Engineering, Brain Control and their impact on our future world
J. Glover, Penguin, 1984

Papers, Journals & Newspapers

Position Papers on Human Germ Line Therapy, Genetic Discrimination, Genetic Privacy and Human Genome Initiative
Council for Responsible Genetics Human Genetics Committee, Cambridge, MA

The Genome Finds Its Henry Ford
Tony Dajer, Discover, January 1993

Embracing Change with All Four Arms: A Post-Humanist Defense of Genetic Engineering
J. Hughes Ph.D. unpublished paper produced at the MacLean Center for Clinical Medical Ethics, Department of Medicine, University of Chicago May, 1993

Scientists Clone Human Embyos
Stuart Newman, Genewatch, January 1994

The Question of Human Cloning
J.A. Robertson Hastings Center Report 24 (2 March 1994)

Genes in Black And White
New Scientist, 8 July 1995

Pissing in the Gene Pool
P. Morales, Processed World 28, 1991

My Genes Made Me Do It
Stanton Peele Ph.D. & Richard DeGrandpre Ph.D.
Psychology Today, July/August 1995

Scope Note 28: Eugenics
Mary Carrington Coutts & Pat Milmoe McCarrick Kennedy Institute of Ethics at Georgetown University

Tampering With The Machinery of God
Tom Paskal, Weekend Magazine, 18 September , 1971

Television Programmes

The Shape of Things to Come
Director: Martin Lavut, Producer: Arnie Gelbart Galafilm, 1995

X-File: Conduit

Case notes by Agent Dana Scully

With Ruby Morris, the missing teenager, returned safely home, this case is now closed. Ruby's whereabouts during her absence are still unknown although her mother has declared further investigation to be unnecessary.

I cannot begin to speculate on how Ruby's eight-year-old brother could have obtained fragments of a highly classified, binary encoded defence satellite transmission, a matter that remains in the hands of the NSA. However, I cannot share Agent Mulder's conviction that the bizarre incident is connected with the disappearance of Ruby, or the proliferation of UFO sightings (including one reported by Ruby's mother in 1967) at Lake Okobogee, where Ruby disappeared.

teenager,
now closed.
sence are
ther has
e unneces-

w Ruby's
obtained
binary
sion, a
he NSA.
ulder's
ent is
by, or
luding
t Lake

THE UFO EXPERIENCE

In *Conduit*, Mulder and Scully search for Ruby Morris – a girl who goes missing whilst camping with her mother and brother near a notorious UFO hot spot. It is, for Mulder, a painful reminder of his sister's abduction.

Howard Gordon, who co-wrote the episode with Alex Gansa, explains their intention to look at UFO phenomena from a more emotional and psychological angle. They achieve this magnificently. Besides Mulder's own torments, Ruby's mother, who had a UFO encounter herself as a teenager, gives moving insight into the life-changing effects of such an experience.

'We were proud of those moments,' says Gordon. 'She's a woman who has been vilified in the broader community for her beliefs. What was nice was the circularity: at the end, when Ruby is returned, the mother enforces her silence because the truth has never got her anything but scorn.

'One woman wrote us a letter saying: thank you for finally exposing to the public what it's really like. It is compared to a religious experience,' muses Gordon.

Chris Carter, shares this analogy, describing himself as 'a non-religious person looking for a religious experience. My scepticism is waiting to be challenged.' Gordon too is largely sceptical, and when he saw a fireball streak across the sky when he was 12, he was never tempted to interpret it as anything other than what it was. 'It was clearly fire. But I think there must be enough strange sightings that are genuinely unexplained – but not neccesarily extraterrestrial.'

Unidentified flying objects have certainly been around a lot longer than identified flying objects. Romans as early as 214 BC described objects as 'altars in the sky', 'gleaming beams in the sky' or 'night suns'. St. Gregory, Bishop of Tours, France, in the 6th century, described how 'there appeared in the sky brilliant rays of light which seemed to cross and collide with one another'. In the Middle Ages, what we would label 'flying saucers' were dubbed 'flying dragons'.

Of all modern explorers delving into prehistoric UFOs, Swiss author Erich von Daniken has had the most success – at least when it comes to firing imaginations and selling millions of books offering 'proof' of ancient astronauts mating with primitive Earthlings and the like. Our favourite debunker, James Randi, however, considers the author of *Chariots of the Gods* a master of hokum.

In his book *Flim Flam!*, Randi completely demolishes most of von Daniken's claims. For example, the underpinning of the blustery Swissman's argument is (rather offensively) that 'ancient heathens' could not possibly have been clever enough to create magnificent structures. And these he goes on to imbue with far more cosmic significance than they actually possess: a sarcophagus lid that he claims depicts an ancient astronaut firing his rocket actually quite clearly shows a typically stylised rendering of a well-known Mayan ruler. The most amusing blunder comes from *Gold of the Gods*, in which von Daniken confidently scoffs at the impossibility of unaided ancients creating visual representations of a human skeleton: 'As we know, Roentgen did not discover X-rays until 1895!'

Unidentified craft and lights continued to be sighted through every period in history, and caused a good deal of alarm and intrigue. They caused even more panic when sighted at times of war, when they were variously dubbed 'phantom airships' and 'foo-fighters'.

Still, the 'original' UFO sighting, the one commonly regarded as having started it all, took place on 24 June 1947 when a pilot, Kenneth Arnold, spotted a formation of odd-looking craft flying over Mount Ranier in Washington State's Cascade mountain range. Weird, since Arnold was hardly the first man to see a UFO, nor even the first man to see a UFO in June of 1947. But then, along came Bill Bequette. Bequette was not the first local reporter in the history of print to take a little literary liberty here or there in the quest for a nice turn of phrase. But when Arnold described what he had seen as moving 'like a saucer would if you skipped it across water', Bequette coined the phrase 'flying saucer' and the UFO era as we know it began in earnest.

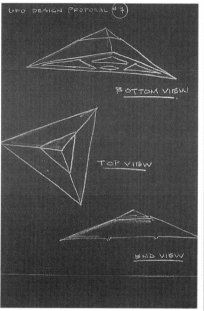

> '*Do you believe in the existence of extraterrestrials?*'
> MULDER
> *The Pilot Episode*

The Extraterrestrial Hypothesis (as the theory is known in circles where people are even aware that there *are* any other hypotheses) posits that these strange airbourne objects are piloted by sentient beings from other planets and it remains the most popular theory. But there are other suggestions. Here are seven of the best of the rest:

THE TIME TRAVEL HYPOTHESIS

The craft are piloted by humans from the future who have discovered the secret of time-travel. Hey, it could happen .

Supporters of this theory point out that many aspects of UFO lore fit better with this hypothesis than with the ETH. It would explain the rumours of a government liaison (why wouldn't we talk to and protect our own?), and the advanced nature of the technology (there's nothing to say that species from other planets should be more advanced than us, but if our future selves could learn to time travel, they sure as hell could knock up some pretty nifty flying machines). If claims of abduction are to be believed, there is no reason why time travellers would be less interested in examining the human race than aliens. Moreover, not all alleged reports of alien sightings describe the beings as little green men, or the more popular 'greys'. About the same quantity of reports describe 'humanoids' (which is, of course, something the episode *Gender Bender* addressed, in a roundabout way).

THE ALTERNATIVE-DIMENSION THEORY
The craft are not from another planet, but another dimension. Supporters include veteran anomalist John A. Keel, who called the visitors 'ultraterrestrials'. Similarly, Jacques Vallee, the innovative astronomer and UFOlogist, pointed out in his fascinating *Passport to Magonia* that UFO lore has a great deal in common with fairy tales and the supernatural.

An off-shoot of this theory is that the things we see are not here, but we are taking a brief peek into another dimension through a tear in reality and getting a glimpse of what is going on elsewhere.

SPACE ANIMALS
One of the wilder theories: these flying things are not piloted craft but living forms. Sir Arthur Conan Doyle's 1913 story, *The Horror of the Heights*, concerned such a beast.

Charles Fort also addressed the idea; numerous Forteans such as Ivan T. Sanderson kept it alive, and Kenneth Arnold mentioned it to the Press after his historic sighting. John Phillip Besor, a psychical researcher, even persuaded the US Air Force's first UFO research project (Project Sign) to take the theory into consideration for a time.

APPARITIONS

There are numerous claimed sightings of 'phantom' buildings, trains, ships, lorries and cars. If these are genuine phenomena, perhaps whatever generates them could also generate more exotic, airbourne apparents.

PSYCHOSOCIAL PHENOMENA

Loren Coleman and Jerome Clark, two influential contemporary anomalists, were the first to suggest, in their 1975 book *The Unidentified*, that the phenomenon was a *human* enigma – a combination of cultural belief and visionary experience. In doing this they were not debunking UFOs, but wondering at the exquisite mystery of the human mind.

TECTONIC STRESS THEORY

Michael Persinger, a neuroscientist, brought a fascinating alternative to the debate when he suggested that tension below the earth's surface brings about electromagnetic charges which may both create the effect of distant lights in the sky, and affect the human brain's own electromagnetic activity. His theory was that this could create hallucinations that are so real as to be virtually indistinguishable from something that is actually experienced. He suggested that the nature of the thing conjured by the brain would be plucked from one's own cultural data-banks – an alien craft, an alien, a ghost, an angel and so forth. Persinger has since begun to prove, in a mind-blowing research programme, that stimulation of certain parts of the brain can and does produce intensely 'real' subjective experiences.

UNEXPLAINED NATURAL PHENOMENA

Paul Devereux is another theorist who works on the basis of tectonic stress, but he suggests a slightly different below-the-crust effect (which he feels may be limited to fault-line areas), and concentrates on the production of 'Earthlights'. Slightly more out-there and difficult to prove, however, is Devereux's suggestion that these energies may have innate intelligence.

'There's a marsh over there. The lights the driver saw may have been swamp gas. . . It's a natural phenomenon in which phosphine and methane rising from decaying organic matter ignite, creating globes of blue flame'
SCULLY

'That happens to me when I eat Dodger Dogs'
MULDER

UFO has become so synonymous with the concept of alien craft that it is often easy to forget what the acronym actually stands for - *unidentified flying objects.*

Roughly 95% of UFO sightings have an explanation of a rational nature of which even Scully would approve. This figure is almost universally agreed upon (give or take a percentage or two) by every official body logging UFO sightings, from civilian research organisations to the British Ministry of Defence.

Donald H. Menzel, one-time director of the Harvard College Observatory in the US, never made any attempt to conceal his disbelief in the entire UFO phenomenon. As far as he was concerned, where there was a UFO sighting, there was some perfectly natural explanation that could turn a UFO into an IFO. He said that while he was on an aeroplane, he had a sighting similiar to Kenneth Arnold's (of a crescent-shaped craft apparently flying in formation) which had turned out to be raindrops on the window. He authored a list, which he described as 'minimal and highly abbreviated', of over one hundred logical explanations of UFOs.

His rationalizations include soap bubbles, spider webs, cigarettes tossed away, failure to wear glasses, or reflection from glasses (so for anyone with less than 20/20 vision it was a case of heads I win, tails you lose to Menzel), ponds, weathervanes and visual after-images triggered by other things (including 'smoker lighting pipe').

It is certainly true that people unfamiliar with the skies get bamboozled a heck of a lot. The most common misidentifications are sightings of planets, stars and (conventional) aircraft lights. But whether Mr. Menzel would have been prepared to stand up in an auditiorium and address the several thousand trained observers – military personnel, civilian pilots and the like – who have seen UFOs, and suggest to them face to face that the object they painstakingly reported as a large, black, triangular craft, accelerating from nought to mach five in under a second, could have been a soap bubble is a matter for question.

Sometimes, though, the explanations *are* mundane. On 23 May 1995, a multiple sighting of an illuminated floating object over West Virginia, Ohio and Kentucky prompted over 70 phone calls to police across the three States, and countless more to local UFO groups. Dispatcher Kevin Fannin of Ohio's Scioto County Sheriff's Department told the *Charleston (Ohio) Gazette:*, 'Some people were just wondering what was going on, and some people were really scared.' It was fortunate, then, that the mystery did not remain unsolved for long. Police soon determined that the UFO was, in fact, the Blockbuster blimp, wending its way on a nationwide promotional tour of the video company's stores.

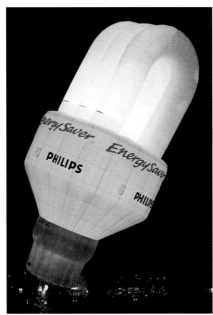

A Virgin balloon lights up the sky – these blimps are frequently mistaken for UFOs

Most people, during daylight hours are able to recognise a blimp or at least arrive at the logical conclusion that, if alien craft do indeed exist, their fusilages are unlikely to have 'Blockbuster Video' emblazoned upon them. Although it must be said that it is not all that common for an advertising blimp to create a mini UFO flap, aerial advertsing vehicles are nevertheless most certainly responsible for great number of UFO sightings in darkenss – and even in daylight.

Virgin Lightships, a subsidiary of the Virgin Group in Britain, owns a fleet of 11 illuminated, airbourne balloons which they hire out for advertising purposes. Six of them are located in America, the rest spread across South America and Europe, and wherever they go, they leave a wake of perplexed observers. The company's spokesman, Christian Brown, receives at least four calls a week from police stations and UFO research groups asking for details on the fleet's time schedule and whereabouts.

'I've been told we account for something like 80% of UFO sightings,' reveals Brown. 'So obviously it is essential to people's investigations to be able to eliminate the lightships early on.' The company had never anticipated becoming so closely involved with the UFO lobby, and as a humorous response (and publicity exercise), built a small flying saucer-shaped air balloon which entrepeneur supremeo Richard Branson, (Virgin's president), flew over one of Britiain's busiest motorways whilst dressed in a silver space-suit. Unfortunately, this resulted in a jamming of police switchboards, and subsequently, a polite but formal request from the police not to fly the balloon again.

All of which brings us back to that unidentified 5%. Many opponents of the UFO phenomenon have insisted that 'unknowns' were merely 'knowns' for which there was insufficient data.

However, one of the United States Air Force's own reports unwittingly skewered this notion. Project Stork, a 1955 classified data analysis venture with the Batelle Memorial Institute of Columbus, Ohio, a respected think-tank, discovered that knowns and unknowns were entirely different beasts, and that there was actually more back-up data provided for the unknowns.

*'This is the essence of science, Scully –
ask an impertinent question, you're on
your way to the pertinent answer'*
MULDER
Conduit

So how about those unknowns? Richard Hall, chairman of the Fund for UFO Research, has chosen some of the more provocative cases from the files of America's major UFO research organisations. We present a sampling in chronological order:

24 April 1964: Socorro, New Mexico (5.45 p.m.)
A Socorro police officer, Lonnie Zamora, heard a roar and spotted a flame in the sky. After speeding to the site, he saw an elliptical object with supporting legs in a gully. Standing near the craft were two humanoid figures. The beings noticed Zamora, quickly entered the craft, and took off, rising straight up in a blast of flame. After a roar the craft became silent and flew off.

The 'footprints' left by the legs of the craft were never definitively analysed, and while only one other couple claimed to see an airbourne craft of similar description, several others in the area recounted seeing a blue flame in the sky at around that time. Investigators have nothing much to go on but the integrity of Officer Zamora is considered extremely reliable.

2-3 July 1965: Antarctica
Meteorological observers at various Antarctic stations reported a series of sightings of coloured lights and objects in the dark, mid-winter skies. One sighting, reported by 17 people, was described as a lens-shaped disc that manoeuvred erratically for about an hour; the Argentine Navy sent out a detailed press release confirming this.

5 March 1967: Minot, North Dakota
Air Defence Command radar tracked an unidentified target

descending over Minuteman missile silos near Minot. Security converged on the area and saw a slow-moving, metallic, disc-shaped craft ringed with bright, flashing lights. The disc hovered 500 feet off the ground, then suddenly began circling the launch-control facility. Just as base operations decided to launch F-106 fighter-intercep-tors, the UFO climbed straight up and streaked away at incredible speed.

26 February 1975: Lake Sorell, Tasmania, Australia (8.45 p.m.)

A former Royal Australian Air Force crew member on a fishing trip with a companion saw three glowing lights in the north-east sky. When they came into view he identified each as an elongated disc with a pulsating red light on its underside. One object began travelling east and stopped over the north shore of the lake. Suddenly, one began whizzing at the witnesses at 'phenomenal speed' before coming to a halt 500 feet up. A brilliant, cone-shaped beam then swept across the terrain. The surface of the lake glowed a florescent blue-white. The object then shot away to the north-east 'at a colossal speed' that the witnesses likened to 'the trajectory of a tracer bullet' and the others followed.

19 September 1976: Tehran, Iran (12.30 a.m.)

Under the Freedom of Information Act, a US Defence Intelligence Agency report on this UFO sighting was released a year later. The Air Force Command Post, responding to citizens' calls about some UFO sightings, scrambled an F-4 Phantom jet from Shahrokhi AFB. (Iran was a US ally at the time.) The Phantom spotted the brilliantly glowing UFO from 70 miles away. As it closed in, all instrumentation and communication went dead, and the

F-4 returned to base. As soon as it turned away from the object, power was resumed.

A second F-4 was sent up. As it closed in, the object moved away, maintaining a distance of 25 nautical miles. The intense light made it difficult to gauge the object's size. Suddenly, a smaller, brightly lit object emerged from within and headed straight at the F-4 at high speed, like a missile. The pilot attempted to return fire, but at that moment his weapons control panel went off. The pilot went into a negative-G dive to escape, and the smaller object redocked with the larger.

While some may assert that there are no UFOs at all, occasionally evidence emerges that *so many* UFOs are out there that we need some sort of interstellar traffic control tower. The Civil Aviation Authority set up a Joint Air Miss Working Group to investigate near-misses between earthly craft. But, as Nick Pope of the Ministry of Defence reports, the JAWG has had several dealings with pilots reporting near-misses with UFOs.

6 January 1995:
A British Airways jet on a flight from Milan to Manchester nearly collided with a brightly lit UFO at 13,000 feet over the Pennines. The triangular craft veered at the last moment to miss the BA Boeing 737, then flew off and disappeared. Captain Roger Willis and First Officer Mark Stuart were informed by air traffic control that no other planes were tracked on radar at the time. Graham Shepherd is an airline pilot who has had two near-collisions with UFOs. (Formerly with British Airways, he requested the omission of the international airline for whom he now works, for reasons you'll soon understand.)

'On 22 March 1967, I was co-pilot on a flight from Gibraltar to Heathrow around 8.30 at night. Over the Bay of Biscay, we noticed a very bright star at about 30 degrees elevation straight ahead of us. We couldn't judge the distance.

'After about ten minutes it moved off to our left, all the time changing colours: greens, reds, blues. . . quite beautiful, actually. Then it started doing very fast acrobatics: figures of eight, looping and very impressive acceleration. It was completely outside the realms of possibility that this was a man-made machine.

'Then it was joined from nowhere by another one. We watched them doing this for five or ten minutes. We questioned Bordeaux radar, and they confirmed unidentified traffic exactly where these things were.

'We didn't report it. It is a written rule that one doesn't discuss what is regarded as an operational matter with the media. The sighting of a UFO by a pilot is regarded as an operational matter.

'Six months later, we were flying in daylight, beautiful weather, from Scotland to London and were given a radar alert. A disc with a bump on top – the archetypal flying saucer came very close to the aeroplane flying at extremely high speed. It was a dull silver, doing about 1,000 miles an hour. When we landed we didn't report it.

'About two years ago I did an interview with Radio 4 about this. It was picked up by the media; I was answering the phone all morning. The British Airways managers gave me a dressing down, formally warning me that any further talk about this kind of rubbish on the radio or TV would result in dismissal. (Shepherd left BA soon after this, for a 'combination of factors'.)

'I've been flying for 30 years; I've spent all my working life in the sky. So when people suggest I might be hallucinating or seeing normal meteorological phenomena, the chances are really low.'

'How did you recognise me?'
MULDER

'Saw your picture once in a trade publication. And, of course, I read your article in Omni *on the Gulf Breeze Sightings'*
MAX FENIG
Fallen Angel

It is widely acknowledged that one well-publicised spate of sightings tends to cause what is known in the trade as a 'flap' – a flurry of other sightings, most of them dubious 'me too's. This, in turn, creates a UFO 'hot-spot' – like *Conduit's* Lake Okobogee. Gulf Breeze, Florida, is likely to be the hotspot of the decade, and weirdly, it seems that the UFOs genuinely just keep on coming.

Unidentified lights and craft have been spotted on and off there since the mid-Eighties, but the real story began in 1988 when local man Ed Walters snapped some pictures of a UFO with his old polaroid camera. They came out disappointingly dark and unclear, but the nature of the polaroid film meant that it could be light-blasted: a process which strips away the top layers of the print and lightens the whole picture. The results were astonishing.

'When I first saw the Gulf Breeze
photos I knew
they were a hoax...'
MULDER
E.B.E

Outside *The X-Files* universe, no solid evidence of hoaxing has been found, but Walters's pictures are such a far cry from the usual blob in the sky – startlingly clear, and rather beautiful – that the general consensus is that it must be a case of too-good-to-be-true.

Representatives from the Mutual UFO Network (MUFON) supplied Ed with one of their cameras, loaded with a marked film and sealed with wax in the presence of a lawyer. It was returned untampered with and the film was developed under highly controlled conditions. Says MUFON's international director, Walter Andrus: 'We didn't expect a single shot . . . he filled the entire roll.'

One of the MUFON 'Gulf Breeze' photographs taken by Ed Walters under carefully controlled conditions

Although the pictures Ed took with this camera were nowhere near as unusual as the ones that had made him famous, everyone was pretty impressed.

While much of the world was prepared to open their minds to the possibility that Ed had photographed something extraordinary, his subsequent claims of closer encounters went beyond many people's boggle-threshold, casting a shadow of doubt.

But the interesting thing about Gulf Breeze is that it does not live or die on the claims or photos of Ed Walters. Since

1988, people have flocked there in the hope of seeing a UFO and most have not been disappointed. There have been more photos and video tapes submitted to the media than anyone knows what to do with.

In the midst of the 1988 flap, on 21 August, the joint Chiefs of Staff met at nearby Pensacola Naval Air Station for a 'secret' conflab, adding much fuel to the conspiracy-theory fire. As did the testimonies of a number of witnesses who claimed to have seen the military retrieval of a crashed saucer taking place before being surrounded by personnel and ordered to leave immediately.

Sceptics point out the proximity of a major airbase, and suggest that the craft seen are covert military projects. Believers counter that it would seem unlikely that the military would test top-secret craft over a densely populated area that is swarming with UFO-spotters and journalists – let alone do it for a decade.

Whatever is going on at Gulf Breeze, it is not simply the work of over-active imaginations. Says UFOlogist Bob Oechsler: 'What is so remarkable about Gulf Breeze is that we are now in the tenth year of consistent activity. Sometimes it's daily activity. I have been able to say since 1988 that if you are sceptical about UFOs you merely need to take a trip to Gulf Breeze. Anyone who takes a trip to Gulf Breeze has a very high percentage chance of seeing one of these things day or night with their own eyes. I know of no other location in the world that has had such consistent activity. And I know of no situation in history that even comes close to what is happening in Gulf Breeze.'

Bibliography
Sources and further reading

Books

UFOs in the 1980s: The UFO Encyclopedia, Volume 1
Jerome Clark , Apogee Books, Detroit, MI, 1990

UFOs from the Beginning Through 1959: The UFO Encyclopedia, Volume 2
Jerome Clark, Omnigraphics, Detroit MI, 1992

Unexplained!
Jerome Clark , Visible Ink Press, 1993

UFOs: Operation Trojan Horse
John A. Keel, G.P. Putnam & Sons, 1970

The UFO Enigma: the Definitive Explanation of the UFO Phenomenon
Donald H. Menzel and Earnest H. Taves. Doubleday, 1977

Flim Flam!
James Randi, Prometheus Books, 1982

Brain Storms and Angels
Nicholas Regush

The UFO Encyclopedia
Compiled and edited by John Spencer for BUFORA Headline PLC, 1991

UFOs - The Definitive Casebook
John Spencer, Hamlyn Books, 1993

Encyclopedia of the World's Greatest Mysteries
John and Anne Spencer, HeadlineBook Publishing, 1995

Alien Worlds
Reuben Stone, Blitz Editions, 1993

Passport to Magonia: from Folklore to Flying Saucers
Jacques Vallee, Henry Regnery and Co, 1969

Arthur C. Clark's A-Z of Mysteries
Simon Welfare and John Fairley, Harper Collins, 1993

Papers, Journals and Newspapers

The Charleston Gazette, 27 May 1995

Equinox journal, Summer 1995

FUFOR's UFO case summaries were provided by Richard Hall, Chairman of the Fund for UFO Research, Washington DC. Mailing address: Fund for UFO research, Box 277, Mt. Ranier, M.D. 20712, USA. The fund is a US non-profit, tax exempt organisation that makes research grants and cash awards to encourage scientific study of UFO reports and related phenomena.

Richard Hall's updated *UFO Evidence II* is due in 1996.

X-File: Space

Case notes by Agent Dana Scully

The investigation into the death of former astronaut Colonel Marcus Aurelius Belt is now closed,
having concluded with a verdict of suicide. Our
This has been a perplexing investigation. Our
initial attempt to look into the suspected sabotage
of a NASA space-shuttle mission was thwarted by
Colonel Belt, and his ensuing conduct and remarks
strongly suggest that he was aware of the tampering that had taken place. However, it also seems
likely that it was Belt who anonymously warned
Michelle Generoo, the Mission Control
Communications Commander who alerted Agent Mulder
and myself, to the impending danger. Moreover, the
ill-fated mission we witnessed would almost
certainly have resulted in tragedy without the
guidance of Colonel Belt.
Agent Mulder and myself agree that Colonel Belt's
unpredictable and apparently schizophrenic behaviour seems to date back to a traumatic experience
in space, although we differ in our interpretation
of what form this experience may have taken.
The identity of the perpetrator of the sabotage
operation remains unknown.

ALIEN TERRITORY

In the episode *Space*, Mulder and Scully meet Colonel Marcus Aurelius Belt, a former astronaut now running the Space Shuttle programme at NASA who is haunted – maybe actually possessed – by a creature he encountered in space.

The cosmic entity resembles the photo of a mountain on Mars beamed back by the 1976 Viking Space Probe that looks like a human face, which some UFOlogists, notably Richard Hoagland, consider to be a structure created by intelligent beings.

Says Chris Carter: 'I'd seen this amazing NASA footage, and I'd come across this picture of the face on Mars, and I thought there must be some way to make a connection between the two of them. I liked the concept, but it was not as well realised as I had hoped. Not one of our better efforts.'

Although Colonel Belt's unpleasant torments have not been experienced by any real-life astronauts, there exist more than a few rumours that some of them have encountered objects in space that cannot be positively identified.

The face. Could this be evidence of intelligent life on Mars?

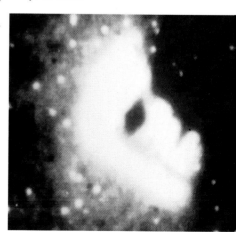

'We send them up there to unlock the doors of the universe – never knowing what could be behind them'

Mulder

The very fact of the American and Soviet space programmes are in themselves evidence supporting the possibility of extraterrestrial spacecraft. After all, if we're out there buzzing around the Galaxy, why couldn't residents of some other planet be doing the same? From an alien's perspective, *we* are the UFOs.

Although it has never been a stated goal of any space mission, every exploration is another chance to detect alien intelligence. Instead of waiting here on earth for them to reach us, we are searching them out on their turf.

The all-time classic space shot was surely the 1969 Apollo 11 mission, in which astronauts Neil Armstrong and Edwin 'Buzz' Aldrin became the first humans to step on to the moon. For years, rumours have spread about what they encountered there, including a rumour that their spacecraft had been chased by a UFO.

In addition, the astronauts supposedly reported seeing two gigantic spacecraft perched on a crater's edge soon after touching down. The story goes that NASA deleted Apollo 11's communication during the re-transmission time delay so it was not broadcast to the general public, but some HAM radio operators claim to have monitored it – as well as a response by NASA instructing the astronauts to photograph what they saw. (HAM radio operators are able to receive the live feed from space rather than the re-transmission via Houston.)

NASA not only denies but condemns such stories, and for such an outrageous claim, a transcript (no tape) really doesn't cut it as evidence. However, the story has been kept alive by a handful of intriguing corroborative comments from former NASA employees.

In his book *Above Top Secret*, UFOlogist Timothy Good quotes Maurice Chatelain, ex-head of NASA's communica-

Buzz Aldrin steps on to the Moon

tion systems, as confirming the encounter and revealing that it was 'common knowledge' within NASA. Good also details a conversation between Neil Armstrong and an unnamed professor at a NASA symposium during which the astronaut came clean, describing the ships as 'far superior to ours, both in size and technology – Boy, were they big. . . and menacing!'

Good admits that the fact that the alleged tape has never surfaced 'could indicate that it's nonsense,' but adds, 'people should also ask the question why Neil Armstrong left NASA as soon as he landed.'

'Holy god! There's something outside the ship!'
SHUTTLE COMMANDER

Another HAM radio operator claims to have monitored and taped the following raw transmission in 1988 from the space shuttle Discovery: 'Uh, Houston, this is Discovery. We still have that alien spacecraft under [observance?]' (The last word is not completely clear.) The transmission via Houston does not contain this statement.

Timothy Good reports that John McLeaish, Chief of Public Information at what was then known as the Manned Space Center in Houston, admitted in 1970 that transmissions from spacecraft are sometimes suppressed from the public by NASA, although he described these occurrences as 'private conversations, usually to discuss medical problems'.

A 1991 Discovery mission yielded another controversy, this one making it all the way up the media ladder to CNN's

Larry King Live. A camera aboard the Shuttle recorded *something* out there performing a high-speed manoeuvre. The tape was enhanced and endlessly analysed. NASA explained it as waste water dumped from Discovery, and said that the motion had been observed countless times before.

By never acknowledging the remotest possibility of an alien encounter, NASA has infuriated believers with its knee-jerk scepticism. On the other hand, the UFO community have infuriated NASA, by taking creative licence with numerous mission reports to make them sound suitably suggestive. For instance, Gemini XIII's Jim Lovell and Edwin Aldrin reportedly observed four objects linked in a row which they said were not stars. This is absolutely true. They were bags of rubbish that they had jettisoned themselves an hour earlier. Other astronauts' descriptions of satellites, light reflecting off clouds and the ocean, and debris from their own craft have been cunningly edited to omit any details which make them sound less like mysterious craft.

Space can be a messy place. There is a lot of stuff up there. And those passing through are more likely than not to spot a UFO – in the literal sense of the phrase – which later becomes an IFO.

'Roger, Houston. We've got some spooky stuff going on up here. . .'
SHUTTLE COMMANDER

But do astronauts believe in UFOs – in the popular sense of the definition? Some do. Several astronauts and cosmonauts have been outspoken about their belief in other life forms in our Galaxy, and some have even gone on record as having seen 'proper' UFOs. Former Mercury astronaut Donald 'Deke' Slayton reported one while on a 1951 test flight and astronaut Gordon Cooper, who, along with Slayton, was one of the original 'Right Stuff' space cowboys, has spoken a number of times of his personal interest and belief in them.

Edgar Mitchell, lunar module pilot on Apollo 14, has said he believes it is likely UFOs exist and that they come from another dimension.

Marina Popovich, a retired colonel of the Soviet Air Force and wife of prominent cosmonaut Paval Popovich, allegedly received and disseminated an infra-red image beamed back in 1989 from the vanished Soviet Fobos 2 Mars probe (before it lost contact) depicting what strongly resembles a 20-kilometre-long alien spaceship. The Russians never officially released the photo.

James McDivitt (left) waves goodbye before leaving on an Apollo mission

Which brings us, inevitably, to the official cover-up charges. The most frequently cited story is that of astronaut James McDivitt, who photographed an unidentified object through his capsule window on the Gemini IV mission. The pictures released by NASA were correctly identified as sun-flares, although McDivitt pointed out that these were not the photos he had taken. NASA admitted this to be the case, announcing that McDivitt's photos had not developed, and that stills from the mission's movie camera were released by accident without his review. McDivitt has never speculated upon the identity of the object he snapped.

At the more outlandish end of the conspriacy spectrum, speculation abounds that the government has photographic evidence of alien civilisations on Mars and has claimed mission failure (i.e. the Hubble Telescope and Mars Observer) in order to withhold it.'

'We at NASA are looking forward to our next Shuttle mission and to further successful explorations of space for mankind and for the future of mankind'
MICHELLE GENEROO

Collecting the Moon's left luggage! Evidence found in equipment left on the Moon proves that bacteria can thrive outside the Earth's atmosphere

During the course of research for *Space*, Chris Carter had a chance to probe a little deeper into the enigma himself. 'We had an astronaut who came in and talked to us – Pete Conrad, a guy who actually walked on the moon,' says Chris Carter. 'We asked him what he thought, and he said, "Oh, you know, maybe, could be. . ." He's an open-minded sort, but he said he had never seen anything definite to prove that there is life off this planet – except for one thing.

'He said that one mission had left some equipment on the moon, and another mission picked it up and brought it back, and when they opened it up they found something very interesting inside. He found out that one of the scientists who had assembled it had probably sneezed during the assembly, and bacteria must have got into the works. When they brought it back they saw that the bacteria had actually grown while on the moon, so therefore life survived out of this atmosphere.'

Bibliography
Sources and further reading

Books

Above Top Secret
Timothy Good, Sidgwick and Jackson, 1987

The UFO Encyclopedia
Margaret Sachs, Corgi, 1981

Papers, Journals & Newspapers

International UFO Library Magazine, April/May 1994

The Quarterly Report, Fund for UFO Research, 1st Quarter 1989

SAGA UFO Special, No.3

UFO magazine, July/August 1994

Television Programme

Larry King Live, Cable News Network, 1992

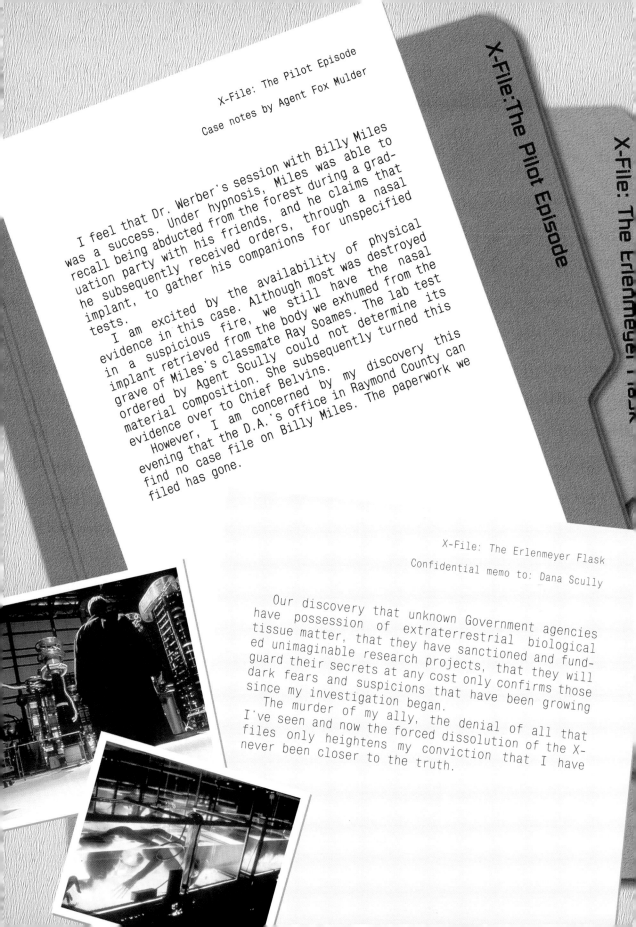

X-File: The Pilot Episode

Case notes by Agent Fox Mulder

I feel that Dr. Werber's session with Billy Miles was a success. Under hypnosis, Miles was able to recall being abducted from the forest during a graduation party with his friends, and he claims that he subsequently received orders, through a nasal implant, to gather his companions for unspecified tests.

I am excited by the availability of physical evidence in this case. Although most was destroyed in a suspicious fire, we still have the nasal implant retrieved from the body we exhumed from the grave of Miles's classmate Ray Soames. The lab test ordered by Agent Scully could not determine its material composition. She subsequently turned this evidence over to Chief Belvins.

However, I am concerned by my discovery this evening that the D.A.'s office in Raymond County can find no case file on Billy Miles. The paperwork we filed has gone.

X-File: The Erlenmeyer Flask

Confidential memo to: Dana Scully

Our discovery that unknown Government agencies have possession of extraterrestrial biological tissue matter, that they have sanctioned and funded unimaginable research projects, that they will guard their secrets at any cost only confirms those dark fears and suspicions that have been growing since my investigation began.

The murder of my ally, the denial of all that I've seen and now the forced dissolution of the X-files only heightens my conviction that I have never been closer to the truth.

TRUST NO ONE

With pleasing circularity, *The Erlenmeyer Flask*, Season One's finale, concludes with a shot of Cigarette Smoking Man in a Pentagon warehouse, just as we had seen him in the closing scene of the series pilot. Our first glimpse of him then – placing a nasal implant found by Scully into a box of other neatly catalogued nasal implants – had been darkly entertaining. But, by the end of the season, and with so much water under the bridge, the same scene – with an alien foetus in place of the nasal implant – became imbued with a deep and chilling resonance. It had become a powerful visual shorthand for conspiracy, cover-up, a shadowy government within a government, unthinkable knowledge, calculated manipulation and control. The stuff of wake-up-soaked-in-sweat paranoid nightmares.

While Chris Carter says he reserves judgement on the UFO issue 'until I see something myself, until I can go up and touch it and kick its tyres,' he does not doubt the existence of government cover-ups. 'I have much more belief in that than anything else,' he says. 'You pick up the paper every day and find out what the Government didn't tell you and what they did. As I think someone once wisely said, "Men and nations will behave wisely once they have exhausted all other avenues." And I think that's the way the Government operates.

'I believe that there were investigations into UFOs by the Government. I think that's pretty clear, and the Government has admitted that much. But is it ongoing? I don't know; I'd like to think it is for my purposes. We on *The X-Files* certainly believe it still is. It's a general government paranoia that we try to bring to light.'

'He's in a delicate position. He has access to information. An indiscretion could expose him'

MULDER

The Erlenmeyer Flask

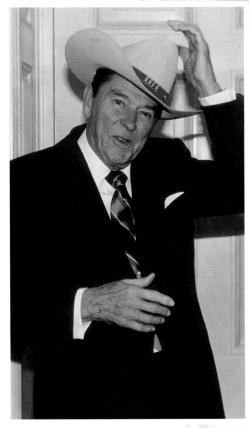

Ronald Reagan made public declarations of his belief in UFO's

During a private White House screening of *E.T.* President Reagan said to Steven Spielberg 'If people only knew how true this really was. . .' Perhaps you've heard this one before. It has lived for over a decade in the glorious neighbourhood of urban legend, side-by-side with tales of persecuted baby-sitters, microwaved poodles and film stars with gerbils lodged in inconvenient places. The difference, however, is that for the first time we can reveal that the Spielberg–Reagan story is absolutely, unquestionably true.

It is reprinted here with permission from Mr. Spielberg's representatives, who were also kind enough to provide us with the correct wording of the president's comment. (In some versions of the story, he is reported as saying, 'There are only about six people in this room who know how true this is. . .'.)

Whether or not Reagan knew some great 'truth', he was certainly not afraid to have his name linked with the concept of extraterrestrial intelligence. He publicly recounted two personal UFO sightings, and on three separate occasions, made public speculations on how a 'threat from outer space' would unify all nations. Both Soviet President Gorbachev and Foreign Minister Edvard Shevardnadze made it known that they shared his feelings.

This could have been merely an eccentric (and rather effective) hypothetical statement on how unity is possible, but some are convinced it was an attempt to hand us a morsel of epochal information, or at least to 'soften us up' for the day when the truth would finally be revealed.

There are degrees of belief: the US Government is more interested in UFOs than they make out; they know who is behind the unidentified craft which seem to dot our skies; they possess craft recovered in crashes; they have alien bodies; they have communicated with live aliens; they have liaised with them and made deals; there are alien bases on earth; it's all over bar the shouting.

But no matter which end of the spectrum a believer occupies, there is one common certainty: the Government is hiding something.

'Under the circumstances, I've given you all I can'
DEEP THROAT

Jimmy Carter appears to have been another believer. During his 1976 election campaign, he confirmed that he and others had observed a large, bright, airborne object change colour for ten minutes one night in Leary,

President Eisenhower was rumoured to have witnessed a demonstration of extraterrestrial flight technology

Georgia, in 1969. He vowed: 'I'll never make fun of people who say they've seen unidentified objects in the sky.' And he promised that if he became president he would make all information about UFOs 'available to the public and the scientists'.

His election pledge remained unfulfilled – not exactly unusual in the world of politics – but official documents reveal that he tried his best. His science advisor wrote to NASA administrator Dr. Robert Frosch in February 1977 suggesting that NASA become 'the focal point for the UFO question'. Frosch replied that although he did not mind responding to public enquiries, 'research activity' or convening 'a symposium' was out of the question.

Some interpreted Carter's statement as an insinuation that he knew 'the truth' and wanted it to remain a secret no longer, while NASA and the Air Force were battling to keep the lid on it. It is equally easy to say that perhaps Carter, like millions of others who have seen UFOs, simply wanted to know the truth himself.

Allegations that the president of the USA is privileged to 'the truth' are nothing new. Gerald Light, a psychic researcher, wrote a letter in April 1954 to a colleague at the Borderland Sciences Research Foundation that kicked off a chain of rumours. 'My dear friend,' it began, 'I have just returned from Muroc. The report is true – devastatingly true!' Light went on to say that he had spent several days at the Muroc Dry Lake Air Force Facility in California (now Edwards AFB), where occupants of several extraterrestrial craft were demonstrating their technology to select groups of scientists, military officials and other fortunates.

He added: 'President Eisenhower, as you may already know, was spirited over to Muroc one night during his visit to Palm Springs recently. And it is my conviction that he will ignore the terrific conflict between the various "authorities" and go directly to the people via radio and television if the impasse continues much longer. From what I could gather, an official statement to the country is being prepared for delivery about the middle of May.'

Needless to say, Eisenhower never gave that address. But what of the rest of Light's charge? There have been many claims of saucer sightings at Edwards AFB, both from insiders and civilians. Former astronaut Gordon Cooper, for instance, has revealed that during his tenure as test-flight manager at the base during the late 1950s, he studied a security film showing a large, unidentified, disc-shaped craft briefly landing on the base, then taking off again before anyone had a chance to investigate.

A number of former Air Force employees have independently relayed the same tale as Light. A retired colonel even claimed to have been present during Eisenhower's visit. However, all have chosen to remain anonymous, and therefore lend insufficient credence to the story.

Eisenhower *had* been in Palm Springs on the dates in question, and on the evening of 20 February, he had apparently disappeared for four hours. At a subsequent press conference, it was announced that he had gone for emergency dental treatment after losing a cap whilst eating a chicken drumstick. Attempts by researchers to find official memos or documents pertaining to the impromptu dentistry have proved fruitless.

One accusation often levelled against those making outrageous claims is that they were enticed to fabricate by the lure of 15 minutes in the spotlight – plus maybe even a few bucks into the bargain. The late Jackie Gleason,

Actor Jackie Gleason was 'visibly shaken' (as the story goes) after visiting a top-secret repository containing alien bodies

however – known as the Great One and one of America's best-known performers – certainly needed neither, nor did he choose to go public with his cover-up story.

It was Gleason's second wife, Beverly McKittrick, who revealed that he returned home one night 'visibly shaken' after having visited Homestead Air Force base in Florida. The visit had, she said, been arranged by President Richard Nixon, with whom Gleason was very chummy, and was conducted under the strictest security. Gleason had allegedly been allowed a peek at a top-secret repository containing alien bodies.

Gleason was approached by various parties, including a movie producer, who sought to verify the story, but chose neither to confirm nor deny it. Spokespersons for Homestead AFB denied everything.

'How do you know he's not just yanking your chain, this Deep Throat character?'
SCULLY

On the surface, government involvement with UFOs is an above-board matter. The British Ministry of Defence welcomes and investigates reports of UFOs. However, according to RAF press officer

David Davis: 'The M.o.D. does not have any direct interest, expertise or role in respect of UFO/flying-saucer matters, or those relating to the existence or otherwise of extraterrestrial life-forms, about which we remain totally open-minded. To date the M.o.D. is not aware of any evidence which substantiates the existence of extraterrestrial craft or life-forms.'

The US Government's first official investigations into UFO sightings began in 1947 with the USAF's Project Sign. After internal squabbles, this venture went into near abandonment a few years later as the UFO-refuting Project Grudge, until a flurry of fresh sightings in 1951 spurred a revival of the programme and it was renamed Project Blue Book.

For years, however, Blue Book primarily served a Grudge-like PR function of dispelling and explaining away any and all incidents, including the notoriously lame 'swamp gas' analysis of some credible 1966 sightings. The public lambasting they took for this dismissive sham helped lead the Air Force in 1969 to pull the plug on Blue Book. Since then, the USA has had no official interest in UFOs. Yeah, right.

Thanks to the 1966 Freedom of Information Act, thousands of documents released by such agencies as the CIA, FBI, Air Force, Coast Guard, Defence Intelligence Agency, Federal Aviation Administration, Navy, North American Aerospace Defence Command (NORAD), and the once super-secret National Security Agency, reveal the American Government's abiding interest in UFOs, contradicting the flimsy official pretence of indifference. And this does not include the documents still held back in the name of national security.

The documents themselves, however, are mainly standard reports of UFO sightings as well as dossiers on the activities of well-known UFO researchers. But some are intriguing. A 1975 NORAD document reveals that a number of high-level military bases in the Mid-west were put on alert after a spate of sightings. A 1969 memo from Air Force deputy director Brigadier General C.H. Bolender states that UFO reports which could affect national security 'are not  part of the Blue Book system'. This could mean, of course, that the impending closure of Blue Book didn't involve curtailing the monitoring of the skies for incoming Soviet missiles etc.; it could also confirm the long-held suspicion that more provocative cases by-passed Blue Book (and therefore public attention) altogether.

'Roswell was a smoke screen.
There've been half a dozen better
salvage operations'
DEEP THROAT

Sometimes such compelling evidence of cover-up turns up – the Roswell autopsy film, the notorious MJ12 documents, or the 'Intelligence leak' of 1988 – that all attention is focused on it. When the evidence crumbles – as it usually does – the suggestion inevitably arises that these tantalising diversions are not merely civilian hoaxes, but acts of deliberate government disinformation, designed to distract attention from the issue at hand and sink the field of UFOlogy into confusion, infighting and disrepute (although many of its members have proven over the years that they can achieve this all by themselves).

The 1988 shenanigans were the most bizarre. UFO researcher William Moore reported that while on a promotional tour for his book *The Roswell Incident*, he was approached by military insiders who revealed the truth and supplied him with a handful of back-up documents, including a brief allegedly written for President Carter.

In October 1988, Moore and two of his informants appeared on the international TV special, *UFO Cover-up – Live!*, where 'Falcon' recounted tales of government-alien liaison and enlightened viewers to the fact that the three aliens given refuge in various American air bases are small, intelligent and terribly fond of Tibetan music. Their favourite flavour ice-cream is strawberry.

Moore was also involved with the notorious MJ12 affair – documents which surfaced giving details of a highly classified group of scientists, thinkers and politicians appointed to handle the Government's knowledge of the extraterrestrial situation. However, there were problems with the format of the documents and most agree that they are not the genuine article. Just who perpetrated the forgery is not known, although Joe Nickell and John F. Fischer, who did a thorough job of debunking the documents in their *Mysterious Realms* subtly point the finger at Moore.

Many, including British UFOlogist Timothy Good, feel that the fallacy of the

documents does not neccesarily mean that the MJ12 committee did not exist. Says Good: 'I personally think there was such a committee. The documents may be fake or they may not be fake. I received a set from an intelligence source in the States. I'm sure the information contained is very accurate.' Good remains convinced that there is a cover-up and his books *Above Top Secret* and *Alien*

Liaison put forward the best evidence for the prosecution.

> *'If you two have no
> evidence, you have no
> case. Who would ever
> believe the story I've
> just told you?'*
>
> DEEP THROAT

G ood is the first to agree that for all the documents proving government interest, tangible evidence of government *knowledge* is harder to come by.

He cites as a 'major milestone' one particular endeavour by himself and two allies, US researcher Robert Oechsler and British peer Admirial Lord Hill-Norton, to gain feedback

from the upper echelons of the American intelligence community.

In 1989, they succeeded in arranging and recording a telephone conversation

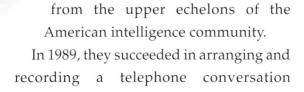

US researcher Robert Oechsler uncovered what seems to be remarkable evidence of American Intelligence knowledge of UFO technology

between Oechsler, a former NASA mission specialist and physicist, and Admiral Bobby Ray Inman. Inman has held a string of mind-blowingly powerful posts including Director of Naval Intelligence, Vice Director of the Defence Intelligence Agency, Director of the National Security Agency and Deputy Director of the CIA. Nominated for Secretary of Defence under Bill Clinton, Inman withdrew his name from consideration a few days later.

Oechsler reached Inman by dropping Lord Hill-Norton's name, and after a bit of chit-chat, Oechsler explained to Inman that the admiral was 'quite furious with his inability to gain knowledge on the issues' and felt that Inman might be able to help in gaining access to answers.

Inman responded that his knowledge in the areas of Oechsler's interest was several years out of date, but suggested he should contact other people, including Everett Hineman, the Deputy Director for Science and Technology at the CIA, who would soon be retiring and may therefore be more open to discussion, or Sumner Shapiro, a former director of Naval Intelligence.

The kicker came just before the end of the chat:

OECHSLER: *'Do you anticipate that any of the recovered vehicles will ever become available for technological research outside of military circles?'*
INMAN: *'Again, I honestly don't know. Ten years ago the answer would have been no. Whether as time has evolved they are beginning to become more open on it, there is a possibility. Again, Mr. Hineman probably would be the best person to put that question to'*

After a cheery 'good luck' wish from Inman to Oechsler, the conversation ended. Later, when Oechsler asked for Inman's permission to discuss their conversation at a conference, Inman's assistant Tom King responded that the admiral 'regards the material subject matter as being covered under national secrecy laws and asks that his name not be used. . . in regard to these matters'.

However, Oechsler and Timothy Good decided to publish details of the conversation in Good's 1991 book *Alien Liaison*. Inman did not deny that the conversation had taken place. Instead, when questioned by a reporter, he asserted that he had thought Oechsler was talking about the recovery of underwater vehicles.

An attempt by another researcher to debunk the conversation only served to increase the intrigue. In reply to a letter demanding clarification of what had taken place, Inman wrote a letter which included the words, 'having no prior knowledge of (Oechsler's) interests, I did not understand until well into the dialogue that his research was about unidentified flying objects.' He added that he had never, in 22 years of service in the intelligence community, 'encountered evidence of extraterrestrial or inter-planetary entities, crafts, vehicles or persons.'

Unwittingly, Inman had lent weight to Oechsler's case. Bob points out that if understanding had only dawned on Inman 'well into the dialogue', one must assume that he understood the subject matter well 'before the end of the conversation – which is when he made his most suggestive remark.

'Trust no one'
DEEP THROAT

Steven Spielberg and E.T.: part of a government conspiracy?

L et us pretend the Government knows the truth. So why won't they tell us? There is the school of thought which says that they *are* telling us – through a subtle process of indoctrination. Bob Oechsler tracked down a copy of a 1960 report commissioned by NASA from the Brookings Institute, America's most venerable think-tank. He says: 'They were trying to determine what the social implications would be of revelations of face to face contact with an alien culture. . .' The conclusions?' The result would be a process called acculturation where human beings worldwide would ultimately become subservient to such a society. . . and in order to avoid that process of acculturation it was deemed that a long-term indoctrination process would be the solution to avoiding that.'

And there are those who think that movies like *E.T.* and *Close Encounters* are part of an indoctrination process. Even, heaven forbid, *The X-Files*.

There again, there is one more explanation for why the Government is saying nothing, possibly the scariest one of all: *There is no conspiracy*. No aliens. Just us, alone in space – for now. Glen Morgan voices one of the most convincing arguments against: 'Scully says that line to the Lone Gunmen, "You know, I think you're giving the Government too much credit." And I think if the Government could barely cover up selling arms to the contras, that (a UFO cover-up) would have been exposed. I just don't think the Government's that good at doing it.'

Bibliography
Sources and further reading

Books

Unexplained
Jerome Clarke, Visible ink press, 1993

Above Top Secret
Timothy Good

Alien Liaison: The Ultimate Secret
Timothy Good, Arrow, 1991

Papers, Journals & Newspapers

The APRO Bulletin, Vol 29, no 8, 1981

Backroads of Nevada Lead to UFO Buff's Dreamland
Patrick Graham, Associated Press newswire, 30 May 1995

Multiple Sightings of Secret Aircraft Hint at New Propulsion, Airframe Designs
Aviation Week and Space Technology, 1 October 1990

George Washington University Relations Department Bulletins
1 November 1994, 15 March 1995

Stealth and Beyond
Jim Schults, James C. Goodall (writing as Al Frickey) Gung-ho, February 1988

Las Vegas Review Journal
20 March 1994, 11 November 1994, 24 May 1995, 14 June 1995

Suddenly Your Briefcase is Classified
Benjamin Wittes, Legal Times, 26 June 1995

Cash-Landrum Case Closed
John Schuessler, MUFON UFO Journal no 222, Oct 1986

The Observer, 4 December 1994

UFO Magazine, July/August 1994, July/August 1995

The Washington Post, 30 May 1995

News Bulletins

ABC World News Tonight, 1 August 1994

Area 51 Frequently Asked Questions, Psychospy

KLAS TV News, November 1989

Internet

Internet: The Internet UFO Group Web site

X-File: Deep Throat

Case notes by Agent Dana Scully

Mrs. Anita Budahas has dropped charges of kidnapping against the military employers of her husband, Colonel Robert Budahas, and has blocked further investigation, although none seems necessary now he has been safely returned.

The secrecy surrounding Colonel Budahas's incarceration in an Air Force medical facility would seem to suggest his involvement in a highly classified experimental project — a hypothesis supported by the peculiar ailments and psychoses he suffered, the stringent security surrounding Ellens Air Force Base, and the hostility with which our investigations were met.

I feel that this may also go some way towards explaining the proliferation of local 'UFO' sightings. I find no evidence to corroborate Agent Mulder's conviction that the experimental craft at the base utilise extraterrestrial technology.

charges of
employers of
as, and has
though none
en safely

Budahas's
l facili-
ent in a
ct — a
ailments
t secu-
and the
s were

wards
'UFO'

gent
ntal
ial

A CELESTIAL FLEET

I n a UFO 'hotspot' in Idaho, a USAF test-pilot is hospitalised under high-security conditions after working on a classified project at a military facility so secretive that officially it does not exist. Such was the premise of *Deep Throat*, and viewers who had even a nodding acquaintance with contemporary UFO-lore clocked the reference immediately: Area 51.

'You want to see something weird Mulder? Ellens Air Base isn't even on my USGS quadrant map. . .'
SCULLY

N inety-five miles north of Las Vegas, beyond the Nevada Test Site and Nellis Air Force range, on the dusty shores of the Groom dry Lake, sprawls the barracks, hangars and airstrip of America's most fiercely secretive military installation.

Like Ellens Air Base in *The X-Files*, it does not appear on any military map. In the 40-odd

A deserted highway leading to the top secret US Air Force base: Area 51, also known as 'Dreamland'

years since the base was built, it has had a variety of nicknames, including

'The Pig Farm', 'Paradise Ranch' and 'The Box'. Users of aviation frequencies refer to it as 'Dreamland', although its airspace is off limits even to military pilots. But most people call it Area 51.

'Ever hear of something called The Aurora *project? The Pentagon has all but admitted they've been testing a secret class of suborbital spy craft over the western US. Maybe these guys are flying those planes'*

SCULLY

Area 51 - the land from which this picture was taken is no longer accessible to the public

Area 51 has been the birthplace and testing ground of numerous highly classified secret projects – the U2 spy plane, the Blackbird spy plane, the SR-71 and F-117A stealth aircraft, and the 'Star Wars' Strategic Defence Initiative. Now, workers are allegedly beavering away on *The Aurora*, a ground-breaking hypersonic craft that can do 5,000 m.p.h.

The Aurora project had piqued Chris Carter's interest in Area 51. He had been hearing experimental craft from Nevada for some time, 'I've tracked their sonic booms in my own home. There's these secret planes that are being tested and the Government won't tell you where they come from, and I've heard the booms. So that's pretty interesting.'

Besides *The Aurora*, speculation has it that the Area 51 team may also be at work on such exotic projects as radar-evading helicopters and weirdly-shaped, pilotless spy planes, funded by the 'black budget' – monies which don't appear in Federal allocations. The shroud of secrecy is entirely understandable.

But secrecy begets rumours. Unsurprisingly, Area 51 is thick with them: that the base receives most of the US Government's 'black' funds; the base's annual budget runs to between a billion and one and a half billion dollars per annum; security measures include high powered telemetry satellite dishes which not only facilitate communication but also fog photographic film; the cafeteria serves free prime rib, frogs' legs, king crab and *filet mignon* daily; the colonels drink mineral water to the tune of $50,000 a month; one has grapefruit flown in specially from Israel at 25 bucks a pop.

Artist's impression of The Aurora *a ground-breaking hypersonic craft that can allegedly do 5,000 m.p.h*

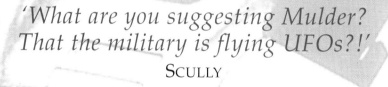

'What are you suggesting Mulder? That the military is flying UFOs?!'
SCULLY

'No. Planes built using UFO technology'
MULDER

Oh yes – the most extraordinary claim of all: that Area 51 houses a fleet of nine recovered extraterrestrial craft, whose propulsion techniques are being closely studied and tested at a facility within the base called S-4.

In the great tradition of urban legend, it is difficult to trace the genesis of these rumours.

'What do you think they are?'
MULDER

'Everybody thinks they're flying saucers. I think it's some new Star Wars cybertech hardware. Who knows? They'll probably roll it out for, like, Desert Storm II. . .'
EMIL

Observers have reported seeing odd lights describing manoeuvres which appear to be well beyond the capabilities of conventional aircraft – exceptional speeds, abrupt mid-air halts and hovering. Some report sightings of triangular craft and discs.

Aviation Week and Space Technology magazine reported on the base in their 1 October 1990 issue, speculating on 'a quantum leap in aviation' and saying: 'There is substantial evidence that another family of craft exists that relies solely on exotic propulsion and aerodynamic schemes not fully understood at this time.' However, editor and author of the piece, John D. Morocco, later scoffed at the suggestion that the craft were anything but terrestrial in origin on public radio. As Area 51's past record had proven, if anything was possible, it was possible there.

In a 1988 article in *Gung-Ho*, (an American military

publication) aviation writer James Goodall had quoted a retired Air Force colonel as saying, 'We have things that are so far beyond the comprehension of the average aviation authority as to be really alien to our way of thinking.' So was that the only kind of 'alien' out at Area 51? It is not hard to rationalize that a 'UFO' seen there, more than any other place on the planet, could well be a state-of-the-art experimental craft.

But still the rumours persist – and not just of strange sightings. According to one-time local news anchorman George Knapp, who is also involved in UFOlogy, 'stories of captured or acquired alien technology have circulated in the area since the mid-1950s and the beginning of the base.' Most were nothing more than rumours – although an insider's claim, in 1953, of a disc-shaped craft whose cockpit was so small that it had to be altered to fit a man, and a daylight sighting of a disc escorted by helicopters in 1978, kept the story alive.

Ten years later, it was stronger than ever. *Gung-Ho* editor Jim Shults acknowledged these stories in 1988, writing: 'Yes, I know I sound crazy, but the rumour is awfully solid! Something remarkable has caused the Russians to suddenly want to play ball, and I personally believe this could be it. . .'

No smoke without fire? Unfortunately, before anyone could investigate the fire, it became entirely obscured by the smoke. What had, for most of the decade, been a relatively thin plume of speculation became, at its close, a billowing cloud.

In 1989, Robert Lazar, a technical engineer, appeared on KLAS TV news and made UFOlogical history. He had, he said, worked at Area 51, sector S-4, in a position that was 38 levels above the top secret 'Q' clearance that he had held at a previous job working on the Strategic Defence

Initiative at Los Alamos National Laboratory. His claims were astonishing. He had been involved in 'reverse engineering' the vehicle propulsion system of an extraterrestrial craft.

He described the craft he had worked on as disc-shaped, approximately 30-35 feet in diameter and 15 feet high with a dull aluminium finish. Inside, he said, 'It looks like it's made out of wax and heated for a time and then cooled off. Everything has a soft, round edge to it – there's no abrupt changes in anything. It looks like it was cast out of one piece.' Lazar said that he was not told how or when the craft – referred to affectionately on base as 'The sport model' – had arrived at S-4, but guessed by its appearance that it had not crashed. It was, he said, in working order, and had been test-flown. He added that knowledge of the project was subject to compartmentalised 'need-to-know' clearance, and that members of Congress, possibly even the president, would not know about it. (Unless they happened to be watching the news, one supposes.)

For a guy making some outrageous claims, Lazar sounded remarkably credible. It was because he appeared, to the layman at least, to truly know his stuff in the science department. In interviews he convincingly described the concept of non-linear travel, facilitated by a gravity field which distorts space and time, and exactly how the craft's reactor generated such a field.

On the technical side, most of Lazar's claims were not *a priori* impossible – just unprovable. And proof that Lazar did work at Area 51 has yet to be satisfactorily refuted. However, his own credibility was severely thrown into doubt when some of his academic credentials failed to check out, and aspersions were cast on his character when he was subsequently arrested on pandering charges for his involvement in a Nevada brothel.

However, many people believe there is truth in his claims. British UFOlogist Timothy Good says, 'Bob Lazar's story is fascinating and I feel it's essentially true. I think he's lied about his credentials – there's absolutely no evidence that he has any qualifications as a nuclear physicist, but he's a very talented engineer, that's for sure.' Indeed, Lazar had built a jet car for fun, and had a particle accelerator in his bedroom – he was that kind of guy. Good muses: 'I think he needed to bolster his image to make the story more credible, but of course, once people realise that he's exaggerated about something, they tend to throw the baby out with the bathwater, which, in his case, I don't think we should.'

Those who believe that the Government is executing an insidious programme to manipulate the public, suggest that Lazar may be an unwitting pawn in this plan.

Lazar himself claims that his prospective employers knew a great deal about his background – including his contacts within the UFO community – when they approached him. Not impossible, then, that they even knew about his fudged c.v. The cover-up theorists conjecture that if someone wanted to disseminate information in a way that would reinforce an idea, Lazar would be just the fella you'd pick for the job – credible enough to command belief and fallible enough to invite doubt.

The problem with government conspiracy theories is that there is one for every occasion: denials? lack of evidence? it's a cover-up; a breach of official confidentiality? indoctrination? claims which invite ridicule? deliberate disinformation.

In some cases, of course, the deductions may be right on the button. But, in essence, conspiracy theorising is just another example of mankind's need to know, to have an explanation for everything. As Jerome Clark, veteran anomalist and deputy president of the J. Allen Hyneck Centre for UFO Studies once wrote: 'The three hardest words for a human being to utter are *I don't know.*'

*'I know Bob worked on top secret projects. Word gets around.
But he was always a patriot first; he took loyalty to his country as
an oath. And now - they treat us like strangers'*
MRS. BUDAHAS

'The Government is not above the law. They cannot withhold information'
SCULLY

Tragically, it is not only *Deep Throat's* UFO elements which have a real-life parallel. The problem with an air base which does not officially exist is that it does not exist within the jurisdiction of the law – a fact against which a young lawyer named Jonathan Turley has been battling since December of 1994.

Turley represents five ex-Area 51 employees and the widow of another, who want to bring suit against the Pentagon and the Environmental Protection Agency for violating federal law over the alleged open burning of toxic waste throughout the Eighties.

> *'. . . I started noticing it about two years ago. Bob developed a rash under his arms. . . then everything just went crazy'*
> MRS. BUDAHAS

I developed a rash, skin rash. I use sandpaper to get the scale off, because its the only way I can remove it,' one of the victims reported during an appearance on an ABC World News bulletin. His voice was disguised and his face in silhouette as he revealed that the open pit burnings had been carried out for 'the destruction of classified material'. He closed by saying: 'The running joke was, the place didn't exist so consequently anything could occur there.'

However, the situation was becoming less and less amusing. At the time of the newscast, many workers were seriously ill, and Robert Frost, who had suffered the same rash, had already died.

Professor Peter Kahn, a hazardous chemicals expert at

Warning sign at the boundary of the non-existent Area 51

Rutgers University, had analysed a tissue sample from Frost's body and told reporters: 'My only reaction is, what on earth has this man been exposed to?'

Nobody knew. The victims, under threat of imprisonment for breach of security, were unable to talk to their doctors about the place or nature of their work.

It has been slow going. A Government statement was issued confirming that there was 'an operating location near Groom Lake', but it insisted that it remain nameless. There were moves to ban the use of the terms 'Area 51' or 'Dreamland' in proceedings, although Turley noted that the former had appeared both in Congressional record and the Pentagon's in-house newspaper.

Next, US secretary of the Air Force, Sheila Widnal, submitted an affidavit saying that the Government felt *any* disclosures (and therefore most of the prosecution or defence's evidence) would be a grave threat to national security. And on 26 June 1995, the *Legal Times* featured an article entitled 'Suddenly, your Briefcase is Classified' which revealed that Turley had been banned from owning or referring to the facility's security manual – despite the fact that it was freely available to the Press, the justice department and even the public, who could download it from the Internet.

As of Autumn 1995, the case is ongoing. Turley told the *Observer*: 'It's like something out of a bad Fifties movie. The Soviets have pictures of it, kids in Nevada play with toy planes that fly from it, and I've got clients who are dying from it. . . but it doesn't exist.'

'This isn't some UFO goose chase you're leading me on, is it?'
SCULLY

Grotesquely enough, art is soon to be imitating life imitating art – *Area 51* the movie, penned by *China Syndrome* co-director Mike Gray is in the works. Already on the market is a CD - ROM game, *Entry Denied*, as well as the toys to which Turley refers – ones made by The Testor Corporation of Rockford, Illinois, who have greatly irritated the Pentagon by manufacturing model kits of secret Government aircraft. Their latest, more fanciful offering is 'The S-4 UFO-model flying saucer'. All this, and the Bill put forward by State Assembly man Roy Neighbours to rename the main road near Groom Lake 'Extraterrestrial Alien Highway', have certainly been newsworthy. But no one has done more than the Government to keep Area 51 in the public eye.

The Little A'Le'Inn in Rachel – the meeting place for UFO researchers

Around the same time as the litigation broke, the Pentagon reclaimed 4,000 acres of land, including 'Freedom Ridge' – the location offering the best and most accessible vantage point of the site. 'We identified this additional land as being needed to ensure the safety and security of operations on the Nellis Range Complex,' said spokeswoman Kim Ransford. 'We don't have UFOs out there. What goes on out there is classified,' added Air Force spokeswoman Major Mary Feltault, in a May 1995 interview with the *Washington Post*, neatly dignifying the rumours with a denial.

In the words of Glenn Campbell, a level-headed Boston computer programmer who acts as unofficial local

A B2 Stealth Bomber is alleged to have anti-gravity capabilites, something not known to be possible at our current standing in technological advancement

spokesperson, it is this sort of thing which has made Area 51 'the most popular secret airforce base in the world'.

'. . . Lots of folks out here looking around. UFO nuts mostly'
MOSSINGER

Today, more people than ever flock to Groom Lake, hoping to check out Area 51 and catch a glimpse of something. The nearest town, Rachel, has a fixed population of one hundred and one hostelry, The Little A'Le'Inn, (*alien*, geddit?) which is not dissimilar to The Flying Saucer Diner of *Deep Throat*, and plays host to thousands of visitors every year.

With Freedom Ridge closed, however, getting a glimpse of anything is difficult. The best vantage point now is at Tikaboo Peak – providing you have your own telescope and don't mind a one and a half hour hike up a remote hill-side. Crossing the military borders can cost a hapless rubber-necker a $600 fine and a rather scary encounter with the 'Cammo - Dudes' – armed private-security patrolmen with walkie-talkies who drive white Cherokee Jeeps with Government plates and wear camouflage fatigues without insignia.

But still the UFO enthusiasts come in droves.

'What are they?'
SCULLY

'I don't know. Just keep watching. It's unbelievable'
MULDER

Belief that the Government has access to UFO technology remains strong. Bob Lazar's claims may have been discredited to some extent, but other odd facts remain.

After the 1988 unveiling of the B2 advanced technology bomber, renegade West-coast scientists from the 'black world', who felt that their civil rights were being abused by attempts to silence them, leaked statements saying that the craft had anti-gravity capabilities – something that is not known to be possible at our current standing in technological advancement. Even some engineers uninvolved in the project claimed that there was something strange about the design and capabilities of some of the new craft.

Since 1972, rumours have abounded regarding a Government project to test-fly a recovered alien vehicle, apparently code-named Project Snowbird. These rumours have often been linked to one of the most significant, bizarre and tragic nuts-and-bolts UFO encounters in history.

At 9.00 p.m. on 29 December 1980, near Huffman, Texas, Betty Cash was driving with her friend Vickie Landrum and Vickie's seven-year-old grandson, Colby, when they saw a fiery object in the sky. They stopped the car, got out and watched it descend and hover no more than 135 feet away from them, flames shooting down from its underside. Frightened, Vickie and Colby had clambered back into the car right away. By the time Betty joined them, the outside door handle was too hot to touch.

As the craft flew onwards, the trio drove behind it. That is when they noticed that it was being 'escorted' by 23 Chinook twin-rotored helicopters.

Shortly after arriving home, Betty developed a blinding

(Below) Betty Cash became desperately ill with suspected radiation sickness after watching a mysterious craft hover no more than 135 feet above her. She and Vicky Landrum (Bottom) sued the US Government for 20 million dollars for the trauma and sickness they claim they suffered as a result of the incident

headache, neck pains, skin-irritation and diarrhoea. Her eyes swelled shut, she vomited uncontrollably and fluid-filled nodules appeared on her scalp. Four days later she was admitted to the burns unit at Parkway General Hospital in Houston.

Colby and Vickie, who had spent less time outside the car suffered from eye inflammation. Colby appeared to have 'sunburn' on his face, and both Vickie and Betty subsequently suffered from hair loss. Betty went on to develop breast cancer, although this may have been unrelated to their experience.

Passed from doctor to doctor (Betty's medical bill totalled $10,000 by February of 1981), a definite diagnosis was not forthcoming, although most agreed that some form of radiation damage had occurred.

Cash and Landrum sued the US Government for twenty million dollars. Representatives from the Air Force, the Army, the Navy and NASA took to the stands and testified that they did not own or operate such an object and it was on these grounds that Judge Ross Sterling dismissed the case. Neither Betty Cash, nor the Landrums, nor independent witnesses who had seen the object and the Chinooks were allowed to testify.

Beyond the media, too, these tales thrive in friend a-friend tradition, and sometimes even straight from the source. Chris Carter reveals: 'There's a guard right here (at 20th Century Fox's Los Angeles offices) at the gate box who told me a very interesting story about the military, and something he had seen while a crewman on a military ship, and how he had been threatened if he ever told anyone. . . he had seen a spacecraft.'

Bibliography
Sources and further Reading

Books

Unexplained!
Jerome Clark, Apogee Books, Detroit, MI, 1990

Above Top Secret
Timothy Good

Alien Liaison: The Ultimate Secret
Timothy Good, Arrow, 1991

Papers, Journals & Newspapers

The APRO bulletin, Vol 29, no 8, 1981

*Backroads of Nevada Lead
to UFO Buff's Dreamland*
Associated Press newswire, 30 May 1995

*Multiple Sightings of Secret Aircraft Hint
at New Propulsion, Airframe Designs*
Aviation Week and Space Technology, 1 October
1990

Stealth – and Beyond
Gung-Ho, February 1988,

Las Vegas Review Journal, 20 March 1994,
11 November 1994, 24 May 1995,14 June 1995

Suddenly, Your Briefcase is Classified
Legal Times, 26 June 1995 (Benjamin Wittes)

Cash-Landrum Case Closed
MUFON UFO Journal, no 222, October 1986

The Observer, 4 December 1994

Area 51 Frequently Asked Questions, Psychospy

UFO Magazine July/August 1994, July/August
1995

The Washington Post, 30 May 1995

*George Washington University Relations
Department Bulletins*
1 November 1994, 15 March 1995,

Television Programmes

KLAS-TV news, November 1989

ABC World News Tonight, 1 August 1994

Internet
The Internet UFO Group Web site.

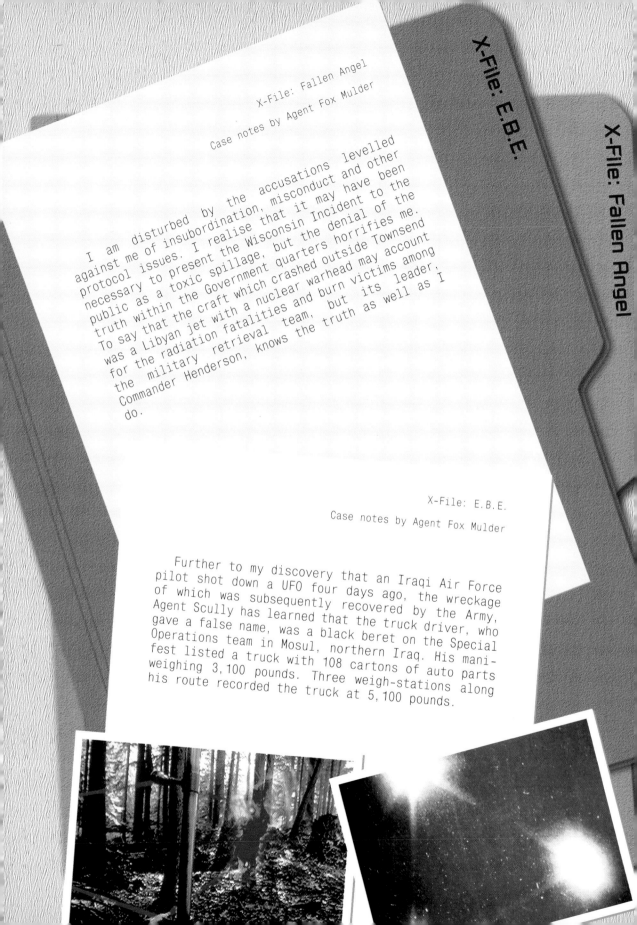

X-File: Fallen Angel

Case notes by Agent Fox Mulder

I am disturbed by the accusations levelled against me of insubordination, misconduct and other protocol issues. I realise that it may have been necessary to present the Wisconsin Incident to the public as a toxic spillage, but the denial of the truth within the Government quarters horrifies me. To say that the craft which crashed outside Townsend was a Libyan jet with a nuclear warhead may account for the radiation fatalities and burn victims among the military retrieval team, but its leader, Commander Henderson, knows the truth as well as I do.

X-File: E.B.E.

Case notes by Agent Fox Mulder

Further to my discovery that an Iraqi Air Force pilot shot down a UFO four days ago, the wreckage of which was subsequently recovered by the Army, Agent Scully has learned that the truck driver, who gave a false name, was a black beret on the Special Operations team in Mosul, northern Iraq. His manifest listed a truck with 108 cartons of auto parts weighing 3,100 pounds. Three weigh-stations along his route recorded the truck at 5,100 pounds.

FALLEN ANGELS

*F*allen Angel leads Mulder and Scully into a web of intrigue following the crash of an extraterrestrial craft and the frantic military clean-up operation which follows. In *E.B.E.*, a similar military retrieval operation (this time involving an extraterrestrial biological entity – an alien) casts a web that is even wider and more treacherous.

'This big rig had overturned and spilled some toxic substance which required the evacuation of an entire town,' says Howard Gordon on the inspiration for *Fallen Angel*. 'So our thought was, what if they just said that and in fact something else really weird had happened?'

Gordon is sceptical of claims that UFOs have landed or crashed on earth but adds 'I'm also open-minded enough to think that there is something to them. I'm mostly

doubtful but think it's possible. Roswell is probably the most interesting case to me, but it's the only one that I've really investigated with any kind of thoroughness. We certainly know there was a cover-up. The question is was it an experimental mission or a UFO?'

Glen Morgan, who co-wrote *E.B.E.*, shares Gordon's uncertainty about the UFO phenomenon. 'That's the one I most want to believe. But in doing all the research, I can't say that I came across anyone who convinced me.' Morgan admits that he enjoyed a little playful sport with the UFO supporters. 'Because we knew there were so many Internet people watching, we would always have someone say things like "Roswell was a smoke-screen", because we knew it would kind of ruffle their feathers.'

Unlike vague sightings of lights or shapes in the sky, or outrageous claims of abduction, reports of nuts-and-bolts UFO encounters seem to be the closest thing to solid evidence that can be offered by the defenders of the Extraterrestrial Hypothesis. Here, we look at three of the most significant.

The Roswell Incident

Mac Brazel: the wreckage found on his ranch in Corona has kept the world talking for 50 years

> *'There still exist secrets that should remain. . . secrets. Truths that people are not ready to know. The world's reaction to such knowledge would be too dangerous'*
>
> DEEP THROAT
> *E.B.E.*

On 2 July 1947 something fell from the sky over Corona, New Mexico. The question is what? Almost half a century later the truth, for many the holy grail of UFOlogy, remains hidden. During a thunderstorm that night, ranch foreman Mac Brazel heard a loud crash. Checking the storm damage in his fields the next morning, he discovered strange, unidentifiable debris scattered across a half-mile swath.

He showed pieces to several neighbours before report-ing the incident three days later to the Chaves county sheriff, George Wilcox. Wilcox then phoned nearby Roswell Army airfield. Major Jesse Marcel, the base intel-ligence officer, along with Sheridan Cavitt, a counter-intel-ligence agent, came swiftly to investigate, and from then on the world went crazy.

On 8 July the investigation resulted in a military press release that shook the world. The intelligence office of Roswell Army airfield announced it was in possession of the remains of a crashed flying saucer.

By noon, Roswell's newspaper and radio station were inundated with calls from the world's media. The press conference at Fort Worth, Texas, where some of the debris had been taken, was eagerly awaited.

But there, surrounded by pieces of what appeared to be a weedy silver kite, Major Marcel and other army personnel posed for pictures and broke the bad news: there had been a big mistake. The 'flying saucer' was actually a weather balloon with a radar target.

The story was dead. Or was it? Some say the 'hidden truth' was about to get even more amazing.

'What can I say? How can I disprove lies that are stamped with an official seal?'
MULDER

Soon after the press conference, more substantial debris was sighted. And accompanying these remnants, according to reports from civilian onlookers, were the corpses of several small humanoids with unearthly features. Whether this seems beyond belief or not, the fact that the Roswell incident has persisted for almost 50 years, with continual revelations of new twists and turns and governmental backpedalling, makes it perhaps the ultimate real-life X-file.

The Roswell incident lives or dies on the testimony of those involved. And never before or since have so many credible witnesses come forward.

Lt. General Ramey and his adjutant Col. DuBrose examine the 'wreckage' found at the Roswell crash site

The debris Brazel found was seen by several people, including his neighbours, Major Marcel, and the town fireman. All marvelled at how light yet durable it was. And it would not burn or break. All agreed this was not the weather balloon that had been shown at the press conference. Most importantly, Major Marcel himself declared that the debris had been switched.

More intriguing still was the call received by Roswell mortician Glen Dennis, from the Roswell airfield mortuary officer requesting three child-sized coffins. He claims a friend of his on the base, a nurse, described the unusual, inhuman features of the bodies to him.

*'I have my orders – and the licence
to execute them. So I suggest you
erase from your memory what
you saw or think you saw.
For your own well-being'*

COLONEL HENDERSON

Fallen Angel

The US Government has admitted that the original debris discovered on Mac Brazel's ranch was switched for the wreckage of one of these balloons

Then there are the claims of heavy-handed threats from the military. The radio station that broadcast the original press release was threatened with closure if it perpetuated the UFO story. Mac Brazel was escorted everywhere by a cordon of military guards in the days following the incident and shocked everyone by changing his version of events, perfunctorily recanting the Army line about the weather balloon when asked. Within a year, he had left Corona and opened a food-storage facility. His neighbours believed he had been hushed with a payment and his son claims Mac took an oath not to tell.

The granddaughter of Sheriff Wilcox says her grandmother told her that military police informed Wilcox that if he ever spoke out, he and his family would be killed.

Despite the thorough work of researchers like William Moore and the eminent Stanton Friedman, and testimony from over 100 witnesses, the Government kept schtum and the mystery remained in limbo for decades

'A lie, Mr. Mulder, is most convincingly hidden between two truths'
DEEP THROAT

E.B.E.

Then, in September 1994, just as a feature dramatization of the Roswell incident was about to première on the American Showtime cable network, there was an odd, perhaps even inexplicable Government confession: the debris *had* been switched at the press conference. What had crashed in 1947 was a test for the Mogul project – Flight #4, to be specific – which was the development of a balloon that could track the progress of the Soviet nuclear programme.

Was this a red herring to distract from the inevitable questions that would be raised by the film? An article by Dave Thomas in the *Skeptical Inquirer* analysed the flight data and opined that despite one's knee-jerk mistrust of a Government that has already admitted to one lie, the explanation seems quite plausible. Most intriguingly, the Mogul balloons bore hyroglyphic markings – a feature mentioned by those who had seen the original wreckage. UFOlogists counter that if it was a test flight – even if it was a failure – it would have appeared in the Mogul flight log, now no longer classified. Yet no Flight #4 appears on the log at Roswell.

The Roswell Incident just keeps on trucking. The summer of 1995 brought two new developments. New Mexico congressman Steve Schiff, who had been trying for some time to get answers to the 48-year-old mystery, had become frustrated with the lack of information coming from the Department of Defence and had instigated the launch of an enquiry through the General Accounting

Office – America's Government watchdog agency.

At the end of July, the GAO's report was returned. The outgoing messages from Roswell Army airfield for the time-period (which would have shown how its military officials were explaining to their superiors exactly what was going on) had been destroyed without proper authority. According to Congressman Schiff: 'The GAO could not identify who destroyed the messages, or why.' This is a particularly odd turn up for the books, since destruction of official documents is an act which itself has to be documented with details of who is doing the trashing and for what reason. Moreover, Schiff explained: 'It is my understanding that these outgoing messages were permanent records, which should never have been destroyed.'

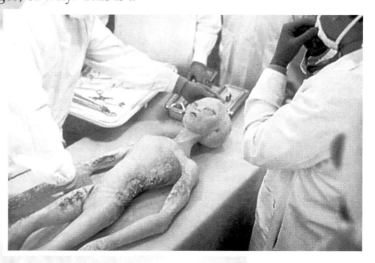

A still from the movie Roswell – *a scene reminiscent of video footage claimed to have been taken at the time of the incident*

'How would you like to have on your front page the first substantiated photograph of an Extraterrestrial Biological Entity?'
MULDER

The event that really put Roswell back in the news, however, was an announcement by Ray Santilli, a British video promoter, that he had secretly bought some extraordinary film footage shot at the crash site by an ex-Army cameraman. In the main, the film depicted the autopsy of what was apparently one of the occupants of the fated saucer.

Was this the hard evidence for which the world had been waiting? Unfortunately not. For a start, checking the authenticity of the film was impossible. Santilli refused to reveal the identity of the cameraman, and although he agreed to requests from several quarters to supply a sample of the film for dating-analysis, it never materialised. A document from Kodak, dating the film-stock at either 1927, 1947 or 1967 was not much help, and became even less help when the story broke that it was the result, not of a proper analysis but of a cursory examination by a rep in a Kodak outlet.

The journalists and UFOlogists who were given a sneak preview of the footage were unconvinced. Although there was no proof that the video was fake (a claim that the type of curly phone cord seen in the background had not been invented in 1947 turned out to be a mistake), the general consensus was that the 'alien' looked absurd or like a severely deformed human. A keen-eyed journalist also noted that for what would have been one of the most important events in the history of the world, there was little sense of this conveyed. The surgeons seemed to be hurriedly slicing away at the body, and unceremoniously dumping organs into buckets without really looking at them, and at one point the cameraman seems to get very interested in someone behind a glass screen

who is wearing a funny hat.

A Channel 4 documentary team showed the video to various witnesses who had claimed to have seen the Roswell E.B.E.s, and were met with mixed feelings, mainly erring on the negative side. When the film itself aired in late August 1995, audiences on both sides of the Atlantic were distinctly under-whelmed.

The film had certainly brought Roswell to mass media and public attention, but it had only served to breed more specula-tion.

Whether it was a hoax or – as the conspirasy theorists suggested – Government disinformation designed to divert attention from the GAO announce-ment, it had distracted from the main issue – the truth behind the unsolved mystery.

'You've got some kind of downed craft in those woods. . . We both know what's out there, Colonel!'
Mulder
Fallen Angel

The Rendlesham Forest Incident

O ne of the best documented and most significant military encounters with a UFO occurred in Rendlesham Forest, near Ipswich, Suffolk, just outside the perimeters of two US air bases, RAF Woodbridge and RAF Bentwaters – site of one of NATO's largest nuclear-weapons stockpiles.

Although the events occurred over several nights, and there is now a dispute over the exact dates, the reliability of the witnesses and the clarity and consistency of their accounts put this one at the top of the British UFO charts.

The report, filed by deputy base commander Lieutenant Colonel Charles Halt and released almost three years after the event under the Freedom of Information Act, ranks high in the annals of credible and amazing UFO incidents.

At approximately 3.00 a.m. on 27 December 1980, two USAF security guards saw unusual lights outside the back gate at RAF Woodbridge. Three patrolmen were sent to investigate. They reported seeing a strange glowing object in the forest, described as metallic in appearance and triangular in shape,

Lt. Col. Charles Halt – one of the key witnesses to the Rendlesham Forest incident

approximately two to three metres across the base and two metres tall, illuminating the entire forest with a white light. It had a pulsing red light on top and a bank of blue lights underneath. It was hovering or on legs. As the patrolmen approached the object, it manoeuvred through the trees and disappeared. It was briefly sighted again about an hour later.

The next day, three depressions were sighted on the ground where the object had appeared, and the area was checked for radiation. Beta/gamma readings of 0.1 milliroentgens were recorded, with peaks at the spot where it had landed.

Later that night, an intense red light was seen moving and pulsing through the trees. It broke into five separate white objects and disappeared. Three star-like objects were then seen in the sky, moving rapidly in sharp, angular motions and displaying red, green and blue lights.

'What she tracked was a meteor. It's aberrant movement was clearly due to instrument malfunction. . . Your report will reflect these facts. Understood?'
COMMANDER CALVIN HENDERSON

Despite the high-weirdness going down, the Ministry of Defence's report was dismissive: 'In view of its reported small size, it is considered highly unlikely that the object was a piloted vehicle. In addition, it is highly improbable that any violation of UK airspace would be heralded by such a display of lights. As such we are satisfied that the incident is of no defence significance.'

Admiral Lord Hill-Norton, former chief of the British defence staff, disputes this conclusion. He told Granada's *Network First* documentary team: 'I have no doubt that something landed at this US Air Force base, and I have no doubt that it got the people concerned into a considerable state. The Ministry of Defence has doggedly stuck to its normal line, that to nothing of defence interest took place.

'Either large numbers of people, including the commanding general at Bentwaters, were hallucinating – and for an American Air Force nuclear base, this is extremely dangerous – or, what they say happened *did* happen. In either of these circumstances, there can be only one answer: that it was of *extreme* defence interest to the United Kingdom.'

Nick Pope, a Ministry of Defence employee who, for three years, was in charge of their UFO investigations, also boggles at the apathetic M.o.D. party-line: 'You had a number of US Air Force personnel at a very important base in Suffolk having seen a structured craft moving through Rendlesham Forest. It almost appeared to be leading them on a merry chase through the woods. It was ahead of them, and at one stage it was directly above them in the clearing and fired down a bright light.

'This activity went on probably over a period of about three nights. On one occasion the deputy base commander came out with his personnel and took readings with a geiger counter. I thought, Okay, yes, but you get background radiation readings everywhere. I gave the Defence Radiological Protection Board the readings from Colonel Halt's memo and said, "What do you think of those readings?" And they said, "Well, ten times the normal reading. What the hell happened there?" '

Larry Warren, then a 19-year-old US Air Force security officer, was one of the witnesses at Woodbridge. He has since brought his story to the media, but only after enduring, he claims, what smacks of a classic government hushup. After attempting to phone home and describe what he had witnessed, he became persona non grata. He was honorably discharged from the Air Force in 1981, but when he changed his mind and tried to reapply several months later, his re-entry was barred. His record had become classified, but he later found out that it showed that he 'cannot fully extend his right arm', which he says is not true at all.

Warren's account differs from Halt's in one significant aspect: he claims the occurrence was documented on video and in stills. None of this material has ever surfaced.

Nick Pope: 'I've heard the stories, but I've never seen any videos or photographs. The story is they were taken to Ramstein base in Germany, but I've certainly not seen any of the material. I've seen Colonel Halt's memo, and he was able to confirm that yes, he was there, that the memo was for real, that it all happened as he described, and that they encountered this strange craft in the forest.

'My conclusions: Type of craft: unknown. Origin: unknown. Purpose of craft: unknown, I guess.'

When the case made headlines three years later, an odd embellishment about an alien encounter was added. Larry Warren claims this was planted to undermine the story's credibility.

At any rate, there seems to be no disagreement over the first-hand reports and the geiger-counter readings. Something strange did indeed occur that December in Rendlesham Forest.

Larry Warren at the alleged landing site of the UFO in Rendlesham Forest

The Belgian Triangle

'Sir, I'm sorry to disturb you at this late hour – but we picked up an unidentified bogey. I thought you should see the replay for yourself'

Lieutenant Bruce Taylor

Before all hell breaks lose in *Fallen Angel* and *E.B.E.*, we see the military tracking strange, unrecognised craft describing seemingly impossible manoeuvres. No fictional conceit, this.

Occurrences of this kind can and do happen. Here, the Ministry of Defence's Nick Pope describes a recent and remarkable example. 'From 1989 and into 1990, there was a huge wave of UFO sightings over Belgium. Hundreds of reliable witnesses saw large triangular objects with lights in the apex and a huge light in the middle, resembling no known craft and capable of hovering, or moving at very slow speeds of 20 or 30 m.p.h., and then moving off at immense speeds – estimated to be thousands of m.p.h. – almost instantaneously.

A flying triangle. But could this one be a USAF innovation?

'And one night in 1990, 30–31 March, everything went absolutely crazy. The Belgian Air Force received 2,700 reports of UFOs, from a mixture of civilians and military. To put that in perspective, we in the M.o.D. get about 200 or 300 reports a year.

'At the same time, two separate NATO radar stations picked up an object on their screens in the place the eyewitnesses were saying. So they scrambled the two F16 fighter interceptors which are held on quick-reaction alert. The pilots closed on the object, then acquired it on their airbourne radars. The air radar was on a different frequency to the ground radar, so even if there are problems with radar systems sometimes, with ghost returns, you've got visual sightings correlated by two different systems.

'The pilots managed six or seven locks-on, but each time they locked on, the object broke the lock and appeared to move off at speeds of several thousand m.p.h. It appeared to be reacting to having been locked on.

'Curiously enough, we (in England) had a wave of similar sightings the same night. I remember I took calls all that morning from people, many of them police officers, saying they'd seen this huge triangular craft. Some of the reports were incredible.

'A family in Staffordshire had seen this thing come very, very low over their house at 1.00 a.m. in the morning with a deep, unpleasant hum – rather like if you stand in front of the speakers at a rock concert, you can feel the low-frequency hum as well as hear it.

'The most bizarre report was from an RAF officer at a nearby military base who had heard there had been some UFO sightings and had gone outside about 1.15–1.30 a.m. To his absolute amazement, he had seen this triangular object fly directly over his base. The disturbing thing was, he said it appeared to be firing a beam of light down at the countryside – the beam was tracking backwards and forwards as if looking for something. And then the beam retracted, and the object passed over his head. He said it was midway between the size of a C-130 Hercules transport aircraft and a jumbo jet. Pretty big.'

'Sir, no known aircraft can manoeuvre like this'
CREW CHIEF KAREN KORETZ

Pope concludes: 'I spoke to our air attaché in Belgium who had spoken to the chief of Air Force Operations and the two F16 pilots involved. Again, all they could say was that there was a structured craft of unknown origin operating over their airspace and it seemed to be able to do nought to mach five or mach seven in less than a second. They didn't have the faintest idea what it was.

'Obviously, there is always speculation about prototype devices. I'm not necessarily privy to every black project, as they call them. But my best assessment is we don't have anything that could even remotely compare to the flying triangle. What the Belgian triangle could do is way beyond what anything we've got can do.'

'You can deny all the things I've seen, all the things I've discovered. . . but not for much longer. Because too many other people know what's happening out there – and no one, no government agency, has jurisdiction over the truth'
MULDER

Bibliography

Sources and further reading

Books

Crash at Corona
Stanton Friedman and Don Berliner, Paragon House, 1992

UFO Crash at Roswell
Kevin D. Randle and Donald R. Schmitt, Avon Books, 1991

Papers, Journals & Newspapers

The Guardian, 25 July 1995

Cosmic Conspiracy: Six Decades of Government UFO Cover-Ups,
Part One
OMNI, Vol. 16, No 7, April 1994 (Dennis Stacy)

The Roswell Incident and Project Mogul
Sceptical Inquirer, July, August 1995 (Dave Thomas)

Schiff Receives, Releases Roswell Report
News Release from the office of Congressman
Steve Schiff, First Congressional District, New Mexico, 28 July 1995

The Sunday Times (Australia), 23 April 1995

The Sunday Times, 30 July 1995

UFO Magazine, July/August 1995

Washington City Paper, 12 April 1995

Television

The Secret History, Channel 4.

Network First, Granada Television

Internet
Paranet Information Service

* Larry Warren has co-written a book with Peter Robbins about his experiences during and after the Rendlesham Forest incident, entitled *Left at East Gate*, which promises to be a fascinating read, and is due out in 1996.

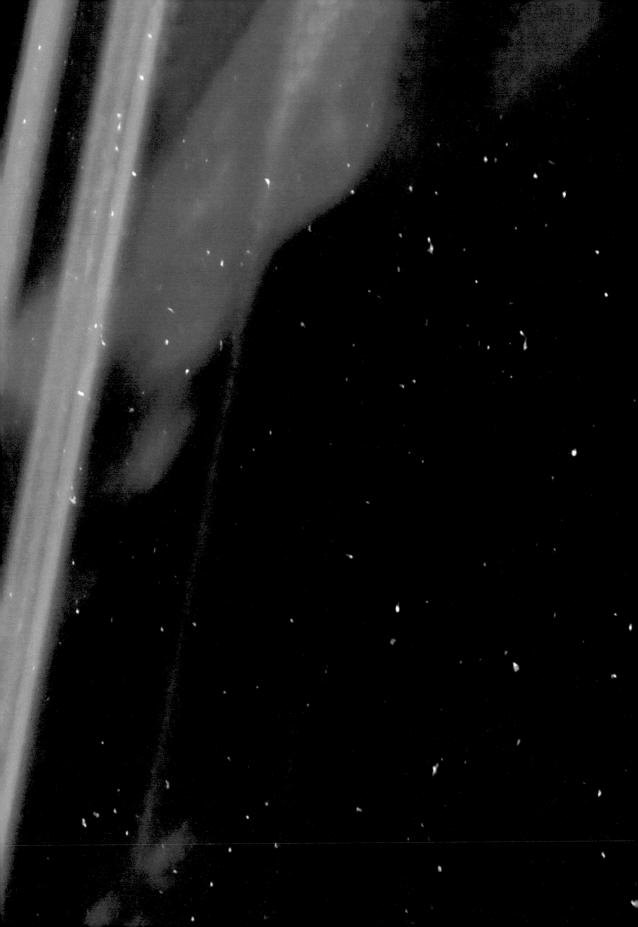

IN SEARCH OF THE TRUTH

These four people have devoted their lives to learning the truth. By doing so, they have risked being disparaged as crazy, which they are not. If it is too much to call them real-life Mulders, it is fair to say they embody various degrees of the Mulder philosophy. Here they are in their own words, describing themselves and their travels through the unknown.

Bob Rickard

Bob Rickard is co-editor, along with Paul Sieveking, of Fortean Times, *which he founded in 1973, the foremost chronicle of the strange. Like all true followers of the innovative anomalist and philosopher Charles Fort, Bob approaches the strange with a sense of wonder, humour and true open-mindedness.*

'I was born in India in 1945 – here's the joke – at a place called Deolali, which gave the English language the word "doolally". It was a place that shell-shocked soldiers were sent to recover and rest. So they would arrive mad, and it was a phrase, you "went doolally".

'When I was in my last year in Art College in Birmingham, I went to my first science fiction convention, and there on a table I saw the four paperbacks of Charles Fort. I read them all in one sitting.

'Fort seemed to give an expression to the way I'd looked at and thought about things. I'd been collecting news clippings like he did, and I appreciated the rather legalistic twists of logic that he applied to analysis – the way he

Bob Rickard, Co-editor of Fortean Times. *'What I've liked about* The X-Files *is that they have encapsulated a very Fortean attitude, a dialectic between doubt and belief'*

attacked establishment, and the way people wanted an explanation as a substitute for trying to think things out.

'The sweep of his criticism of the modern world was devastating, because without attacking too much it seemed he revealed science to be as rigid as religion. He thought that in every age there was something dominant. In earlier times it was religion; everything was judged or seen or interpreted in terms of the dominant religion of that era. In to the modern age, science superseded religion, and so you got scientists behaving like priests, expecting people to believe dogmatically. But scientists rarely extend the same rules of evidence to subjects outside their area, and there is a lot of misunderstanding about what is called paranormal or strange phenomena because of that.

'The Academy of Sciences in Paris in the 18th century sent a famous astronomer called LeBoissier to investigate an account that had been sent in of a meteorite falling in a field. Le Boissier goes out and talks to these peasants. (I think he ended up being guillotined; I'm not surprised, because he had an educated nobleman's scorn for the peasantry.) He went to see what these peasants were talking about, and he saw this rock in the field. He said it's obvious the meteorite is iron: lightning struck it and revealed it in the earth in the blast. And he came up with the great phrase: "There are no stones in the sky, therefore no stones can fall from the sky." And that was the report he sent back to the Academy of Sciences. In the meantime, there were further accounts of meteorites falling which were dismissed as the nonsense of peasants. It was quite a few decades later that the first study of lights in the sky gave credence to the idea of meteorites.

'Most of the big scientific advances have come not because of painstaking work *within* science but because somebody made a leap to something that was outside the norm, understood how it worked, and then brought it within our sphere of knowledge. What Fort attacked in science was complacency and dogma. These are the enemies of Forteans as well.

'I like to think we are true sceptics in the Greek sense, not in the modern American sense. If you mention the word sceptic in America – with a 'K' that is – it automatically means an attitude that you are dismissing anything non-scientific. The original sceptics questioned things in order to discover things about them, which is similar to the attitude that Buddha asked his disciples to follow. He said if you want to know, you must question your teachers, your parents, your rulers, and everybody – otherwise you won't know. Sure it's uncomfortable, but as Fort said, "I don't know how to find out anything new without upsetting people".

'What I've liked about *The X-Files* is that they

Charles Fort at his super checkers board

have encapsulated a very Fortean attitude, a dialectic between doubt and belief. It alternates, and even the characters who traditionally doubt are allowed their moments of belief, and vice versa. If you like, they are the yin and yang of Forteanism, Mulder and Scully. I think the writers have understood the dynamics of looking into the unknown far better than many scientists do.

'We like to think of ourselves as observants. I wish we had more resources to actually go out and investigate, because I think data is an important part of it. Too many Forteans rely on a newspaper report. We tell our readers: don't believe it, even if you read it in the *Fortean Times*. But you have to trust people sometimes.

'The honest investigators are able to investigate a case and point to aspects of it which aren't explained, data which is contradictory or unsatisfactory, questions that are still unanswered. There are some investigators that do that, and I see this reflected in some *X-Files* stories. Sometimes a single piece of data or an event is interpreted differently by Mulder and Scully, and there you have, in a microcosm, the dilemma facing most of us.

'There's a quote I like: "For every expert there is an equal and opposite expert." We are often introduced on the radio as "expert on the unknown" – which is absolute nonsense when you think about it.'

Timothy Good

A highly-respected researcher into the UFO phenomenon, he has done much to lend weight and credibility to the extraterrestrial hypothesis and the concept of a world-wide cover-up. He is the author of many books on the subject. His next, Beyond Top Secret – The Worldwide UFO Security Threat, *is due out in 1996.*

'In 1955 my cousin in the States, Edmund Berkley, who is a pioneer in the computer field, sent me a book by Major Donald Keyhoe called *The Flying Saucers are Real.* I was immediately excited because I've always been passionate about aircraft. So here was a book describing reliable sightings by airline captains and military pilots, scientific personnel and so forth, and I was intrigued.

'From about 1960, I began to do my own independent investigations. From 1963 onwards, as a musician with the London Symphony Orchestra, I went travelling, so I was was able to investigate cases abroad.

'I have had several UFO sightings myself, the first on 1 August 1963 when, together with my mother and brother and other neighbours in Beckenham, south-east London, we observed for about an hour and 20 minutes a very bright light in the sky. Through binoculars it had a triangular shape, like a huge translucent tetrahedron. The official explanation was that this was a balloon sent from Germany, but I made enquiries later and I'm not satisfied it was a balloon, because it was stationary. There's a photograph in *Above Top Secret* of the object taken through a telescope from Hertfordshire. I went to the astronomer who took the photograph – who is also a pilot, by the way – and he told me that the thing was absolutely stationary within the field of the telescope. There's no balloon on earth that can do that. I know some of

them have little gas jets to manoeuvre and position, but there's no way any conventional object could have stayed as still as that for such a long time. It was apparently about 400 feet in diameter. The United States Air Force sent up jets, but it was never satisfactorily explained.

Timothy Good, a highly respected UFO researcher and author. 'The X-Files has done more than any other fiction series to stimulate interest in UFO phenomena'

'The last sighting I had was very frustrating because normally I don't go anywhere without a movie camera or a camera with a telephoto lens, but I had nothing with me on that occasion – of course! I'd been shopping in the high street, came back up my road and saw this brilliant point of light in the sky. It was completely cloudless, by the way. I knew it wasn't a planet or star, so ran home and on my return it had gone. I was very very frustrated about that. The next day a journalist from the *Kentish Times* phoned and said, "Had any reports of UFOs yesterday afternoon?" I said, "Why? Tell me more". It transpired that about 40 witnesses at Orpington hospital, on a construction site, had been passing around binoculars and watching as this elongated, triangular-shaped object hovered and then shot off to another part of the sky, then periodically split up into as many as four or five separate objects, which then regrouped. This had gone on for more than an hour.

'The significant thing about this particular sighting is that about ten days later, outside the twin United States Air Force bases of Bentwaters and Woodbridge, in Suffolk, over a period of about four or five nights, numerous Air Force security personnel reported a landed craft which was triangular shaped, the description is very similar to that of the thing seen over here [See *Fallen Angels*]. This was either the same or a similar object to the one I had a fleeting glimpse of for a few minutes.

'There have been several attempts by various governments to educate the public to some extent. In the former Soviet Union, for example, in the Museum of Scientific and Economic Achievments, there is a display cabinet of information about UFOs which always draws tremendous enthusiasm from the crowds.

'We talk about governments covering up information, but it seems that very few people in government have the faintest idea what's going on. The real information is restricted to relatively small groups within the military and scientific intelligence community.

'The deception, from an intelligence perspective, has been handled very capably, by the Americans at least. They've gone about debunking it extremely skilfully. You hardly ever get a serious investigative journalist to push questions. First of all, you have the tabloids sensationalising it. This, in turn, affects the attitude of the broadsheets. They don't want to touch it, and if they do, any commentary on UFOs is laced with patronising remarks.

'Journalists should be aware that the way this issue is treated by the media affects the way the Government responds. I know there are those in the intelligence community and in other areas of authority who would be far more forthcoming if it weren't for the ridicule they know is going to be heaped on them by the papers.

'I hope the information in my books gets out to a wider public. You see, the thing about the politicians is they have no mandate from the electorate to do anything about this subject. They're not going to put their nose out of joint unless there's a huge lobby of people demanding to know what's going on. And that might happen one day.

'*The X-Files* has caught the public imagination. And it has led to an airing of the subject as far as the local papers are concerned. I subscribe to a press-clipping agency, so every week I get tons of stuff like: This is Little Piddlewick's X-Files. It makes people think of the possibilities. The same thing happened with *Close Encounters* in 1978. On the negative side, it led to a deluge of UFO reports in Britain – suddenly, everybody was seeing flying saucers. Obviously, 90% of them were explainable. But at the same time, it got debate going. *The X-Files* has done more than any other fiction series to stimulate interest.'

Professor Robert Morris

Professor Bob Morris is holder of the Koestler Chair of Parapsychology at Edinburgh University. Highly respected by sceptics and believers alike, he is one of the foremost scientific researchers working in the field today.

'I suppose I have been interested in the subject since childhood. My parents had a device set up before I was born to assess ESP. I asked if ESP really did exist, and they answered that they didn't know because science had been ignoring it. What I am trying to say to science is: "Lets try to understand what's going on, even if there's nothing really new there."

'The study of ESP is the study of new means of communication between organisms and their environment. There are a variety of tests that we can use to investigate ESP, for instance the Ganzfeld technique, which is a mild sensory deprivation procedure. ESP may involve attending to very weak signals and we try to heighten perception of these signals by eliminating other signals. When we undertake research we try to look at the best kind of environments for ESP. Through our research we appear to be finding out that we do have access to more means of communication than we currently understand.

'People are trying to collect information at present to see if animals experience ESP, and there is some evidence for it. We need to study and understand animal patterns more closely to make sure that any apparently psychic animals are not just using some cues that we humans might not think about.

'It has been suggested that children may be more perceptive because they haven't been too heavily socialised yet and their minds are more open. Perhaps people grow out of it. We are also looking at creative people being more perceptive. They process information more flexibly, their thoughts are not so fixed and new information may stand a better chance of being noticed.

Bob Morris, Professor of parapsychology at Edinburgh University with Arthur Koestler. 'I tend not to become discouraged in parasychology because even if it's self deception. . . we are going to learn something'

'Serious researchers do not regard themselves as explorers of the supernatural. We are investigating naturally occurring acts, within ourselves – nothing supernatural.

'Sorting out the difference between ESP frauds and

genuine ESP experiences is a complex problem and that is partly why parapsychologist's research goes so slowly. A lot of people are disappointed that some researchers are dragging their feet a bit. That's because we know that there are traps and pitfalls.

'Learning about how magicians communicate has been very helpful, we value their expertise. Some magicians are disappointed that researchers pay so little attention to the ease with which they do things. Magicians are not adversaries – they have important expertise for us. It is extremely important for us to understand the tricks of the trade, how we can be deceived by clever frauds and, in all innocence, by ourselves.

'I tend not to become discouraged in parapsychology because even if it's self deception, that's no problem: we are going to learn something, no matter what happens.'

John Spencer

John Spencer is a psychical researcher, affiliated to the Society for Psychical Research and the Association for the Scientific Study of Anomalous Phenomena. He is also chairman of the British UFO Research Association (BUFORA) and author of many books on a wide range of paranormal subjects. John's personal belief is that the key to the enigma of supernatural phenomena lies here on earth, with the human race. While he keeps an open mind, he does not at present subscribe to theories of spirits or extraterrestrials.

'My approach is to try to be as open-minded as I can while also being sceptical. I'm not ready to dismiss things just because I don't like the sound of them, but I will challenge the evidence as much as I can.

'Recently we were in a public building, in a controlled

environment – everyone sitting facing each other, the room sealed and in a team of three. We were pelted with stones appearing from nowhere. You would hear this whizz build-up and. . . crash. You could see the stones bouncing, but not where they came from.

'After we'd been pelted by four stones – in fact, one hit one of us quite nastily on the side of the head – I wanted a different team who didn't know what to expect to go in. On the way, one of them, Chris Waltham, realised he'd forgotten his torch, so he went back for it. I took the team in and sat a couple of them down. Chris came in very excited and said, "Look! I got hit by this, guvnor, in the corridor!" He had this stone.

'There were a total of eight stones. The last one I found very compelling. It was only a small room, and we heard this build-up right above me, and I think I saw the path of the stone. It bounced down. I grabbed it immediately. And just like it says in all the books, it was red-hot. It burnt me. But it cooled down very quickly. Somebody else who picked one up said the same. Someone that understands fossil rocks is going to have a look at them, but my understanding of apports is that once you get an apport, you get what you get. It's just going to be a pebble, and that's it.

'With poltergeist effects, too, no-one knows. There are three front-runner theories. One is that they are totally generated from inside a living person, like a PK (psychokinesis) effect, possibly a particular expression of stress and anxiety. The second theory is that it's an entity from beyond, little hobgoblins sitting on another dimension that sling things at you, which I have a bit of a problem with. And the third is a combination of the two: some entity that's always going to be there but can't get through unless there is a condition of stress. And I would add that you can have that third situation with a *natural* energy which just happened to be triggered by stress. So a stressful person alone wouldn't do it, but if they were in the right conditions for other energies that we're not familiar with, that link could happen.

'There's a theory that it's projected thought forms taking on a life of their own. We were in a poltergeist-infested house with one researcher who was totally sceptical until he visited that house and things moved. The people who owned the house were not there. So even if it was psychokinesis, they weren't around to create it!

'It's very tempting to rationalize whenever you get a pattern you can't understand. The analogy I used once in a talk I was giving consisted of asking people to come up with a device which could create six-sided objects, a thousand of them a second, and they all have to be completely different. They were getting into this thing about a really complicated computer program, and I pointed out that snowflakes come down like that. Would you have to think that there was an intelligence behind them?

John Spencer, psychical researcher and chairman of the British UFO Research Association.'When everything we don't currently understand is understood, there'll still be people like us writing books about something we can't conceive at the moment'

'Part of what we do is record the details of what happens. If we can guess what all the components are, maybe we could manifest a genuine ghost by creating the right conditions.

'In terms of detecting ghosts, we go from the ludicrously over-equipped to no equipment at all. In a castle, we have taken in infra-red, radar, night vision, a computer monitor called EMU – environmental monitoring unit (it has 16 devices which pick up movements of air and, movements of temperture, and sends them all back to a computer which flags any movement), video cameras, still cameras, motion-triggered cameras, you name it.

'And the sum success of that lot is about five or six minutes of slightly thought-provoking stuff. That's it after years of work.

'I think the danger of science is that we depend on it. It's become a religion; if science can't explain it, there must be something wrong. But the idea of science is right: everything must have cause and effect. Therefore, by one definition the paranormal has to be rational, and once you understand all the criteria you can replicate it, you can predict it, and so on.

'But if science is saying, "See, all this is rubbish", then it's not good science. Scientists are wrong to say that the world is as we know it and that's the end of it. The director of the US Patent Office in 1899 resigned with the words, "Everything that can be invented now has been invented". Wonderfully stupid man, but so assured. How lovely to live like that.

'Ghosts are a bit beyond our understanding at present, but they will be understood one day. In a number of years we'll know all the criteria, have all the answers. What we're doing as a species is dragging ourselves along by looking at the next area of something we don't understand, investigating, solving it, looking at the next one. When everything we don't currently understand is completely understood, there'll still be people like us writing books about something we can't conceive at the moment, the next paranormal. The X-Files of tomorrow.

THE REAL X - FILES

'Hey, Spooky!'
'Seen any little green men lately?'

T he smartly-suited young man wends his way down the drab corridor of the government building, ignoring the customary salutations of his co-workers. It is not difficult. He's had years of practice. Besides, he has more important things on his mind. There's that disturbing new wave of UFO sightings, for one. Not to mention the threat of more trouble from his superiors, whose discomfort with his unconventional beliefs seems to increase daily.

Nick Pope,
Whitehall's very own
Fox Mulder

But this is not *The X-Files*. This is real life. The young man is not Fox Mulder, but Nick Pope, employee of the British Ministry of Defence. Pope is a higher executive officer – the ranking equivalent of an Army major – who has worked at the M.o.D.'s imposing London headquarters at Whitehall for ten years. Between the summer of 1991 and the summer of 1994, he was appointed to a post offi-

cially entitled Secretariat Air Staff, Department 2A – better known to insiders as 'The UFO desk'. It was an experience which was to change his life.

'When I was asked if I wanted to become the Government's expert on UFOs, I was extremely interested,' recalls Pope. 'I thought it sounded a fascinating job. I didn't have any idea what I would find or what it would entail, but I certainly thought, yes, I'd very much like to do it.'

Pope entered the job without any prejudices about the subject. 'I was open-minded. I didn't really know that much about it – my opinion of UFOs was based on little more than having watched *Close Encounters*. But as I found out in the end, truth really is much, much stranger than fiction. I came in as an open-minded sceptic and I ended up a believer.'

However, as Pope was soon to discover, a believer was not the kind of person the M.o.D. wanted manning Desk 2A. Officially, the brief of the officer in charge of Desk 2A

The imposing Ministry of Defence building may not house alien artifacts, but its Secretariat Air Staff Department 2A is the closest we have to a real life X-Files division

is to investigate reports of UFOs in order to ascertain whether there is any threat to the UK's defence – an initiative which comes from an era in which an unidentified flying object could well turn out to be a foreign aircraft, reconnaissance device, or missile. Unofficially, as Pope swiftly learned, the officer at the post was expected to do little more than send out standard letters dismissing sightings and write up reports confirming that there was no threat.

Pope had no intention of going by the book. He says: 'The reason for the M.o.D.'s involvement is to look for any potential threat to the defence of the UK. Now, what I argued was that was a moveable feast. What did it mean? I think some of my predecessors had interpreted it as meaning that unless there's actually hard evidence of something hostile, it's not our business to investigate UFOs. I disagreed. I took the view that you couldn't make a valid judgement on whether there was or was not a threat until you'd made some effort to find out what it was. Particularly since, as I soon found out, we were talking in many cases about structured craft of unknown origin penetrating the UK air defence region. I wasn't prepared to say, "Oh well, I'm gonna assume there's no threat there." Many people would have been more comfortable if I had, but you know, I was paid to do that job, and I wasn't going to turn a blind eye.'

Pope's approach did not win him any brownie points. 'The parallels between myself and Fox Mulder are quite extraordinary. I was a bit of a maverick, a loose cannon within the department, viewed with a mixture of suspicion and distrust by others. I had exactly the same sort of problems as Fox Mulder has, I guess.'

The connection did not elude Pope's colleagues, and it wasn't long after *The X-Files* began to air in Britain that Pope acquired the nickname 'Spooky'. By that time, however, he had become inured to teasing, it being such a constant occurrence. UFO researcher Timothy Good, who refers to Pope as 'The real Fox Mulder', can attest to this. On his first meeting with Pope at the Ministry, a passing group of sober-looking civil servants broke into a spontaneous rendition of *The Twilight Zone* theme tune.

The Pope/Mulder similitude does not end here. Pope explains: 'I got drawn into various other oddities. Because I did UFOs, everything that was slightly weird and didn't have a normal home would come to me. I got quite a bit about crop circles, and even the odd ghost story. One was a report of a ghost at an RAF base – I think I referred them to a civilian ghost hunter – obviously there's no official interest in ghosts. But, like Fox Mulder, anything weird and wonderful would come to me.'

So what was it that turned this once sceptical young man into a real-life Mulder? 'There wasn't any one absolutely blinding revelation. It was the drip-drip effect. I began to see so many cases which just couldn't be explained. When you added together all the eye-witness testimony – much of it reliable stuff from trained observers such as pilots and military personnel and police officers – with all the photos, the videos, the radar tapes, the radiation traces on the ground, they made for a really convincing case, as far as I was concerned.

'Ninety-five per cent of UFO sightings are misidentifications, cases where there is insufficient data, or hoaxes – although I must say I've had an absolute minimum of hoaxing to handle. But there's a hard core of 5% which I would classify as "genuine unknown" – cases which appear to defy explanation after as much analysis as possible. Five % of the total numbers seen is a lot – you've got to factor in that for every 100 people who see a UFO, perhaps only one or two will ever get round to reporting it. There were enough of these unexplained cases to make me think, there's something there. And if you accept that there's a hard core of 5% that defies explanation, you've got to ask what they are.'

Pope asked himself that question and it took great courage to make his conclusions public. 'There are all sorts of weird and wonderful theories, but I guess I've got to come off the fence. I have now come down on the side of the Extraterrestrial Hypothesis. On the basis of the extraordinary cases I've seen and the accounts I've heard from people, I have come to the conclusion that the most logical explanation is that somewhere out in the universe people are beginning to do what we ourselves are beginning to do now:  reaching out into space to try and contact another civilisation. And I do think that a small number of UFOs, the *real*

UFOs, are ET space craft. And that has made me very unpopular.'

Pope is passionate and unflinching in his beliefs, and is unafraid to criticise the British Government for it's *laissez faire* attitude toward UFOs. 'There needs to be an awareness that there is a core phenomenon that appears to go beyond human understanding and experience, and that we can't simply write it off as weather balloons or hoaxes. We must make an effort to find out what it is – people (in the Government) know too little about something that they damn well should know about. You've got to figure from a common sense point of view that if a craft slips through your defensive screen of radar and air defence fighters, that its technology is probably above yours. In other words, the attacker seems to be more advanced than the defender – and that makes me very worried.'

His assessment of the situation is that UFOs are a 'potential threat'. 'We don't know anything about them. Until we can say who they are and what they are and what they want, I guess the jury is still out.'

He feels that extensive research should be a governmental priority. 'The sad thing is that we've got all the resources in place – we've got radar, we've got access to satellite imagery, we've got people who can go out and talk to people. It just needs to be targeted and focused and given a proper remit. I did my level best to investigate all the sightings that came my way. But there was a limit to what I could do. I was one man struggling against the tide.'

Regardless, Pope took his investigations extremely seriously, processing as much raw data as possible in the form of telephone calls, letters and reports from the public, the police, the military and the Civil Aviation Authority. He was also unique in being the first officer at Desk 2A to have cultivated a friendly working relationship with the UFO lobby. 'I initiated an active dialogue. The idea was to be there for each other, to know that you can phone each other up and say "Hey, we're beginning to get reports of a wave of sightings over Cornwall, what have you got? What do you think?" And if we found explanations, of course we'd tell each other and we'd both be able to switch inquiries off and concentrate on the real UFOs.'

The lobby found Pope to be a useful ally. His position gave him access to military specialists, radiation experts and other valuable human resources, and the authority to impound radar tapes and make inquiries at civil airports, RAF bases and observatories. Despite his good relationship with the UFOlogy community, Pope admits: 'There are areas where I and all these people have to agree to disagree.' Primarily these areas concern belief in the concept that the world's governments know more about the UFO situation than they are letting on.

Pope reserves judgement on the situation in America. 'I know the conspiracy theorists say that the US Government is up to its eyeballs in crashed saucers and dead and live aliens, but it's not a world on which I have any window. Unfortunately I couldn't get access to any American opposite number, although I did try.'

However, he is adamant that there is no cover-up in Great Britain. 'I am satisfied that there isn't one and I think it's inconceivable that in three years I wouldn't have caught a hint of something.' His fruitless searches for classified UFO-related documents further bolster his certainty. 'My clearances are very high – not because of the UFO thing, but because I did one or two duties connected with the Gulf War. Now, someone like Tim (Good) will always argue that of course it's not simply a question of classification, it's "need-to-know", and he's quite correct – just because you're cleared to a certain level doesn't give you access to everything on that level. But I would have thought that I'd have had the combination of clearance *and* need-to-know, given that I was doing the UFO job.'

Pope is aware that some of his allegations can sound suggestive. For instance, there were times when he was, he suspects, 'deliberately given other work just to take me off an investigation.' He asserts: 'I know some people say that's because they were covering something up. But honestly they did not know about flying saucers. If they were covering up anything it was their own ignorance and predjudice about the subject.'

However, Pope's experiences were not without a touch of *X-Files*-style intrigue. He reluctantly confesses: 'I don't really want to get into this, but I had a sort of Deep Throat. Not neccesarily someone directly involved, but yeah, I had a Deep Throat character. A sympathiser who I would sometimes consult, who would offer an opinion. Someone in a senior position? I don't think I can really get into that, but I think you could say: well-placed to discuss one or two of the more interesting options.'

After the military style, the M.o.D. regularly appoints its employees to new tours of duty, and in the summer of 1994, Pope was promoted to a position in a financial department. 'An awful lot of people were glad to see the back of me, I can tell you,' he laughs. 'I had mixed feelings. Everyone loves promotions, of course, but there was no way I was ever going to come across a job that was as interesting as investigating UFOs for the Government again. I was very sad to leave.'

But although they took the man out of the UFO department, they couldn't take the UFO department out of the man. Pope's involvment with the UFO lobby continues, and his future plans include a book, provisionally entitled *Open Skies, Closed Minds*, scheduled to be published in 1996. 'The aim of the book is to get people talking about the

whole issue and it's also addressed to the establishment – the military, the civil servants, the politicians. I want to focus people's attention and offer an effective case for the prosecution: to say there is something unknown here that defies explanation and merits urgent investigation.'

Further down the line, Pope would love to become more directly involved in helping to set UFO research firmly on course for the future. He would like to see a coalition between the independent UFO organisations, allied to world governments and able to draw upon their resources, and perhaps run under the auspices of the UN. 'And yes, I would love to think that I could be one of the people involved in putting together this study or organisation,' he admits.

In the meantime, Nick Pope, like Fox Mulder, remains

convinced that the truth is out there, and he is not going to give up searching for it.

While Mulder's desire is not just the truth, but also a resolution to the mystery of his sister's disappearance, Nick Pope's purpose is surely more straightforward. Or is it? 'You could say that, like Fox Mulder, my interest is not purely an academic one and I'm driven by some more personal motivations. My *primary* motivation is the intellectual belief that there is a genuine unknown phenomenon, and my belief in the people's right to know, but a part of my motivation is a desire to explain some anomalous events in my own past.'

He is reluctant to go into detail but offers: 'The very furthest I would want to go is to say that there are some events in my past which some people in the UFO lobby would say are some of the factors that are present in cases of abduction. But I want to stay on the fence until I know what happened to me.'

STRANGE BUT TRUE

It goes without saying – though let's say it anyway, for the benefit of anyone not able to distinguish between television and real-life – that the FBI has no X-Files department. And, as both the fictional Fox Mulder and the very real Nick Pope have discovered, beliefs which extend beyond the realm of accepted science are about as welcome to the powers that be as the proverbial turd in the swimming pool.

It is not merely scepticism behind the authorities 'desire to avoid anything with a faintly paranormal odour'. Chasing after an elusive explanation – which, even if found, may make no sense in terms of universal order as we know it – is a time-consuming, expensive and futile exercise when you are in the business of upholding the law.

Civilian investigators may have time on their hands and a vested interest in unlocking the mysteries of the unknown, but the authorities have neither.

This is not to say that the FBI and British police archives are entirely free of mysteries.

The Thornton Road Stones
Birmingham, England 1981

Towards the end of 1981 and well into the following year, residents of five houses in Thornton Road, Birmingham, complained of stones being thrown at their windows at night.

The stones yielded no fingerprints, so teams of officers were posted at Thornton Road with surveillance equipment, infra-red scopes and image intensifiers, in the hope of catching the culprit. The stone-throwing continued, but no one was spotted, giving rise to speculation that there may be some paranormal force involved.

Probably, the truth will never be known. But the unfortunate fact remains that the fruitless investigations cost Birmingham CID over 300 man-hours and a large slice of their financial resources before they were finally abandoned.

The Mad Gasser Of Mattoon
Mattoon, Illinois 1944

On 1 September, the police were called to investigate a very odd incident. At about 11.00 p.m. Mrs. Bert Kearney had been woken up by a pungent smell in her bedroom which she described as 'sickening sweet'. The odour had grown stronger, and she realised, to her dismay, that her legs and lower body were becoming paralysed.

Her screams woke neighbours, who came to her aid, but no explanation could be found. However, Mr. Kearney, returning from work at 12.30 a.m., caught a glimpse of a man standing at their window, whom he described as, 'Tall, dressed in dark clothing and wearing a tight-fitting cap. 'The man had fled as he approached.

Later it transpired that Mrs. Kearney was not the first victim of the character who was later dubbed 'The Mad Gasser of Mattoon' – in fact there had been two similar incidents the previous night.

Neither was Mrs. Kearney the last victim. Over the next nine days, the police logged 19 further 'gas attacks', some felling two or three people at a time. All the victims experienced the same sickly sweet odour, nausea and paralysis from the waist down which lasted between 30 and 90 minutes.

It wasn't long before Mattoon was in a state of panic – a situation aggravated by the frequent melodramatic

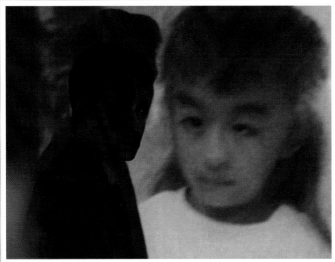

reports appearing in the local newspaper. By 6 September, the police chief, E.C. Cole, had posted all ten of his officers on round-the-clock duty.

The police soon had the assistance of two FBI agents from Springfield, Illinois, and a crime specialist from the State Department of Safety, who declared: '(This is) one of the strangest cases I have encountered in many years of police work.' But, despite this extensive application of the State's resources, the gasser could not be found.

As the attacks continued to escalate, the situation became politically embarrassing for city officials. When local businessmen announced plans for a protest rally on the 9 September, the police commissioner issued a statement urging citizens to pull themselves together. Whilst he acknowledged that 'a gas maniac exists', he suggested that the level of panic was disproportionate to the threat, and put many of the alleged attacks down to 'hysteria'.

The only solid evidence was a white cloth, which, on the night of the 5 September, a Mrs. Buelah Cordes found lying outside her front door. Sniffing it, she had experienced not just the now-familiar symptoms but also facial swelling, bleeding from the mouth and an inability to speak.

On the 11th, however, the authorities learnt that the analysis of the cloth had revealed nothing, and despite reports of two more attacks the previous night, the investigators began to conclude that the Mad Gasser did not exist at all. All gas attacks reported to the police that night were dismissed as false alarms, including one in which a doctor, arriving at a victim's house, had noticed the smell himself.

In a press conference the following day, Police Chief Cole announced: 'Local police, in co-operation with state officers, have checked and re-checked all reported cases and we find absolutely no evidence to support stories that have been told. Hysteria must be blamed for such seemingly accurate accounts of supposed victims.' He added that the peculiar smell, and the stain on Mrs. Cordes's cloth may well have been due to carbon tetrachloride carried on the wind from the nearby Atlas Diesel chemical plant.

A spokesman for the plant quickly replied that they did

not use carbon tetrachloride, and the only gas they did use was odourless. Even if this had been the case, why had residents not noticed the smell before 31 August? Who had left the cloth on Mrs. Cordes's porch? And, if it was hysteria fuelled by fear of the gasser, how could the attacks which had taken place *before* the first newspaper report be explained?

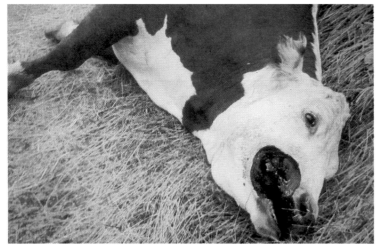

The victims were far from satisfied with the authorities' conclusions, but with charges of delusion levelled at them, the onus was now on them. As Fortean researcher Loren Coleman eloquently noted: 'The victims, in a dilemma worthy of Kafka, had to answer for their own victimisation.'

CATTLE MUTILATIONS

The 'Mad Gasser' case is not the only one in the FBI's repository which has the hint of an X-File about it. Autumn of 1973 marked the dawn of America's cattle-mutilations phenomenon, which was to plunge the authorities up to their collective necks in high-weirdness.

There had been isolated cases of animals found dead under mysterious circumstances in the late Sixties, but it was in 1973 that the trend began in earnest with a spate of reports from farmers in Minnesota and Kansas.

Reports stated that the dead animals, mainly cattle, showed no signs of bullet or knife wounds, but were missing various combinations of body parts – including eyes, ears, lips, rectum, sex organs and glands – all of which had been removed cleanly and precisely. Odder still, there was never a footprint or any other evidence of human presence to be found – even in the case of one carcass which had been discovered in a mud-hole. Furthermore – as Agent Mulder mentions in his discourse on cattle mutilations in *Eve* – there were also numerous claims that animals had been entirely exsanguinated, without a drop of blood spilled.

Local police were as baffled as the farmers. An announcement from Albert Thompson, sheriff of Lincoln County, Minnesota, that the cows had died of diseases and subsequently been chewed by 'varmints' was met with derision, despite a Kansas pathology report which determined black-leg (a common cattle ailment) as the cause of death for some of the cows they examined. These claims could not explain the apparently surgical nature of the mutilations, and other channels of inquiry were kept open.

Police Agencies in four States pursued the idea that Satanic cults were involved, and in 1975, the US Treasury Department's Alcohol, Tobacco and Firearms Division assigned Agent Donald Flickinger to hunt for a

network of slaughter-happy Satanists who were allegedly operating state-wide. The claim turned out to be largely the invention of a convicted bank robber who was scamming for transfer to a smaller jail from which he could make a break – which he did.

In the same year, the Colorado Bureau of Investigation had the honour of examining the only piece of hard evidence to date – a blue satchel containing medical gloves, a bloody scalpel and a cow's ear, discovered next to a rancher's mail box in Lincoln County, Colorado. However, this was not the breakthrough they had been hoping for – no fingerprints were found and the ear could not be matched to any reported mutilation.

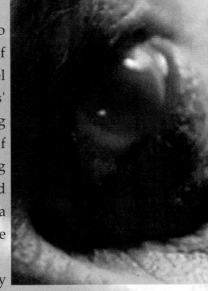

The blue satchel, not so very dissimilar from those of government issue, added fuel to the conspiracy theorists' fire, which was already being fanned by reports of unmarked helicopters flying low over mutilation-sites, and by the winds of paranoia which had been blowing since Vietnam and Watergate.

By the late Seventies by which time the unexplained cattle death tally was allegedly in the thousands and spanned almost every farming State, there were more theories than answers. Depending on whom you asked, cattle mutilations could be explained by mass-hysteria, clandestine government experiments, aliens up-to-no-good, and aliens merely claiming their side of the bargain in an alien-technology-for-cow-parts deal they struck with a covert government faction. To make matters more complex, every school of thought had their own experts to lend weight to their claims. An investigator claimed to have received death threats while exploring the link between animal mutilations and germ-warfare experiments; a veterinary pathologist stated that some animals appeared to have been dropped from a height and sliced-up using sophisticated laser equipment; a physicist announced that he had spoken with Native Americans who told him: 'The "star people" know what they are doing and must be trusted.' In 1979, in the midst of the speculation and confusion, New Mexico Senator Harrison Schmitt made a request for a federal investigation into what he referred to as 'these mysterious killings'. The FBI stepped in, supplying a $40,000 investigation grant to the First Judicial District of New Mexico.

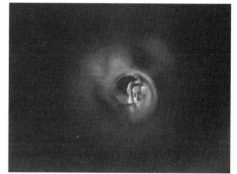

Kenneth Rommel, an ex-federal agent, headed up the year-long enquiry, which ended with a 297-page report concluding that the cases investigated had been the work of predators and scavengers.

There were the inevitable claims that Rommel had clearly not studied any of the 'classic' examples, but as far as the authorities were concerned, the case was closed.

Fortunately, these cases, with their long, expensive, and ultimately inconclusive investigations, are a rarity. Although the public report strange happenings far more often than one might imagine, it is usually simple for the police to get a measure of the situation and bail out as soon as they realise that there is little that can be done either to explain or prevent further occurences.

Still, it is safe to say that over the years, the police have most likely had some involvement in just about every category of paranormal experience.

UFO sightings, for instance, are frequently phoned in to police stations. Callers are routinely referred to local UFO groups or, in Britain, sometimes to the Ministry of Defence.

The remains of an apparent victim of spontaneous combustion

Police in Maidstone, Kent, are well used to strange sightings near Blue Bell Hill. On 8 November 1992, motorist Ian Sharpe was surprised but relieved to learn this, having arrived 'white-faced and shaking' at the station after accidentally driving over a woman who appeared in his path, and then being unable to find any trace of her.

Bizarrely, the public sometimes even call the cops with regard to apparent poltergeist activity. On 31 August 1977, WPC Carolyn Heeps was dispatched to investigate a disturbance at a house in Enfield, where she found an appalling mess and a distressed woman named Mrs. Hodgson telling of books and toys flying around and furniture moving. WPC Heeps herself saw a chair move three or four feet of its own volition, and promptly found her name forever linked with 'The Enfield Poltergeist', a case which became Britain's most famous contemporary account of paranormal activity. Still on the force, Heeps wearily reveals that 18 years down the line, she still receives monthly invitations to discuss the events with the media.

Other police officers have found their lives changed in a more positive way by an anomalous experience. John Haymer, a retired scenes of crime officer with Gwent CID, is today one of the world's leading authorities on spontaneous human combustion. His involvement can be traced back to 6 January 1980, when he was called to investigate a household fire and found 73-year-old Henry Thomas dead in a chair, his torso reduced to ashes but his feet, socks and slippers untouched. All evidence pointing to the fact that the torso itself was the seat of the fire.

Other investigative bodies, such as the world's aviation

authorities also have their fair share of X-Files.

Disappearance Of An Aircraft
Australia, 1982

There are a number of well-docu-mented cases of aerial disasters which allegedly involved UFOs, but the 1982 case investigated by the Australian Department of Aviation is one of the strangest.

At 6.19 p.m. on Saturday 21 October 1978, a 20-year-old amateur pilot named Frederick Valentich departed alone from Moorabbin Field in Melbourne in a rented Cessna. At 7.06 p.m. he was over Cape Otway, flying well below the range of Melbourne's radar systems, when he radioed Melbourne's Tullamarine airport to enquire about a large, low-flying aircraft in his flight path.

Air-traffic controller Steve Robey made investigations and told Valentich that he must be mistaken: there should be no craft in the vicinity. Keeping his cool, Valentich told Robey that the craft was now flying over him, circling him and diving at him, at unidentified high speeds.

The transcript of their exchange is truly unsettling:

Goings on at the Hodgson household in Green Street, Enfield, as furniture and toys were thrown around the rooms. This picture shows the children John, Margaret and Janet

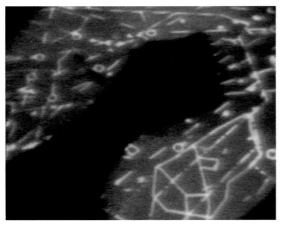

'It's not an aircraft... It is... Ah... as it's flying past me it's a long shape. I, er, cannot identify more than that... such speed.'
'... And how large would the, er, object be?'
'It seems like it's, er, stationery... What I'm doing right now is orbiting and the thing is just orbiting on top of me also. It's got a green light and a sort of metallic like... it's all shiny on the outside... Ah, it's just vanished.''...Would you know what kind of aircraft I've got? Is it a military aircraft?' '... Confirm the, er, aircraft just vanished?' 'Say again?'

Valentich sighted the craft once again shortly afterwards, and at the same time, began to encounter engine trouble. He told Robey that the object was hovering above him. The control in his voice faltering, he radioed: 'It *is* hovering and it's *not* an aircraft.' He attempted one more communication following this, but stopped dead. Robey heard twelve seconds of metallic sounding noises before radio contact was lost.

No wreckage or body was ever found, although this is not neccessarily sinister – the ocean is a jealous keeper of its haul.

The Department of Aviation conducted an investigation into the incident, and as if the tragedy was not peculiar enough already, had to contend with the plethora of weird theories that abounded.

Some said that Valentich was interested in UFOlogy and may have set out to perpetrate a hoax. Others suggested a dramatic suicide bid. When the investigators discovered that he had only filed a one way flight plan and had filled the Cessna with far more fuel than he needed to reach his destination, it was put forward that Valentich may have faked his own death and flown into the antipodean horizon to a new life. Other theories included delusion, an encounter with a covert experimental military craft, a Bermuda Triangle-type affair (a couple of subsequent reports even managed a little creative stretching of the 'triangle' to fit Cape Otway into it!) and of course there was your common hostile aliens theory.

The ADA evaluated all the theories and published their report in May 1982, concluding that the whereabouts of Valentich and his Cessna were not known, and the reason for his disappearance had not been determined.

While most official bodies do all they can to avoid directly addressing paranormal possibilities, there is an exception to be found: the legal system. Particularly in America, the guardians of the scales of justice appear game for anything.

Besides the cases which have been detailed elsewhere in this book – which have taken channelling and testimony from beyond the grave – there have also been a number of cases involving such ethereal complaints as ghosts and bad vibes.

In 1983, an elderly Californian woman filed suit against an estate agent and the former owner of the home she purchased, who had not told her that, ten years prior to the sale, it had been the site of a multiple murder.

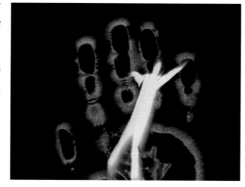

Several years later, a Wall Street stockbroker went to court with a claim that his new holiday home in Martha's Vineyard – Agent Mulder's home turf, no less – was haunted by the ghost of a confederate soldier. He felt this should have been disclosed prior to purchase. The defence's arguments included the fact that the ghost was friendly.

In reaction to cases like these, the State of Connecticut passed a bill concerning 'Psychologically Impacted Property' – informally known as 'The Ghost Buster Bill' – which became effective on 1 October 1990. The act was urged by The Connecticut Association of Realtors and prohibits lawsuits against real estate owners or agents who fail to disclose to buyers that their property was 'psychologically impacted'. Purchasers may apply in writing to be informed of such 'psychological impairment', however, and the owner must give a truthful disclosure or point-blank refusal. The bill's hearing at the House of Representatives makes for fascinating reading.

Representative Farr of the 19th District voiced his concern over how specific the questions to the owner had to be: 'Do you have to ask, is this house haunted? ... Was there ever a suicide? ... Was there ever a tragedy? I am not exactly clear under the amendment to what degree of specificity you have to ask that question.' Representative Jaekle of the 122nd was more concerned about spook-enthusiasts, volunteering: 'Potential ghost hunters now see this law, and say, boy, all I have to do is say maybe I'm a buyer.' Representative O' Neill of the 98th wanted to know whether 'unexplained psychological phenomena' would be taken into consideration, adding that he was 'an individual who has grown up in an area of the country where unexplained psychological phenomena have a direct bearing on my whole life.'

The law was passed at 199 votes to 29.

Bibliography
Sources and further reading

Unexplained!
Jerome Clark, Visible Ink Press, 1993

Mysterious America
Loren Coleman, Faber and Faber, 1983

Alien Liaison: the Ultimate Secret
Timothy Good, Random House, 1991

Mute Evidence
Daniel Kagan and Ian Summers, Bantam Books, 1984

This House is Haunted
Guy Lyon Playfair, Sphere Books, 1980

Death By Supernatural Causes
Jenny Randles and Peter Hough, Grafton Books, 1988

Paper, Journals & Newspapers

Act Concerning Psychologically Impacted Property
Connecticut General Assembly Senate proceedings, 1990,
Vol. 33, part 4

Fortean Times, Issue 73, 82

Operation Animal Mutilation
Report of the District Attorney, First Judicial District, New Mexico, June 1980

THE (X) FILES™

The X-Files Book of the Unexplained, Volume II
Coming in 1996. . .

The essential companion to Volume I, featuring:

Stills and coverage of *The X-Files* seasons II and III, exclusive
interviews with the people who bring you *The X-Files*, and all the in-
depth information any truth-seeker could desire on a plethora of
paranormal, folkloric, supernatural and natural mysteries,
including:

Vampires ,Voodoo , Psychic Abilities, Urban Mythology, Freaks of
Nature, Near Death Experiences , Genetic Puzzles, Deviant
Behaviour, Strange Science, The Search for Extraterrestrial
Intelligence, The Alien Abduction Phenomenon, Mystery Spots,
Paranormal Disturbances, Animal Enigmas, Bizarre Rains,
Conspiracies, Subliminal Mind-Control, Demonic Possession,
Covert Tests And Experiments , More Weird Nature

And that's just for starters. . .

Don't miss it!

CREDITS

Art Director – Aniz Damani
Type & Graphic Design – Colin Eyre & Jake Siney

PICTURE CREDITS

Crash 401 – Associated Press
Moses Dow by Mumler – Images Colour Library
(Charles Walker Collection)
Arthur Conan Doyle – Fortean Picture Library
Cottingley Fairies – Fortean Picture Library
Greg Sheldon – Fortean Picture Library
Mr Chinery – Mirror Syndication International
Fate Magazine cover – Fortean Picture Library
Tibetan Wheel of Life – Mirror Syndication International
Studio image of reincarnation – Mirror Syndication International
Dr White examining mammalian brain
– Alexander Tsaras/Science Photo Library
Cryonics experiment on a hamster
Peter Menzel – Science Photo Library
Mary Lurancy Vennum – Mary Evans Picture Library
Drawings by F. Thompson – Mary Evans Picture Library
Japanese Macaques Monkeys – Planet Earth Pictures
Nostradamus and Catherine de Medici
– Mirror Syndication International
Aberfan Disaster – Mirror Syndication International
Skylab – Mirror Syndication International
Benedetto Supino – Rex Features
Carol Compton – Mirror Syndication International
Grandma Ceccini – Topham Picture Library
Venus fly-trap – G.S.F. Picture Library
Copepod – Planet Earth Pictures
Skin of Vu Quang Ox – Lars Thomas/Fortean Picture Library
Bigfoot – René Dahinden/Fortean Picture Library
Urquhart Bay, Loch Ness – Nicholas Witchell/Fortean Picture Library
Alice Penfold – Range Picture Library
Yogi with head buried in the sand – Klaus Aarsleff

Quest Publications publish UFO magazine:
1st Floor, 66 Boroughgate, Otley nr. Leeds, LS21 1AE, England

THE X-FILES EPISODE GUIDE: SEASON 1

*The X-Files #***101**   PILOT   **OAD:**10.9.93

When a number of high school classmates begin mysteriously dying, Agents Scully and Mulder are called in to investigate

The X-Files # 102   **DEEP THROAT**   OAD: 17.9.93

Mulder and Scully investigate the strange disappearances of a group of Army test pilots

The X-Files # 103   **SQUEEZE**   OAD: 24.9.93

A mysterious serial killer is on the loose and Mulder and Scully must find him before he kills again

The X-Files # 104   **CONDUIT**   OAD: 1.10.93

When a young Iowa girl mysteriously vanishes without a trace, Mulder confronts his feelings about his own sister's unusual disappearance

The X-Files # 105   **THE JERSEY DEVIL**   OAD: 8.10.93

Scully and Mulder investigate a series of murders thought to be the work of a half man half beast living in the New Jersey woods

The X-Files # 106   **SHADOWS**   OAD: 22.10.93

Mulder and Scully investigate a series of unusual murders committed by an unseen force

The X-Files # 107   **GHOST IN THE MACHINE**   OAD: 29.10.93

Scully and Mulder must stop the ravages of a sophisticated computer before it kills again

The X-Files # 108   **ICE**   OAD: 5.11.93

Mulder and Scully travel to the Arctic to investigate the unexplained deaths of a research team on assignment there

| *The X-Files # 109* | **SPACE** | OAD: 12.11.93 |

A mysterious force is sabotaging the United States' Space Shuttle program and Scully and Mulder must stop it before the next shuttle launch

| *The X-Files # 110* | **FALLEN ANGEL** | OAD: 19.11.93 |

Scully and Mulder investigate a possible UFO crash site which Mulder believes the Government is trying to cover up

| *The X-Files # 111* | **EVE** | OAD: 10.12.93 |

After two bizarre, identical murders occur at the same time on two different coasts, Mulder and Scully are called in to investigate

| *The X-Files # 112* | **FIRE** | OAD: 17.12.93 |

Mulder and Scully encounter an unusual assassin: a man who can start fires with the touch of his hand

| *The X-Files # 113* | **BEYOND THE SEA** | OAD: 7.1.94 |

Scully and Mulder seek the aid of a death row inmate with psychic abilities to help them stop a killer on the loose

| *The X-Files # 114* | **GENDERBENDER** | OAD: 21.1.94 |

Scully and Mulder seek answers to a bizarre series of murders committed by one person – who kills both male and female

| *The X-Files # 115* | **LAZARUS** | OAD: 4.2.94 |

When an FBI Agent and a bank robber are both shot during a bank heist, the robber is killed but the Agent begins to take on the criminal's persona

| *The X-Files # 116* | **YOUNG AT HEART** | OAD: 11.2.94 |

After a criminal whom Mulder helped put away dies in prison Mulder finds that the criminal has come back to haunt him

The X-Files # 117 **E.B.E.** OAD: 18.2.94

Scully and Mulder discover evidence of a government cover-up when they learn that an unidentified space craft shot down in Iraq has been secretly transported to the US

The X-Files # 118 **MIRACLE MAN** OAD: 18.3.94

The agents investigate a mysterious young faith healer who seems to use his powers for both good and evil

The X-Files # 119 **SHAPES** OAD: 1.4.94

Mulder and Scully travel to an Indian Reservation to examine several mysterious deaths caused by an unknown beast-like creature

The X-Files # 120 **DARKNESS FALLS** OAD: 15.4.94

Mulder and Scully investigate when loggers in a remote Pacific Northwestern forest begin mysteriously disappearing

The X-Files # 121 **TOOMS** OAD: 22.4.94

Mulder becomes personally involved when Eugene Tooms, a serial killer who extracts and eats human livers, is released from prison

The X-Files # 122 **BORN AGAIN** OAD: 29.4.94

Mulder and Scully investigate a series of murders all linked to an eight-year-old girl

The X-Files # 123 **ROLAND** OAD: 6.5.94

Mulder and Scully investigate the murder of two rocket scientists when they are linked to the retarded janitor

The X-Files # 124 **THE ERLENMEYER FLASK** OAD: 13.5.94

Mulder and Scully discover evidence that the Government has been testing unknown substances on humans – with disastrous results